WITHDRAWN

Voices of Melancholy

Lucas van Leyden 'Portrait of a Young Man' (1519)

Voices of Melancholy

Studies in literary treatments of
melancholy in Renaissance England

Bridget Gellert Lyons

Assistant Professor of English
Rutgers University

Barnes & Noble, Inc.

NEW YORK

PUBLISHERS & BOOKSELLERS SINCE 1873

CALVIN T. RYAN LIBRARY
KEARNEY STATE COLLEGE
KEARNEY, NEBRASKA

First published 1971
© *Bridget Gellert Lyons 1971*
First published in the United States, 1971
by Barnes & Noble, Inc.
No part of this book may be reproduced
in any form without permission from
the publisher, except for the quotation
of brief passages in criticism

ISBN 0 389 04168 8

Printed in Great Britain

to
Rosalie Colie

Contents

Illustrations

Frontispiece Lucas van Leyden 'Portrait of a Young Nobleman' (1519)
Reproduced by permission of the Prints Division, The New York Public Library, Astor, Lennox and Tilden Foundations

Between pages 78–9
1 Dürer 'Melencolia I' (1517)
Reproduced by permission of the Prints Division, The New York Public Library, Astor, Lennox and Tilden Foundations

2 Henry Peacham 'Melancholy' from *Minerva Britanna* (1612)
Reproduced by permission of the Trustees of the British Museum

Between pages 94–5
3 'Inamorato' from the Frontispiece (by C. Le Blon) to Robert Burton's *The Anatomy of Melancholy*. (This engraving first appeared in the 3rd edition of 1628.)
Reproduced by permission of the Pierpont Morgan Library

4 'Democritus Abderites' from the Frontispiece (by C. Le Blon) to Robert Burton's *The Anatomy of Melancholy*
Reproduced by permission of the Pierpont Morgan Library

Facing page 118
5 Salvatore Rosa 'Democritus' (1650)
Reproduced by permission of the Metropolitan Museum of Art, Purchase, 1917, Joseph Pulitzer Bequest

Preface

The medical idea of melancholy as one of the four humours governing the human temperament is now entirely obsolete; it was in the process of becoming so at the very time that English writers of the Renaissance were creating literary masterpieces based upon it. This seeming contradiction is a reminder that the scientific value of a conceptual scheme is not necessarily a measure of its literary usefulness. It has been said, in fact, that scientific propositions become especially susceptible to literary treatment at the point where they lose their validity as science;[1] their transformation into imagery involves the blurring of those categories that make them applicable only to one particular system of ideas.

In our time we have seen the weakening, in scientific terms, of such words as 'neurosis' or even 'schizophrenia'. Since we have become accustomed to assume that all men are in some deep way neurotic—that it is the condition of mortality and our fate as the children of parents—the term, though certainly not meaningless, has lost the kind of scientific precision that would make it applicable to a particular, identifiable group of sufferers who can be restored to a 'normal' condition. While science has developed a more exact language for dealing with mental disorders, literature has appropriated the concept of neurosis and of the unconscious to express concerns that are central to our vision of the world— our lack of freedom, or our unawareness of the motives for our actions. The applicability of psychological notions to literary forms like the novel and the drama has been obvious; we need only think of the literary allusions that pervade Freud's formulations, or of the stripping of familial illusions that creates dramatic climaxes in so many contemporary plays, to see the reciprocal influence between psychological ideas and the forms, conventions and structures of literary works.

Since Renaissance medical tradition was less clearly differentiated from literary or philosophical concerns to begin with, melancholy had even more direct usefulness for writers of that time than neurotic behaviour has had in ours. The melancholy syndrome as it was described in numerous books about the humours was adaptable to a larger related issue: the situation, and particularly the manner of expression, adopted (rightly or wrongly) by the man who felt socially or philosophically alienated from the world around him. To describe the behaviour of melancholics, writers developed stock characters which were based both on observation of real people and on the content of a well-developed medical and philosophical tradition. The availability of established, identifiable characteristics simplified (and sometimes over-simplified) the artistic problem of dramatizing melancholy, a condition that was by definition inappropriate to the situation in which the sufferer found himself. The writer's attitude towards melancholy alienation could be expressed by the context into which he put the melancholic, and this was largely a function of literary form: satiric, comic, or tragic.

Melancholy came to be associated with each of these genres. It was to stock figures, chiefly, that Jonson and Shakespeare limited their treatments of melancholy in their early comedies. Although stereotyped behaviour, rigid and mechanical, was more suited to comedy than to tragedy, the fusion of a variety of stock roles could create an illusion of flexibility and depth in tragic characters, of which Hamlet is the outstanding example. Marston experimented with ways of making melancholy appropriate to the rough, crude style of satire. Finally, the unprecedented range that Shakespeare had introduced into the dramatic presentation of melancholy and the associations that Marston had established between melancholy and satire were exploited in another medium by Burton. Since Burton wrote what was ostensibly a medical book at a time when humoral psychology had questionable value as medicine, the problem of melancholy was substantive as well as literary for him. Melancholy had become an all-embracing word for disease, often denoting illnesses that involved all four humours; and Harvey's discovery in 1628 of the circulation of the blood finally destroyed the physiological assumptions on which humoral psychology rested, although it took some time before a new psychology replaced the old. Burton exploited the obsolescence of melancholy as a medical category in building his variable *persona*, and in extending the idea of melancholy metaphorically until it included all of life, even while retaining its original meanings as a medical term.

The groundwork for any exploration of the literary usefulness of melancholy has been well laid by the many scholars who have studied the background of the subject, notably Erwin Panofsky and Fritz Saxl in their seminal study of the origins of Dürer's engraving, 'Melencolia I',[2] and also Lawrence Babb, whose researches have located many of the places where melancholy appears in Elizabethan and Jacobean literature.[3] I am heavily indebted to these scholars throughout, and have made my own treatment of background material as brief as possible, in order not to repeat unduly what they have already done. My focus is on the literary possibilities that melancholy provided, and that made it the basis of great dramatic, lyric and prose works of the period—*Hamlet*, 'L'Allegro' and 'Il Penseroso', *The Anatomy of Melancholy*. I have been concerned with the literary styles and conventions that grew out of humoral melancholy, rather than with philosophical pessimism in a more objective sense, although the two subjects may overlap where dissatisfaction and disgust are seen partly as expressions of a particular mental condition. I have not attempted to deal with the external causes of 'Jacobean pessimism', of the darkening mood that has so often been attributed to English letters at the turn of the seventeenth century, but have considered attitudes towards melancholy chiefly in their relation to literary forms.

The general movement of the book is from simpler to more complex treatments of melancholy, from superficial to more analytic uses of the syndrome. My first chapter is the simplest and deals with the simplest treatments of melancholy, to be found in the expository books on the subject, medical and behaviour books. These books give us the basic information about melancholy, but do not provide a point of view adequate to 'explain' sophisticated literary treatments. Further, even the substance of these books is often contradictory and confusing, a fact which Burton exploited in his climactic essay. My second chapter, on melancholy in literary contexts, isolates examples from the range of literary devices—imagery, 'voice', genre—developed to express the subject. The chapter on Marston concentrates on a writer who repeatedly experimented with forms for melancholy, and whose failures, as much as his successes, throw light on such important works as *Hamlet, The Anatomy of Melancholy*, and 'Il Penseroso'. These works, treated in detail in my last three chapters, extend and analyse established traditions to make them more coherent and meaningful. As for chronology, Burton's *Anatomy* (1621) and Milton's poems (late 1620s or early 1630s) do come at the end of my sequence, reflecting their distance, I think, from such earlier works as Marston's formal satires (1599) or *Hamlet* (c. 1600). The preceding chapters, however, deal with a shorter time-span and occasionally blur chronology to show how Marston and Shakespeare combined and complicated existing formulas or stereotypes to make them more expressive. For the availability of a wide range of literary devices associated with melancholy ultimately made possible the greatest works on the subject— works that exploit both the existence of established forms and their limitations in order to reveal what we still recognize as the meaning of melancholy.

One section of the chapter on *Hamlet* has appeared as an article in *Studies in Philology*, and I am grateful to the editors for permission to reprint. I want to thank Joseph A. Mazzeo for the assistance he gave me while directing the Columbia dissertation on which this study is based, and also Paul Delany for his suggestions. I am very grateful also to my husband, Robert Lyons, and to the following scholars and friends who have given me a great deal of valuable help and personal encouragement: Maurice Charney, Roy Fisher, David Kalstone, Richard Poirier and Thomas Van Laan. My manuscript improved immeasurably as a result of their efforts on my behalf, and the defects that remain are mine alone.

My greatest debt is to my friend and unofficial teacher, Rosalie Colie. She first suggested the idea of this project to me when I was in graduate school, and she has supported it and me with unstinting generosity ever since. This book could not have been written without her, and it is dedicated to her with much affection and gratitude.

Note on the Text

All references to Shakespeare's plays are to Peter Alexander's edition (London, 1951); all references to Burton's *Anatomy of Melancholy* are to the 3-volume Everyman's Library edition (London, 1932); and all references to Milton's poems are to Merritt Y. Hughes's edition, *John Milton: Complete Poems and Major Prose* (New York, 1957).

I have regularized u and v, i and j, and s's in all of my quotations. The dates I have given for plays are those assigned by the editors of the texts I have used, or those given by Alfred Harbage, *Annals of English Drama 975–1700*, rev. Samuel Schoenbaum (Pennsylvania, 1964).

I have used the following standard abbreviations for scholarly journals:

HLQ   *Huntington Library Quarterly*
MLN   *Modern Language Notes*
MLQ   *Modern Language Quarterly*
MP   *Modern Philology*
PMLA   *Publications of the Modern Language Association*
PQ   *Philological Quarterly*
RES   *Review of English Studies*
SP   *Studies in Philology*

One

The Expository Books and their Background

The Background

When Shakespeare, Burton and other Renaissance writers gave melancholy the complex meanings and associations it has in their work, they were drawing on a tradition that had been developing throughout classical antiquity and the Middle Ages, and whose diverse origins made it an especially fruitful subject for literature. These sources were medical and religious, astrological or themselves literary, and though they were related to each other at some points, they were sufficiently distinct to provide a wide range of imagery and attitudes. Melancholy was classified as a disease, condemned as a vice, or exalted as the condition and symptom of genius. But all these diverse traditions about melancholy expressed, implicitly, the idea of its social importance— it was a physical and psychological condition that expressed an orientation towards the world and society—and this made it particularly susceptible to literary treatment.

The word 'melancholy', or black bile, has its origins in Greek medicine. The concept of the four humours derived from that of the four primary elements (fire, air, water and earth) to which they corresponded. Hippocrates set forth the analogous idea that the body was composed of humours, and that a proper balance of these constituted health:

> The body of man has in itself blood, phlegm, yellow bile, and black bile; these make up the nature of his body, and through these he feels pain or enjoys health. Now he

enjoys the most perfect health when these elements are duly proportioned to one another in respect of compounding power and bulk, and when they are perfectly mingled. Pain is felt when one of these elements is in defect or excess, or is isolated in the body without being compounded in the body with all the others.[1]

Each humour, through its qualities, corresponded to a particular element and season: sanguine 'blood', for example, warm and moist like air, was akin to spring and increased at that time, while cold and dry melancholy, which had affinities with earth, was especially prevalent in autumn or winter. Its characteristic symptoms were defined as 'fear or depression that is prolonged'.[2]

The humoral theory, which Galen enlarged upon in the second century A.D. and which the Renaissance inherited, can be very briefly summarized.[3] According to Galenic thought, blood (and the humours which composed it) was manufactured from food, whose properties determined which of the humours would be produced in greatest quantity. While all four humours had functions that made them necessary to the body, the sanguine humour, warm and wet like blood itself, was considered the best and most life-giving of the four, while the melancholy humour, whose coldness and dryness had affinities with old age and death, was thought of as the worst, the incompletely digested portion of the blood, the sediment and the dregs. Many diseases, including cancers and other tumours, epilepsy, ulcers and paralysis, as well as melancholy depression itself, were thought to be caused by an excess of melancholy humour, although the body was provided with a special organ, the spleen, for the purpose of purging such excess.[4]

All the humours existed not only in their natural state, but could also assume dangerous and virulent 'burnt' forms. Although Galen did not say that burnt humours like phlegm or choler actually became burnt melancholy, he pointed out the similarity,[5] and later writers were to equate all of the burnt humours with 'melancholy adust', occasionally specifying different symptoms according to which humour had originally been burnt. It was partly because of this equation that melancholy became such an all-embracing word for illness in the Renaissance.

One of Galen's most important contributions to humoral

theory was his idea of 'temperaments', physiological personality types governed by the dominance of one or another of the humours. To some extent the theory of temperaments contradicted the notion of one perfect balance which had underlain the purely humoral idea of health. Galen listed eight different kinds of humoral equilibrium, all healthy up to a point, and one ideal temperament which now became more of an abstraction than a reality, a well-tempered type possessed of perfect physical balance and of all moral virtues.[6] Although Galen regarded the other eight temperaments mainly as physical types, the idea of the temperaments (or 'complexions') as basic dispositions or configurations of character-traits was eventually what made humoral medicine most attractive for literary and artistic purposes, providing paradigms of human behaviour that did not necessarily involve disease.

The philosophic and literary tradition of melancholy that the Renaissance inherited from antiquity, though originally connected with medical theories, placed an entirely different—and more positive—value on the melancholy condition. Starting from the view of madness that prevailed in Greek tragedy, in which the gods punished presumptuous heroes like Hercules and Ajax by making them mad or enraged, philosophers treated madness as a heroic disease. While Plato's idea of divine *furor* or inspired madness (in the *Phaedrus*, for example) did not include melancholy, his concept of divine frenzy later became associated with it in one of Aristotle's Problems (No. XXX, 1).[7] 'Why is it', the Problem asks, 'that all those who have become eminent in philosophy or politics or poetry or the arts are clearly melancholics, and some of them to such an extent as to be affected by diseases caused by black bile?' Hercules (an epileptic) and Ajax are mentioned among the heroes, while Empedocles, Plato and Socrates are examples of 'men of recent times'. The answer is that melancholy is like wine in its effects, stupefying and debilitating in excess, but exhilarating in small amounts. Though black bile in its natural cold state caused stupidity, disease or despondency leading to suicide, it could also, when heated, produce ecstasy or inspiration similar to Plato's divine frenzy, and when moderately heated it would result in the kind of superiority suggested at the beginning of the Problem: 'Those, however, in whom the black bile's excessive heat is relaxed towards a mean, are melancholy, but they are

3

more rational and less eccentric and in many respects superior to others in culture or in the arts or in statesmanship.' The Aristotelian formulation became the basis for the theory of heroic melancholy in the Renaissance.

The two faces of melancholy, opposite but related, appeared also in astrological literature, and were reinforced by mythological and astrological presentations of Saturn. The connection between the planets and the major vices of men was an ancient one,[8] but the actual association between the medical humours and planetary powers was the work of Arabic writers of the ninth century. They connected the melancholy humour with Saturn, the sanguine with Jupiter, the choleric with Mars, and the phlegmatic with the moon or Venus. Qualities of melancholy, its coldness and dryness, were attributed to Saturn, while 'saturnine' qualities, the planet's slow motion resulting from its great distance, were transferred to the melancholy temperament. Once the connection between the planets and the humours had been made, the traits of the humours became indistinguishable from the attributes of the corresponding planets.

The contradictory qualities that were attributed to Saturn the planet were a result of the diverse mythological origins of Saturn the god. As the ancient Kronos, he was king during the Golden Age and a beneficent god of agriculture, but he was also deposed, castrated and exiled by his son, and sent to live in a dark prison beneath the earth. He was associated with sea journeys and travel because of his own journey to Latium. A further confusion that entered into the character attributed to Saturn was the frequent identification of Kronos with Chronos, the god of time, who was naturally associated with old age and death. Through the amalgamation of melancholy characteristics with these mythological identities, Saturn acquired a well-defined personality and set of powers: he presided over melancholy complexions, qualities, diseases and organs (like the spleen), as well as over trades connected with the earth, over travel and the command of ships. He was associated with authority and political intelligence in both their good and bad aspects: benign rule, tyranny or intrigue. He was the type of the crafty, envious, secretive, self-contained, miserly person, seldom angry, but long in bearing a grudge, and he was generally inimical to love. In his most maleficent aspect he was associated with dark prisons, drownings and suicide.

4

In the view of Italian Neoplatonists like Ficino, however, who revived the Aristotelian concept of heroic melancholy, Saturn was the planet associated with the highest contemplation (as it had been in Dante's 'Paradiso', though with more emphasis on the contemplation of natural mysteries). He was the planetary patron of scholars, who suffered from melancholy both as a result of their solitary, thoughtful occupations, and as a condition of their genius. The planet's influence was partly to be feared—Ficino's *De vita triplici* contains long sections on dietary, talismanic and other means by which those born under Saturn must try to mitigate its effects[9]—but at the highest level of his mind, the Saturnine man was enjoined to practise the contemplation that was his genius, and to submit himself as completely as he could to Saturn. Saturn could, therefore, be both the cause of illness and, in a higher sense, the cure, and it symbolized the most fundamental contradiction of melancholy itself.

One other tradition must be mentioned because of the influence that it had on Renaissance writing about melancholy: that which viewed passions such as sadness, fear and grief from the standpoint of moral philosophy. The stricter Stoic philosophers had condemned all passions (or 'perturbations') as alien to the truly wise man, an extreme position that more moderate Stoics like Cicero and Seneca could not entirely support. Cicero went to some length in the *Tusculan Disputations*, however, to dispel the Greek notion of the far-reaching mental effects of humoral melancholy, 'just as if the truth were that the mind is influenced by black bile and not in many instances by the stronger power of wrath or fear or pain. . . .'[10] Reason should moderate and govern the passions, an idea that Cicero (contrary to many later writers who were not too much troubled by the contradiction) saw to be somewhat at variance with humoral theory.

In the Middle Ages medical knowledge about the humours and moral notions about the passions, two divergent formulations of experience that writers of the Renaissance were to reunite, developed along different lines. The medical tradition, perpetuated by such physicians as Constantinus Africanus and by the medical school of Salerno, concerned itself mainly with causes, symptoms and cures. At the same time, moralized accounts of the passions, including those associated with melancholy, were included in descriptions of the major sins. Even though the

5

passions of grief and sadness could have a positive value for Christians that they did not have for Stoic philosophers, Christian writing about *tristitia* generally connected it with sinfulness, and eventually associated it with the specific sin of *acedia*. This was originally a spiritual illness that beset monks, hermits and others who had chosen the religious life, afflicting them with weariness of spirit, indifference to their salvation, despair and a tendency to be busy about everything except their proper task. Later the word came to mean sloth and laziness primarily, but it generally retained some of its original meaning.[11]

The process by which *acedia* was reinterpreted and combined with the idea of Saturnian melancholy during the Renaissance can be seen in the visual arts as well as in the verbal ones; it was merely one example of the way in which medieval concepts like the seven deadly sins were combined with new forms taken from classical originals. The authors of *Saturn*, for example, have found sources for several features of Dürer's 'Melencolia I' in medieval representations of Acedia,[12] while Guy de Tervarent has shown that Dürer's engraving was largely inspired in its composition by Giovanni Bellini's painting of Acedia as a brooding figure in a drifting boat. Moreover, Bellini's painting was itself influenced by Saturnian representations, just as his other panels of the sins incorporated appropriate classical motifs.[13] The advantages that Dürer saw in combining a variety of distinct but related formulations and images of melancholy became just as obvious to the writers who dealt with the subject.

Expository Books about Melancholy in the Renaissance

In the sixteenth and seventeenth centuries, melancholy was discussed in a variety of English and Continental books about such overlapping subjects as the humours and temperaments, the nature of man, or manners and behaviour. Since these treatises emphasized medical, ethical or religious problems in various degrees, I have chosen the term 'expository books' (rather than the more usual designation, 'medical books') to describe them. Among the many treatises available, I shall consider a few of those that were written in English or translated into English,[14] because these probably had the widest contemporary influence. What all of these various treatises have in common is that they treat melancholy from a point of view outside literature. Their primary purpose is to convey information rather than to create an imaginative world, even if the images and allusions through which they describe their subject or illustrate it have much in common with those that were current in literary works.

Many of these books had as their aim the transmission and popularization of medical lore, and had few pretensions to artistry or originality even in their presentation and arrangement. Works like Philip Barrough's *Methode of Phisicke* (1583) are merely lists of diseases along with their symptoms and cures, arranged alphabetically or in no particular order, with melancholy as one of the many disparate items. Andrew Boorde's *Breviarie of Health* (1552) represents another genre, the alphabetical medical dictionary, geared (as similar dictionaries of legal and other specialized vocabularies were) to the reader interested in the subject who was not versed in the ancient languages or Arabic. The most popular of all treatises on health in the sixteenth century, Elyot's *Castel of Helth* (1539),[15] is a somewhat random arrangement of topics connected with diseases and their cures, humours and spirits, with occasional moral comments and modifications of the ancient texts to English conditions. The general continuity between such books and the medieval (and therefore classical) medical tradition is illustrated by the similarity to its original of Stephen Batman's version (1582) of the medieval encyclopedia, *De proprietatibus rerum*, and by the popularity of the many sixteenth-century translations of the medieval *Regimen sanitatis Salerni*.

Melancholy was also discussed as one of many subjects in a very different kind of treatise, the philosophic book that was primarily about the nature of man and the governing of the passions, about ethical conduct and social relations. Most of these books did not appear until the end of the sixteenth and the beginning of the seventeenth centuries, at the time that literary writers were also examining the social and ethical implications of melancholy. Pierre Charron's *Of Wisedome* (1606), and Pierre de la Primaudaye's *French Academie* (1594),[16] for example, both of which discussed melancholy, devoted more attention to such social questions as marital and filial obligations or the duties owing to princes and magistrates. Coeffeteau's *Un tableau des passions*

7

humaines (1621) proclaimed its ethical orientation in its title, as did Thomas Wright's *Passions of the Minde in Generall* (1601). It is not surprising, in view of the purposes of such books, that their writers also tended to see the phenomenon of melancholy in its ethical rather than its clinical aspect, or along the lines laid down by Aristotle in his discussion of virtues and by medieval writers about *acedia*, rather than along those laid down by Galen. Charron discussed the feelings of sadness, heaviness and restlessness that were central to melancholy in the following terms:

> Sadness is a languishing feebleness of the spirit, and a kinde of discouragement ingendred by the opinion that wee have of the greatnesse of the evils that afflict us. It is a dangerous enemie to our rest, which presently weakeneth and quelleth our soules, if we take not good heed, and taketh from us the use of reason and discourse, and the meanes whereby to provide for our affaires, and with time it rusteth the soule, it corrupteth the whole man, and brings his vertues a sleepe, even then when he hath most need to keepe them awaked, to withstand that evill which oppresseth them. . . .[17]

In most of these highly moralized treatises sadness acquired much of the meaning of 'accidie', a word that dropped out of the English language in the sixteenth century.[18] Melancholy, discussed as the emotion of sadness or grief, was treated principally as one of the passions, the products of the sensitive ('appetitive') part of the soul that should be controlled by reason.

It followed naturally that works treating the passions and humours primarily from the standpoint of ethical conduct should have stressed the religious, and especially the social and philosophical, cures of sadness and grief. Trust in God, acceptance of the admonitions of friends, realization that the loss that had been suffered was common to all men, and recognition that the goods that had ambitiously been sought were transitory or not worth having—all these were recommended for restoring peace of mind. The principal cure was one that Cicero had discussed in the *Tusculan Disputations*, with added religious overtones: a recognition that excessive grief was against reason, and that it was an impious unwillingness to accept God's law as revealed in nature:

8

Now it [immoderate grief or sadness] is not onely contrary and an enemy unto nature, but God himselfe: for what other is it, but a rash and outragious complaint against the Lord and common law of the whole world, which hath made all things under the Moone changeable and corruptible? If we know this law, why doe we torment ourselves? If we know it not, whereof doe we complaine, but of our owne ignorance, and that we know not that which Nature hath written in all the corners and creatures of the world?[19]

The 'vulgar sort' were to be diverted from the cause and occasion of their sorrow by delightful distractions, which generally included good company, pleasant surroundings and travel, music and plays. But for noble spirits, philosophy must be the remedy against sorrow and melancholy:

. . . disdaining of evils, accounting them not evils, or at leastwise very small and light (though they be great and greivous [sic]) and that they are not worthy the least motion or alteration of our mindes; and that to be sorrie for them, or to complaine of them, is a thing very unjust and ill befitting a man, to teach the Stoickes, the Peripateticks, and the Platonists. This manner of preserving a man from sorrow and melancholike passion is as rare, as it is excellent, and belongs to spirits of the first ranke.[20]

The central idea was that melancholy and grief were caused by our subjective opinion of what was evil, and could therefore be controlled by reason and by a change of attitude: 'Pour en guérir, il faut premièrement oster, ou au moins diminuer l'opinion du mal qui nous afflige. Ce qui nous est bien aisé de faire, puisque cela dépend de nostre opinion.'[21] It was for Hamlet to show that things were not that simple, even for 'spirits of the first rank'.

Between the two poles of approach to the subject of melancholy taken by the philosophical and the purely medical books lay the treatises that dealt more specifically with the workings of the mind and its diseases: Bright's *Treatise of Melancholie* (1586), Huarte's vocational book, *The Examination of Mens Wits* (1590), one section of Laurentius's *Discourse of the Preservation of Sight*

9

(1598), and Lemnius's *Touchstone of Complexions* (1565). The lines of demarcation are somewhat arbitrary, since the ethical content of these books is also very evident; they too insist that reason govern the passions, and they stress the connection between temperance and health. But it was also their purpose to describe rather than merely to advocate patterns of conduct. For that reason they had both a more sympathetic attitude towards melancholy and a more clinical one (regarding it as a disease and not merely a vice), than did the books of a more philosophical cast. Bright's *Treatise*, for example, had a theological aim—to distinguish between humoral melancholy and genuine conscience, and to show the relationship between the two—but in the process of making his distinctions, he described melancholy causes and cures at great length, sympathizing with the sufferings of his friend 'M', for whom the book purported to be written. Lemnius in particular expressed great feeling for melancholics, saying that all who see them 'to be so lamentably fallen from the judgment of right witte and reason'[22] must pity them, and warning that all might fall into the same plight. Wright, probably the most medically minded of the writers primarily interested in ethics and behaviour, was also the most sympathetic towards the melancholic, recognizing melancholy as a universal disease: 'What Maladies grow by cares and heavinesse, many can testifie, and few there bee, which are not subject to some melancholy humour, that often assaulteth them, troubling their minds, and hurting their bodies. . . .'[23] It may have been partly from such hints of identification and sympathy with their subject on the part of some of these writers that Burton created his literary *persona* of the melancholy man dissecting the subject of melancholy and pitying its victims.

The rhetorical position that many of these authors took as their readers' (or patients') counsellors and physicians, helping them to mitigate the dangers of a melancholy temperament or the sufferings entailed by melancholy illness, very largely also determined their view of Aristotelian or heroic melancholy. Many of them included the idea for the sake of completeness, but it was at odds with their most central assumptions about health as the adjustment of physical humours and the acceptance of conventional social roles. Laurentius's picture and valuation of the restless melancholy mind was typical:

This disquieting and distracting of themselves ariseth of the diversitie of matters which they propound and set before themselves, for receiving all maner of formes, and stamping them with the print of dislike; they are constrained often times to change. . . .[24]

Bright included the Aristotelian idea in his *Treatise*,[25] but he specifically condemned the loneliness, restlessness of mind and curiosity that the proponents of heroic melancholy exalted, because he considered them conducive to religious melancholy: the melancholic 'of a sudden falleth into that gulfe of Gods secret counselles . . . and measuring the trueth of such depth of misteries by the shallow modill of his owne wit, is caught & devoured of that which his presumptuous curiositie moved him to attempt to apprehend'.[26] According to Wright, men should seek to live well rather than to pursue 'hidden matters';[27] Boorde thought that curiosity resulted in melancholy madness;[28] and Charron contrasted wisdom with science, calling the latter 'melancholic and presumptuous'.[29] These practical writers were concerned with health and behaviour, with the alleviation of suffering rather than with an exaltation of its value, and with the proper role of man in society, rather than with a critique of that society.

Very different attitudes prevailed among those who exalted Aristotelian melancholy. The authors of *Saturn* have pointed out that the new value put on melancholy by the Florentine Neoplatonic circle was not due to the recovery of Aristotle's text, which had been known and quoted, sometimes even with qualified approval, by medieval writers. What had changed was the value placed on some of the traditional attributes of the melancholy personality: the propensity for lonely study and for tenaciously (or 'curiously') searching into obscure questions.[30] It took a writer like Huarte, therefore, who had a different attitude towards social norms from that expressed in the other expository books, and a theory of genius derived from the 'Tuscan' Neoplatonists, to endorse the Aristotelian view with consistency and enthusiasm. The purpose of his book was to show the circumstances under which the best 'wits' were formed, and the best wits belonged to those who had left the beaten path in order to study nature and penetrate her mysteries:

Wits full of invention are by the *Tuscanes* called goatish.
. . . These never take pleasure in the plains, but ever
delight to walke alone thorow dangerous and high
places, and to approach neere steepe down-fals, for they
will not follow any beaten path, nor go in companie. A
propertie like this, is found in the reasonable soule
when it possesseth a braine well instrumentalized and
tempered, for it never resteth settled in any contemplation, but fareth forth with unquiet, seeking to know
and understand new matters. . . .[31]

Huarte praised not only the temperatures and qualities of melancholy, because they were favourable to the understanding, but
also the experience of suffering that produced those temperaments,[32] and that isolated the sufferer from the common herd.
He was romantic in a way that the medical writers of that or any
other age could not easily be.

Although the expository books did not explore the ambiguities
of melancholy, as Shakespeare and Burton did, there are many
ways in which they were literary, or in which their authors shared
common interests with literary writers. We have already seen
that many of the treatises, though to varying degrees, viewed
their subject morally, stressing such topics as the control of
passions by reason and the necessity of temperance for health.
In discussing such problems, the authors drew on the cultural
tradition of their time, citing Biblical sources and Christian
writers or ancient philosophers as often as medical authorities.
Since subjects like the humours and temperaments touched upon
almost all aspects of life, these books hardly digressed when they
included passages on the nature of man and his place in the
universe, on the praise or dispraise of man and his reason, on the
(usually four or seven) ages of man, or (with a consideration of
bodily temperatures as a starting-point) on the characters of
different national groups.

All of these were favourite literary subjects as well. The vogue
for literary 'characters' at the beginning of the seventeenth
century, for example, can be seen in the portraits of temperamental types in some of the medical books. Laurentius's sketch
of the melancholy man is similar to the characters of Overbury,

Hall or Earle (all of whom included portraits of melancholics and malcontents in their collections of types):

> The melancholike man properly so called . . . is ordin-
> arilie out of heart, alwaies fearfull and trembling, in such
> sort as that he is afraid of every thing, yea and maketh
> himselfe a terrour unto himselfe, as the beast which
> looketh himselfe in a glasse; he would runne away and
> cannot goe, he goeth oftentimes sighing . . . with an
> unseparable sadness, which oftentimes turneth into
> dispayre; he is alwaies disquieted both in bodie and
> spirit, he is subject to watchfulness, which doth consume
> him on the one side: for if he think to make truce with his
> passions by taking some rest, behold so soone as hee
> would shut his eyelids, hee is assayled with a thousand
> vaine visions, and hideous buggards, with fantasticall
> inventions, and dreadfull dreames . . . he cannot live
> with companie. To conclude, hee is become a savadge
> creature haunting the shadowed places, suspicious,
> solitarie, enemie to the Sunne, and one whom nothing
> can please, but onely discontent, which forgeth unto
> itselfe a thousand false and vaine imaginations. . . .[33]

Stylistically, this passage has the features that Morris Croll called typical of the 'character'; the formulaic 'he' is set against syntactic variation and novelty.[34] The melancholic is presented both as a constant type and as one on whose portrayal the author can exercise some inventiveness. This potentially satiric style of characterization also has possibilities for drama, because it equates psychological feelings with observable behaviour by introducing both in the same manner.

The expository authors, like writers who had purely literary aims, often made use of a type of reasoning that was analogical rather than logical, drawing on the traditional correspondences between man and the universe, or between man's body and the body politic. A basic correspondence between the humours and the cosmos had always been inherent in the notion that the primary elements or qualities were common to both, and in the specific correlations that followed, such as the one between earth and melancholy. Other traditional analogies, such as those

between man's reason and the prince or magistrate of a commonwealth, or between reason and a fortified tower, abounded in
these works. Bright's proof of the proposition that the soul is
simple, unmoved and unchanged, even though its effects are
diverse and its instruments corruptible, consisted of a series of
analogies or images drawn from 'art' and nature: the clock whose
motion is always straight though its wheels turn at different
speeds; the varying but unified motions of the planets; the
instrument whose flaws may alter the music but not the nature
of the 'artificer'; and the sun, which may be eclipsed and altered
in its appearance by clouds, but not changed in its nature.[35]
This is a poetic rather than a scientific method; it obviously
resembles the technique of contemporary poems like Donne's
'Love's Growth', which illustrates the idea of increase by a
sequence of natural, cosmological and social analogies.

The physiology of the humours as described in the treatises was
partly metaphorical, just as descriptions of emotions in dramatic works still retained some of the concreteness of their physiological origins.[36] To take a famous example from *Macbeth*,
Malcolm's advice to the grief-stricken Macduff, 'Give sorrow
words. The grief that does not speak/Whispers the o'er fraught
heart and bids it break' (IV, iii, 209–10), is based on the belief
that the heart of a bereaved sufferer who could not unburden
himself by speech was literally oppressed and suffocated by
humours, a phenomenon that Ford dramatized also in the 'silent
griefs which cut the heart-strings' of Calantha at the end of *The
Broken Heart*. The physiological basis of this metaphor is established, for example, by Coeffeteau, who, before dealing with the
virtues of being able to unburden oneself to friends, describes the
suffocated heart that was found in the dissection of a dead
melancholic.[37] In the expository books, such concepts as the
darkening of the mind by black melancholy humour, and the
parallels that were drawn between outer and inner darkness in
explaining the phenomenon of fear, had both a physiological
basis and a connection with a complex of images derived from
the original career of Saturn. The melancholy man was described
as haunting dark places, as being shut up in caves and dens, and
as fleeing the light of the sun.[38] The heart that was oppressed by
gross and heavy melancholy humours was imprisoned, just as
the melancholic himself was.[39] There was no clear line of distinc-

tion between fact and image, or between the state of the melancholic's mind and the landscape that he inhabited or projected. Finally, it was the purpose of several of the treatises to entertain as well as to instruct, and here again the borderline between them and other forms of literature was a narrow one. The *Regimen sanitatis Salerni* recommended Doctor Merryman as one of the healers and preservers of health, and works like Samuel Rowlands's *Democritus, or Doctor Merry-man his Medicines, against Melancholy humours* (1607), a collection of tales, pretended to have a serious purpose by taking this recommendation seriously.[40] The expository books, on the other hand, often included for the entertainment of their readers tales of melancholic delusions—of people who thought they were God, or nothing, or that they were made of glass or butter, or that they could not eat because they were dead, or of the man who thought that he had no head and was cured with a cap of iron, or of the 'Sienois gentleman' who was cured of his dread of flooding the whole town when he urinated by being told that the town was on fire, and that he would be a public benefactor.[41] Walkington's *Optick Glasse of Humors* (1607) went furthest in admitting that its subject matter was primarily the occasion for rhetorical display:

> I am well sure thou wilt here expect . . . vulgar things uttered after a new sort without affection: that I should bee a rich and eloquent merchant of exoticke and new found phrases: that I should intraverse and interlarde my speeches with right Athenian jewells, illuminate the eye of thy understanding with the lustre of Rhetoricall colours. . . . And so farre as each thing is consonant and harmonicall with judgement, I will tender my devoire, to be sutable unto thy scholerlike expectation. . . .[42]

The manner as well as the substance of his Preface expressed Walkington's stylistic pretensions (though perhaps not his lack of 'affectation'). He went on to say that although some people might have preferred him to write on a mythological subject, he had decided to 'mingle my delight with more utilitie, aiming not onely at witte but wisedome'. This too was a double aim that was claimed by many contemporary poets.

While several of the expository treatises had much in common with the literature of the period, they were none the less bound by the necessities of their subject-matter, and by the obligation to transmit various formulations of it. Bright's concentration on the single subject of melancholy, for example, though rich in suggestive imagery, did not enable him to produce a work of any literary coherence; he felt compelled to include material that was not always consistent, or that was at odds with his point of view, without any articulated awareness of such contradictions. The writers who were to treat melancholy as a literary subject would be bound not so much by their sources as by different necessities— those growing out of their vision of the world and the form in which they were presenting it.

Two

Literary Uses of Melancholy

Melancholy Character Types: from Life to Literature

The expository books showed their affinity with literature by describing melancholy in terms of paradigms of social behaviour. Satirists and dramatists filled out the paradigms, embodying the stereotyped, antisocial postures of the melancholic in conventional costumes, gestures and language. The contemplativeness of the melancholy temperament received formal expression in the solitary meditations of the stage melancholic; delusions and madness in a particular kind of visionary speech; calculation and shrewdness in the machinations of the villainous plotter; discontent in the justified or unjustified alienation of the satirist or revenger. Since so much melancholy literature was limited to the manipulation of stereotyped figures, and since even the best of it made use of the familiar attributes (if only to combine them in new ways or to demonstrate their inadequacies), it is worth looking briefly at the actual conditions from which the literary 'malcontent' type arose.

The melancholy figures which became common on the Elizabethan stage appear to have been based originally on the disaffected or discontented people who made their presence felt in London towards the end of the sixteenth century. Such people were labelled as melancholy, or malcontents, or 'melancholy malcontents'. The melancholy malcontent took a stand against the world which was not an essential part of melancholy in its medical sense: he was primarily one who was discontented, sometimes to the point of mutiny and rebellion, with the existing social and political order. The earliest instances of the word 'malcontent' cited in the *OED* show its original connection with the almost interchangeable word 'rebel'; the citation from the 1587 edition of Holinshed's *Chronicles*, for example, contains a significant change from an earlier version: 'The onelie place wherein all the mal-contents [ed. 1577 Rebels] had their refuge.' The substitution probably indicates a new recognition of the complex subjective aspect of rebellion. Shades of opinion were now seen to be almost as important as outright political action, because the one led easily to the other. Furthermore, other examples in the *OED* show that dissatisfaction with self, with family authority, and with political authority were seen to be intimately connected; all were subsumed in the word 'malcontent'.

Politically, the malcontent was often associated with the two extremes of religious opinion, Puritanism and Catholicism. In *The Metamorphosis of Ajax* (1596), for example, Sir John Harington, describing a dream in which he defended two gentlemen against the charge of being malcontents, distinguished between legitimate discontentedness, caused by bereavement or other sorrows, and political disaffection:

> . . . but understanding it as I know you would be understood, that they be *Mal-content* as ill affected to their Prince, I dare say you lye in plaine English. . . . when you would make Mal-contents then your pollicie gives out first that they be so. Oh take heed of such a one, he is a dangerous man. A Puritan, why so? He will not sweare nor ride on a Sunday, then he wishes to[o] well to the Scottish Church, note him in your tables. An other is a Papist. How know you? He said he hoped his grandfathers soule was saved.[1]

As this quotation shows, a malcontent was defined not only by his own activities and attitudes, but also by the degree of rigour with which his society demanded conformity, and the extent to which self-serving individuals were willing to aggravate fears of dissent. The more exacting criteria of political obedience against which the malcontent's activities came to be measured now included religious conformity, and therefore a more deep-rooted attitude towards life than had hitherto been involved in political obedience.

The court, as the centre of patronage and success, was also the focus of melancholy or malcontentedness among those who were unable or unwilling to achieve the success it offered. A memoir by Dudley North, written in 1637–9, but describing events of the early century, shows that the loss of court employment, together with other causes, could induce a lifelong melancholy:

> . . . the losse of the brave Prince Henry, on whom I had laid my grounds, with much sicknesse soon after casting me down, and increasing my disease, I became unable to make use either of my naturall parts, or time and expence bestowed in Court; thoughts beget melancholy, and that, thoughts alternatively.[2]

For others, the competition for court patronage, as well as the atmosphere of political intrigue, led to a less introspective malcontentedness, as the pamphlet, *Leycester's Commonwealth* (1584), shows:

> For now [as opposed to the first years of Elizabeth's reign], there are so many suspitious every where for this thing and for that: as we cannot tell whom to trust. So many melancholique in the Court, that seeme malecontented: so many complaining or suing for their friends, that are in trouble . . . so many tales brought us of this or that danger, of this man suspected, of that man sent up, and such like unpleasant and unsavery stuff. . . .[3]

In 1600 a celebrated political malcontent who was soon to become actively rebellious, the Earl of Essex, was described by Camden as deliberately surrounding himself with other malcontented types:

> The Earl of Essex is now returned to London and it is much noted how his doors are set open to all comers. Sir Gelly Merrick, his steward, entertaineth at his table many captains, men of broken fortunes, discontented persons, and such as saucily use their tongues in railing against all men.[4]

The 'men of broken fortunes' who were political rebels, railers or both, would be represented on the stage by such figures as Webster's Flamineo and Bosola.

The court was also the centre of literary patronage, and some of the most discontented figures of the period were unappreciated writers. Young men of letters, caught between the decay of the patronage system and inadequately developed commercial publishing, found it especially difficult at this time to make a living, and there was a general surplus (described by Bacon in a letter to James I) of well-educated young people without occupational opportunities.[5] Much of Nashe's *Pierce Pennilesse* (1592), for example, concerns his misery and sense of neglect amid the new-rich and the social upheavals of the period, feelings shared by most of the 'university wits':

> I cald to minde a Cobler, that was worth five hundred pound, an Hostler that had built a goodly Inne, & might dispende fortie pound yerely by his Land . . . and have I more wit than all these (thought I to my selfe)? Am I better favoured? and yet am I a begger? What is the cause?[6]

Nashe was none the less absolutely unsympathetic to what he considered to be the true malcontent. This was a dangerous type in his view, as well as a poseur and an upstart:

> Some thinke to be counted rare Politicians and States-men, by being solitary: as who would say, I am a wise man, a brave man, *Secreta mea mihi: Frustra sapit qui sibi non sapit*; and there is no man worthy of my companie or friendship: when, although he goes ungartered like a malecontent Cutpursse, and weares his hat over his eies like one of the cursed crue, yet cannot his stabing dagger, or his nittie love-lock, keep him out of the legend of fantastical cockscombs.[7]

What distinguishes the two kinds of discontent, one presented subjectively and the other with hostility, is a shift in social attitude, which views the 'malcontent's' behaviour as unwarranted, and as false theatricality. The malcontent's manner, moreover, is inappropriate to his protest. Though hungry, he tries to 'make his backe a certaine kind of brokerly Gentleman', and he goes to the eighteenpence ordinaries in order to be seen with courtiers, obviously envying and emulating what he pretends to disdain.

He even has the temerity to take on a superior melancholy pose, and Nashe asks whether it isn't 'pitiful' that such a fellow, who hardly has enough to eat,

> should take uppe a scornfull melancholy in his gate and countenance, and talke as though our common welth were but a mockery of government, and our Maiestrates fooles, who wronged him in not looking into his deserts, not imploying him in State matters, and that, if more regard were not had of him very shortly, the whole Realme would have a misse of him, & he would go (I mary would he) where he should be more accounted of?[8]

The kind of melancholy that Nashe condemns is not only wilfully 'taken up' in such external manifestations as gait and countenance, but it is also childishly and petulantly self-regarding, implying superiority to one's surroundings through an unwillingness to come to terms with them. The same attitude towards the malcontent is expressed in Robert Greene's autobiographical 'Repentance' (1592), where the author ridicules himself for his youthful protest, his stylized pose of superiority, and his disdain (dispelled with the first sign of success) for the society that seemed to have no place for him:

> At my return into England, I ruffeled out in my silks, in the habit of *Malcontent*, and seemed so discontent, that no place would please me to abide in, nor no vocation cause mee to stay my selfe in: but after I had by degrees proceeded Maister of Arts, I left the Universitie and away to London, where ... I became an Author of Playes, and a penner of Love Pamphlets, so that I soone grew famous in that qualitie. ...[9]

Sketches like those of Nashe and Greene depicting the affected style of a malcontent type who was a feature of the life of their time point clearly to the more explicitly literary or fictional treatments of such types in satire and comedy.

Melancholy Types in Satire and Comedy

The evolution of melancholy and malcontent types in literature, the portraiture of stylized and predictable figures who expressed unhappiness, alienation or rebellion, was the work of writers who depicted the malcontent as the butt of satire, of comedy, or as the subject for usually satirical 'characters'. These genres tended to give formal expression and imaginative coherence to social values that were seen as reasonable and normative; they shared, in other words, the assumptions behind the more casual imagery of the expository books. Although, as we shall see, there was some differentiation among malcontent types like the traveller or political schemer, and melancholy ones like the scholar (who could also be malcontent), or the lover, they all assumed the same visible style—a style that was closely linked with representations of melancholy.

The malcontent was sombre in expression and dressed in black, sometimes sumptuously and sometimes carelessly. His arms were often folded (or 'wreathed'), and his eyes cast down on the ground with a hat pulled over them. As Edward Guilpin described this last mannerism in his satire, *Skialetheia* (1598): 'And if he be so mad to walke the streetes,/To his sights life, his hat becomes a toombe.'[10] This could be the pose of love-melancholy also, or of other kinds of grief. A portrait of Donne painted in 1595, with an inscription that identifies it as the portrait of a love-melancholic, shows the poet dressed in black, with hat and folded arms.[11] Malcontent portraiture was similar to the emblematic treatment of Melancholy as an abstraction, and the two clearly tended to overlap. John Willis's *Art of Memory*, for example, which uses the emblems of Peacham and Alciati as mnemonic devices, suggests that Melancholy be remembered as 'a man very sad, who having his armes wreathed up, and his hat pulled downe in his eyes, goeth up and down in a discontented manner'.[12]

Some distinctions among malcontent types seem to be justified, despite the fact (which has been recognized by the scholars who have tried to find and establish such categories) that they tended to overlap in the social scene, as well as in literature.[13] The division of malcontents into recognizable types became a feature of some satires, however, whose bite consisted precisely in the contrast

22

they drew between the facility of their distinctions and the malcontent's claims to individuality and profundity. Guilpin's *Skialetheia*, for example, contains two portraits of malcontents, both of whom are depicted as drawing attention to themselves by a portentous style that is supposed to defy the easy identifications that Guilpin makes:

> But see yonder,
> One like the unfrequented Theater
> Walkes in dark silence, and vast solitude,
> Suited to those black fancies which intrude,
> Upon possession of his troubled breast:
> But for blacks sake he would look like a jeast,
> For hee's cleane out of fashion: what he?
> I think the *Genius* of antiquitie,
> Come to complaine of our varietie,
> Of tickle fashions: then you jest I see.
> Would you needs know? he is a malecontent:
> A Papist? no, nor yet a Protestant,
> But a discarded intelligencer. . . .

(sig. D₆r)

William Rankins's *Seven Satires* (1598) organizes the foibles and villainies of men according to planetary influences connected with the days of the week, the Saturnian types being Machiavellian plotters and atheistic villains.[14] Robert Anton made even more exact distinctions later in his *Philosophers Satyrs* (1616), also organized according to planetary influences, in which he isolates several Saturnian types: plotting revengers, discontented scholars, travellers ('Italionated *antick shapes*') and those discontented figures (sometimes travellers) who thought that they were suited for affairs of state, while their 'planetary' irrationality was exactly what disqualified them.[15]

The traveller, a type of which Jaques is called an example by Rosalind in *As You Like It* (IV, i, 19–34), was a young man who had done a kind of educational grand tour on the Continent. He returned to England with smatterings of foreign culture, languages (and, his detractors said, foreign vices), and he was dissatisfied with everything that he saw in his own country. Though he was ridiculed especially for his foreign mannerisms, his attitude could merge with that of two other stock figures. Because in some

versions he was depicted as having been contaminated by Catholicism, and therefore by subversive tendencies, he could become
associated with the political malcontent or plotter,[16] and because
he sometimes complained of his lack of suitable employment, his
portrait could be conflated with that of the conceited young man
whose merits were not properly appreciated by the world. We
have seen that Greene's malcontent phase took place after his
return to England from abroad.

The malcontent type that Nashe and Greene outlined was
given a voice in satiric vignettes like Marston's sketch of the
traveller, Bruto:

> And now he sighs, 'O thou corrupted age,
> Which slight regardst men of sound carriage!
> Virtue, knowledge, fly to heaven again,
> Deign not mong these ungrateful sots remain.
> Well, some tongues I know, some countries I have seen,
> And yet these oily snails respectless been
> Of my good parts.'[17]

Marston makes Bruto's lamentations an expression of affected
gravity and disdain, exaggerating the contrast between the
abstractions that Bruto invokes (virtue, knowledge) and his
real self-regard. Skilful versification, the lengthened syllables
of 'oily snails', for example, and the irregular monosyllabic
emphasis on 'of my good parts' (especially on the 'my') create a
voice expressing comically exaggerated disdain and conceit.
Since Marston is never too confident of his irony in the satires,
however, he intersperses direct comments and insulting epithets
(like 'O worthless puffy slave!') to clarify his position about the
malcontent traveller. Bruto is given an amalgam of packaged
attributes—his complaints about the 'age' are the stock-in-trade
of the malcontent, who, as Hall pointed out in his character of the
type, is a praiser of the past—and in the end, despite his delusions
of uniqueness, his style fails to correspond to any underlying reality:

> What art thou but black clothes? Sad Bruto, say,
> Art any thing but only sad array?
>
> (*CS*, II, 147–8)

Two other melancholy types were particularly important in
the literature of the period, the love-melancholic and the scholar.

The love-melancholic had the oldest literary history of all these stock figures, since his style and attributes were part of the convention of medieval courtly love. He was in some ways not a typical melancholic, because his condition was neither humoral nor 'causeless', but easily cured by obtaining the object of his desire.[18] Although the feelings connected with rejected love, seriously explored, were central to the Petrarchan conventions of so many Renaissance love lyrics, the male love-melancholic on the stage was almost always (until later plays, like Ford's) a figure of fun. Only women were invested with genuine pathos in that role; men were made to express, through their standardized costumes and the patterned ways in which they behaved, a certain amount of self-indulgence. While characters like Viola in *Twelfth Night* could simply sigh and pine and drop hints about their pains, those like Romeo before his meeting with Juliet (I, i, 138–61), Armado in *Love's Labour's Lost* (I, i, 233–7), or Valentine in *Two Gentlemen of Verona* (II, i, 15–28) behaved in the stylized manner that had become customary for the part, and that borrowed features from the style of the malcontent:

Valentine Why, how know you that I am in love?
Speed Marry, by these special marks: first, you have learn'd, like Sir Proteus, to wreath your arms like a malcontent; to relish a love-song, like a robin redbreast; to walk alone, like one that had the pestilence; to sigh, like a schoolboy that had lost his ABC; to weep, like a young wench that had buried her grandam; to fast, like one that takes diet; to watch, like one that fears robbing; to speak puling, like a beggar at Hallowmas.
(II, i, 15–25)

The externally visible symptoms of the condition were what made it so ludicrous and so easily reducible to stock similes; as Speed tells Valentine (whose name to an extent defines the limitations of his role): 'not an eye that sees you but is a physician to comment on your malady' (II, i, 35–6).

The love-melancholic was unconscious of his appearance or too much absorbed in it, either preening himself and paying extraordinary attention to his beard and clothes, as Benedick does when he ruefully and self-consciously begins to play the part of the lover in *Much Ado About Nothing*, or going around ungartered, slovenly and generally distracted, as Valentine and Proteus are described as doing at the beginning of *Two Gentlemen of Verona* (II, i, 63–9). Other attributes and postures were derived from the lover of the courtly-love tradition: sighing, pallor, an inability to eat or sleep. Because the medieval lover or Renaissance sonneteer had voiced his complaints in poetry, the love-melancholic on the stage was ridiculed for his penchant for literature; the writing of sonnets, as in the case of the king and courtiers in *Love's Labour's Lost* or of Matthew in *Every Man in his Humour*, or the love of poetry or melancholy love songs were his inevitable and, therefore, comic marks.[19]

The figure of the scholar was the product of two traditions linking melancholy with studious activity. One, which we have already touched upon, was the Aristotelian notion that melancholy and philosophic contemplation were linked, and the accompanying astrological idea, of which much was made in the Renaissance, of the artist or the man of genius as 'born under Saturn'. Even artists who appeared to be fairly sanguine, like Raphael, were associated with Saturn, while others, like Michelangelo, exploited the affinity in their work.[20] The other tradition postulated a reciprocal connection between studious activity and the melancholy temperament in its undesirable, Galenic sense. Melancholy men were thought to be naturally inclined to solitary study, while such mental concentration, if unrelieved by exercise, 'wasted' the vital spirits that mediated between body and soul. As Bright explained in his *Treatise*:

> Of actions of the minde, over vehement studies, and sadde passions, do alter good nourishmentes into a melancholicke qualitie; by wasting the pure Spirites, and the subtillest parte of the blood: and thereby leaving the rest grosse and thicke (pp. 30–1).

The traditional studiousness of the melancholy man ('Exceeding studious, ever solitary,/Inclining pensive still to be, and musing . . . .'[21]) was conventionalized on the stage in much the same manner as the portraits of other melancholy types. The most distinctive mark of the studious stage-melancholic was that he entered reading a book, a gesture that could be showily theatrical or genuinely expressive (or, in a few of the best examples, both). The book that he was reading was generally related to the subject of his preoccupations. Dowsecer's affected ruminations about the decay of the world in Chapman's *An Humourous Day's Mirth* (1597), for example, are touched off by his reading of Cicero (Sc. vii),[22] while tragic instances of this kind of short-hand identification of the broodings of melancholics became very common: the reflections of Marston's Antonio in *Antonio's Revenge* (1600) about the inadequacy of Stoic philosophy are set off by his copy of Seneca (II, ii);[23] the meditations on hell-fire of Webster's guilty Cardinal in *The Duchess of Malfi* (1614) are prompted by the theological tract which he enters reading, and which, as a prop, identifies him as melancholy even before his soliloquy begins (V, v, 1–7);[24] Hamlet's satiric bent is expressed by his entrance (II, ii, 168) with a volume that has been tentatively identified as Juvenal's Tenth Satire or Erasmus's *Praise of Folly*.[25] The traditional affinity between melancholy and scholarship could make the melancholic useful as a focus for contemporary intellectual problems; this was equally true of tragic figures like Hamlet or of comic ones like Marston's Lampatho Doria in *What You Will* (1601).

Like satiric vignettes and character sketches, comedy ridiculed stock melancholy figures; it did so by making their style appear mechanical, unreasonable and inappropriate. Jonson's comedies are important in this connection, because they are articulate both about what constitutes a 'humour' and about the function of comedy. Jonson regarded melancholy both as an affectation and an affection, part of the lower function of the mind that comedy should hold up to ridicule and that reason should control. The idea is embodied in the structure of his masque, *Hymenaei* (1606), in which the four humours and the affections comprise the unruly 'antimasque' that is overcome by Reason. In his satiric comedies the same attitude is expressed by reasonable spokesmen. Melancholy for Jonson is a 'humour' in his own sense of the term, 'a gentleman-like monster, bred in the speciall gallantry of our time, by affectation; and fed by folly'.[26] The old physiological humours were in the background, but, because humoral imbalance had always been thought of as giving rise to different temperaments, the word 'humour' came to denote for Jonson dominant traits of characters whose mechanical compulsiveness or affectations made them suitable as satiric or comic types.[27]

Jonson's humours form part of his comic picture of a world of follies. Since they are viewed in the Stoic way as a kind of flux that should be subordinate to the stability of reason, they are analogous to the motley parade of humanity in the satiric landscape, dispassionately viewed by the reasonable satirist.[28] Images expressing such a view of the humours can be found, for example, in *Cynthia's Revels* (1601):

> Oh how despised and base a thing is man,
> If he not strive t'erect his groveling thoughts
> Above the straine of flesh! But how more cheape
> When, even his best and understanding part,
> (The crowne, and strength of all his faculties)
> Floates like a dead and drown'd bodie; on the streame
> Of vulgar humour, mixt with commonst dregs?
>
> (I, v, 33–9)

In the same play, after Mercury and Crites conspire to put the other characters 'out of humour', Mercury says:

> And good men, like the sea, should still maintaine
> Their noble taste, in midst of all fresh humours,
> That flow about them, to corrupt their streames,
> Bearing no season, much lesse salt of goodness.
>
> (V, i, 13–16)

Men's reason and 'goodness' should keep them from drowning in the flux that the humours represent.

The humours that the satirist must try to eliminate, by squeezing them as one would a sponge, or by soaking them up as a dry crust soaks up moisture,[29] retain, through this kind of imagery, their original connection with bodily fluids, while Jonson extends their range of meaning to include a variety of affectations and behavioural quirks that violate reasonable norms. The artificial poses of humour characters, including melancholy ones, are often contrasted with more real concerns and attributes. Since melancholy, frequently a product of idleness and exacerbated by it, was a fashionable courtly ailment,[30] Stephen, the country gull in *Every Man in his Humour* (1598), desires it as an attribute of gentlemanliness. His clumsiness at it, and the innocence with which he considers the external features of the condition essential to it ('Have you a stoole there, to be melancholy upon?' III, i,

100), are in keeping with his comic eagerness to enter into what should properly be a misery to be avoided. The whole pose is contrasted with the true melancholy he feels at being laughed at (I, ii, 79–80), and the real distemper that he displays, ready to 'eate the very hilts for anger!' (III, i, 181–2) when he discovers that he has been cheated.

The artificial styles of the melancholy humour characters are distorted as well as unreal. When Amorphous, the traveller in *Cynthia's Revels*, is described as 'one so made out of the mixture and shred of formes, that himselfe is truly deform'd' (II, ii, 85–7), the judgment against him is aesthetic as well as moral. His style is not consistent within itself, and in a play that begins (as *Every Man out of his Humour* does also) with the presentation of 'characters', his is not a good 'character', consonant with the laws of reason and artistry that the satiric spokesman, Crites, represents. In even so genial a comedy as *Every Man in his Humour*, moral laws of reason and aesthetic criteria are analogous;[31] therefore the pretensions of the would-be gentleman, Stephen, are analogous to the stolen verses of the 'melancholy' poet, Matthew. This is a parallel that the two longest speeches of Kno'well Senior in the original version of the play, one on true gentlemanliness and one on true poetry, made very clear. In the satiric comedies, the well-temperedness of the satirists is a metaphor for the reason and harmony that they project; Crites in *Cynthia's Revels* is described as a man in whom the four humours are perfectly mingled (Induction, 88–91), and in *The Poetaster* (1601), Jonson expressly repudiates the connection between the satirist and melancholy: 'This (like Joves thunder) shall their pride controule;/ "The honest Satyre hath the happiest soule" ' (V, iii, 374–5).

While Jonson's predilection was for making his satirists images of temperamental balance, he appears to have acknowledged, in *Every Man out of his Humour* (1599), the problem of reconciling such harmony with the angry feelings that had to be expressed in satire. In that play he splits the personality of his satirist. Asper, a 'free spirit . . . constant in reproofe', becomes, for the purpose of lashing the humours of others during the course of the play, the malcontent Macilente, a travelled scholar 'who (wanting that place in the worlds account, which he thinks his merit capable of) falls into such an envious apoplexie, with which his judgement is so dazzled, and distasted, that he grows violently

impatient of any opposite happiness in another'.[32] The melancholic's propensity to see evil in the world, to be 'envious and jealous,
apt to take occasions in worse part',[33] were similar to satiric
feelings, and Macilente simply acts out on the stage the affinity
of the malcontent for satiric expression that the character-writers
described discursively: 'His life is a perpetual satyr, and he is still
girding the age's vanity, when this very anger shows that he too
much esteems it.'[34] Satire itself could therefore be a 'humour', as
the character of the bad satirist, Carlo Buffone, the 'scurrilous,
and prophane Jester' and irresponsible railer in the same play,
shows, and as Macilente demonstrates when, having purged his
own envious humour by stripping the humours of others, he can
turn back into Asper.

For other playwrights, the satirist was often a malcontent and
the butt of comedy. While Macilente's envy has real follies and
crimes to work on, satirists could also be mocked by being mis-
placed in comic worlds. The most famous example of such a
figure is Jaques in *As You Like It* (1599), whose name expresses
the melancholy dregs and excrement that the Duke accuses him
of disgorging into the world in his satire (II, vii, 64–9). In accordance with the melancholy humour (in both the medical and
Jonsonian senses) that defines him, he is a solitary character,
fleeing the companionship even of the forest exiles who have
themselves been outcast from society, and thereby demonstrating
the inflexibility of a role that requires withdrawal and solitude
for melancholy, antisocial meditations. Moreover, he tries to
invest the role of the licensed jester, of the mocker of other
people's pretensions, with the utterly incompatible self-assertions
and rhythms of heroic speech:

> Invest me in my motley; give me leave
> To speak my mind, and I will through and through
> Cleanse the foul body of th'infected world,
> If they will patiently receive my medicine.
>
> (II, vii, 58–61)

Jaques' complaints and meditations, like those of other melancholy satirists who are mocked in comedies, appear ridiculous
not only because of their incongruous grandeur, but also because
of their mechanicalness. In Marston's *What You Will* a stock
meditation on the misery of man by the melancholy scholar,

Lampatho Doria, is maliciously set in motion, like the actions of a puppet or a trained dog, by the Epicurean scholar, Quadratus:

> *Quadratus* What, art melancholy *Lampe*? Ile feede thy humour, Ile give thee reason straight to hang thy selfe: Mark't, mark't: In heavens handiwork theirs naught—Beleeve it.
> *Lampatho* In heavens handiwork ther's naught
> None more vile, accursed, reprobate to blisse
> Then man, and mong men a scholler most. . . .
>
> (pp. 256–7)[35]

Jaques' famous meditation on the seven ages of man is really the same kind of set speech or expression of a 'humour', triggered off accidentally by a metaphor of the Duke's:

> *Duke S* Thou seest we are not all alone unhappy:
> This wide and universal theatre
> Presents more woeful pageants than the scene
> Wherein we play in.
> *Jaques* All the world's a stage. . . . (etc.)
>
> (II, vii, 136–9)

Jaques' pretensions are, therefore, contradicted by the mechanical nature of his responses; his elaborate denial of stereotyped attributes only makes us aware of the extent to which he is a stock theatrical figure:

> I have neither the scholar's melancholy, which is emulation; nor the musician's, which is fantastical; nor the courtier's, which is proud; nor the lawyer's, which is politic; nor the lady's, which is nice; nor the lover's, which is all these; but it is a melancholy of mine own, compounded of many simples, extracted from many objects, and indeed, the sundry contemplation of my travels; in which my often rumination wraps me in a most humorous sadness (IV, i, 10–18).

The gap between his insistence on an heroic melancholy individuality and the roles that are actually available to him is emphasized by the labels given him by other characters: 'Monsieur Melancholy', 'a traveller!' (III, ii, 276; IV, i, 19). Where Jaques expresses his desire to play the fool on his own terms, preserving

his identity and wisdom behind his motley, the Duke mildly
suggests that the fool's role may be definitive (II, vii, 42–9).

Comically treated, the licensed satirist is degraded merely by
being allowed to vent his spleen or deplore the 'age' by the
King or Duke who represents the power of society in the play's
world. Such a satirist has only one mode (the malcontent's vein)
in which to express himself, while the court demonstrates its
beneficence by the very act of permitting or even encouraging
criticism of itself. The malcontent voice, which presupposes
some radical evil, is therefore bound to sound excessive and
mechanical—it is labelled and reduced, even by being praised—
as it is turned into entertainment, consonant with the mood of the
play, by generous authority figures. In Chapman's *An Humourous
Day's Mirth*, for example, the King praises the melancholy
Dowsecer's laments ('no . . . humour . . . but perfit judgement',
Sc. vii, 87), defending Dowsecer's sanity and integrity by calling
him a man 'rarely learned, and nothing lunatic/As men suppose,/
But hateth company and worldly trash . . . and his rare humour
come we now to hear' (Sc. vii, 15–22). Dowsecer's complaints
about fashions, the falseness of women, the affectations of travellers and courtiers, become a kind of show, and their predicta-
bility indicates their limitation as a 'humour', even if a 'rare one'.
Although Duke Senior in *As You Like It* is critical of unbridled
satire, his praise of the educational or entertainment value to be
derived from Jaques' malcontentedness—'I love to cope him
in these sullen fits,/For then he's full of matter' (II, i, 67–8)—
functions in the same way.

The melancholy meditation could be reduced to comic pro-
portions in other ways besides by simply being given, in its aggressive forms, licence to display itself. It could be wordy and windy
nonsense in the first place, like Dowsecer's speech about the
decay of the world:

> For acorns now [no more] are in request,
> But [when] the oak's poor fruit did nourish men,
> Men were like oaks of body, tough, and strong;
> Men were like giants, then, but pigmies now. . . .
>
> (Sc. vii, 82–5)

Such a speech is facile in its elaboration of commonplaces that
have nothing to do with the action of the play. Even more

obviously, characters who are defined as fools or low-comic types could be made to parody the style of more serious malcontents. In *An Humourous Day's Mirth*, Labesha, like Dowsecer, enters reading a book, quoting Latin, and expatiating on life in terms that are even more ridiculously empty and meaninglessly elaborated than Dowsecer's:

> *Felix quem faciunt aliena pericula cautum.* O silly state of
> things, for things they be that cause this silly state.
> And what is a thing? A bauble, a toy, that stands men
> in small stead. . . (Sc. xii, 35–8).

In *As You Like It*, Jaques himself reports the Fool's meditation on time, which parodies his own manner:

> 'It is ten o'clock:
> Thus may we see,' quoth he, 'how the world wags:
> 'Tis but an hour ago since it was nine,
> And after one hour more 'twill be eleven;
> And so from hour to hour we ripe and ripe,
> And then from hour to hour we rot and rot
> And thereby hangs a tale.'
>
> (II, vii, 22–8)

Jaques' delighted amazement that a fool can be so 'deep contemplative' that he can 'rail on Lady Fortune in good terms,/ In good set terms—and yet a motley fool' (II, vii, 16–17), points, of course, not to the wisdom of the fool, as Jaques suggests, but to the foolishness of stylized melancholy railing in 'good set terms'.

The main source of comedy connected with the melancholic or malcontent, however, was the one that Jonson exploited in characters like Stephen and Matthew; it lay in the lack of correspondence between the melancholy style and the feelings that it purported to express. The most obvious device to reveal the artificiality of the style was to show it as one that was taught or wilfully assumed: 'I'll be very melancholique, i' faith', says Sir John Daw in *Epicœne*, and he has to be instructed by his mocking companions on how to proceed from there, that he must 'walke alone' and use similes like 'melancholique as a dog' (II, iv, 139–48). The rigidity and falseness of the pose was exposed by the ease

33

with which it could be cured or cast aside, as (on the lowest level) Labesha's melancholy is when he finds a spice cake, cream and a spoon. Dowsecer abruptly drops his misogyny and satire the moment he sees Martia's picture, and Marston's Lampatho Doria renounces his scholarly melancholy, as Quadratus has planned that he should, when he meets the courtesan, Meletza. In Dowsecer, we are told, the heat of vanity is expelled by the heat of love, while Lampatho is really the happy fool whose ignorance he has pretended to envy because it is supposedly so opposite to his own burdensome state:

> *Quadratus* Why now could I eate thee, thou doost please mine appetite. . . . God made thee a good foole, and happy and ignorant, and amarous, and riche, and fraile, and a Satyrist, and an *Essayest*, and sleepy, and proud, and indeed a foole . . . (p. 279).

Presented in this way, the melancholy role is a rigid and unnatural one, with little relationship to real desires and aptitudes.

The mere existence of a melancholy style, moreover, had comic possibilities of the kind recently alluded to by an American song-writer: 'I feel that if a person can't communicate, the least he can do is shut up.'[36] Jaques is ridiculed for the avidity with which he seeks food for his gloomy thoughts and for the enjoyment with which he presents them. Since melancholy reflections constitute the essence of his limited role, they paradoxically make him 'merry' by sustaining his dramatic existence. When he boasts that he can 'suck melancholy out of a song, as a weasel sucks eggs' (II, iv, 12–13), his metaphor is entirely accurate; he has become skilful at staying alive even in a world that offers him little food. While the melancholy state is a solitary, painful and undesirable one, the cultivation of style implies everything opposite: the desire to communicate, conscious intention in the choice of costumes, gestures or language, and a certain energy of self-presentation. It is this contradiction that comic writers exploited in their creation of melancholy types.

Melancholy Types in Tragedy

Melancholy malcontents in tragedy could be either the active plotters of villainous deeds or the victims of such plotting; far apart as these roles seem, each enacts one aspect, as we shall see, of the melancholic's affinity for satiric expression. The possibility of villainy had always been connected with melancholy through the sinister personality and influence of Saturn, and through the tenacious, plotting, revengeful nature that was attributed to melancholy types:

> I confesse this, that oftentimes the melancholicke man by his contemplative facultie by his assiduitie of sad and serious meditation is a brocher of dangerous machiavellisme, an inventor of strategems, quirks and pollicies. . . .[37]

Destructive shrewdness animates characters like Aaron in *Titus Andronicus* (1594), who is born under Saturn but actually derives great enjoyment from his villainies, or Don John, the Saturnian villain who tries to turn *Much Ado About Nothing* into a tragedy, or the dimly-sketched figure of the melancholy villain Lazarotto in *The First Part of Hieronimo* (1605):

> A melancholy, discontented courtier,
> Whose famish'd jaws look like the chap of death;
> Upon whose eyebrows hangs damnation;
> Whose hands are wash'd in rape, and murders bold.
>
> (I, i, 114–17)[38]

Disenchantment with the world and disillusionment over their failure in it are understood to make such characters amenable to any kind of villainy, and often their past is alluded to only in the vaguest way to provide the clue to their dramatic function. When the melancholy villain places himself at the disposal of a more powerful and established evil person whose commands he executes, he plays the part of the 'tool villain'[39] that Bosola becomes for Ferdinand in *The Duchess of Malfi* or that Vindice pretends to be when he wants to ingratiate himself with the Duke's heir, Lussurioso, in *The Revenger's Tragedy* (1606).

The potentiality for villainy in dramatic malcontents often developed from their function as satirists who gave expression to the evil in the world around them. The ambiguity of the satirist's role, which he needed all of his rhetorical ingenuity to control in formal satire, grew out of the fact that he necessarily created the vision of evil that he described, even if he was successful in conveying the illusion of objectively rendered pictures. Dramatists like Marston, Tourneur and Webster, for whom the malcontent character often took over a satirist's function, could be more open in suggesting the sources of the satiric vision than formal satirists could, and the degree to which the malcontent was actually responsible for the evil with which he was obsessed determined the extent of his villainy.

In *The Revenger's Tragedy*, for example, Vindice's moral judgments on the court, delivered at the outset, are largely justified by the intrigues, incest, rape and subversion of justice that the scenes following his opening speech acquaint us with in an almost programmatic way. But there is a fine line that he frequently oversteps between the observer of action or moralizer upon it, and the instigator of scenes that will prove his points or pictorialize them. The 'unsunned lodge, wherein 'tis night at noon', for example (III, v, 18–19),[40] where he arranges the amorous interview between the Duke and the 'country lady', is a kind of emblem that he stages for the unnatural overturning of time—youth and lustful age, daylight and night—that the play's 'revels' exemplify also. Examples could be multiplied: the temptation to which his mother succumbs, thereby illustrating the evil of the 'time', is one that Vindice puts her to himself, playing the part of the tempter or bad angel. The evil that he sees is not entirely the product of his imagination, but he brings it into relief by his manipulations.

This point about the malcontent satirist is made even more clearly by the more obviously villainous Flamineo in Webster's *The White Devil* (1612). His obscene remarks about the lovemaking of his sister and Brachiano at the beginning of the play colour a scene that he creates himself, both by his comments on its moral value and by his preceding directions to the principals. When Vittoria and Brachiano speak in order to reveal their passion or their murderous intentions towards Isabella and Camillo, they amply justify his satirical cynicism about human affairs:

> Excellent devil.
> She hath taught him in a dream
> To make away his duchess and her husband.
>
> (I, ii, 256–8)

But it is Flamineo himself who translates their wishes into reality by carrying out the murders or issuing orders for their execution. Just as Vindice shows a little too much pleasure in the evils that he feels called upon to avenge, so Flamineo, doubling as malcontent and pander, reveals the nature of both roles as ones that translate a diseased imagination into reality.

Besides the malcontent plotter and manipulator, the other important type of melancholy character in tragedy was the man who, at least initially, was the victim of the plot, who had been demented by his suffering in the course of the action, or (as in the case of Marston's Antonio) whose unstable or melancholy frame of mind temporarily incapacitated him for the role that the drama, in conventional terms, cut out for him. The medical tradition regarding melancholics, while stressing their studiousness and pensiveness, rarely insisted on any radical incapacity for action, although Bright's *Treatise* mentioned it:

> Nowe contemplations are more familiar with melancholicke persons then with other, by reason they be not so apt for action, consisting also of a temper still and slowe according to the nature of melancholie humour. . . .[41]

The connection in drama, however, between melancholy or mad 'passion' and temporary inactivity was a natural one, since the expression of such emotion seemed to imply an irremediable situation.

The prototype of the melancholy or mad victim is Kyd's Hieronimo, whose passionate action and speeches in *The Spanish Tragedy* (*c.* 1589) illustrate one function of madness as a state that allows for the rendering of extravagant emotions. Before an audience, his exaggerated gestures and complaints, his preservation of the bloody handkerchief with which he wiped up his son's blood, such actions as digging in the earth and crying:

> Away! I'll rip the bowels of the earth,
> And ferry over th'Elysian plains,
> And bring my son to show his deadly wounds.
>   (III, xii, 71–3)[42]

cause the other characters to speak of him as melancholy and mad (III, xii, 89, 99). In his madness Hieronimo equates his private cravings for revenge with cosmic and mythological forces:

> Well, heaven is heaven still;
> And there is Nemesis, and Furies,
> And things called whips,
> And they sometimes do meet with murderers;
> They do not always 'scape; that's some comfort.
> Ay, ay, ay; and then time steals on,
> And steals, and steals, till violence leaps forth
> Like thunder wrapp'd in a ball of fire,
> And so doth bring confusion to them all.
>
> (III, xi, 40–8)[43]

Madness allows here for a mixture of the elevated and the colloquial, mythological allusions reduced to personal concerns ('that's some comfort'), and occasional obsessive repetitions or incoherences ('Ay, ay, ay') joined to large abstractions (violence, time) that are given personified and imagistic force.

The ambiguity of Hieronimo's madness, feigned for political purposes and also 'real' (expressed in soliloquies), is analogous to the indeterminate nature of the supernatural machinery of the play. Revenge is both a personified abstraction and a plausible motive leading to a causal sequence of action. Hieronimo's madness, his confusion of distinctions between the real and unreal, are therefore the means by which those scenes where Revenge and Andrea's Ghost appear in order to control the action can be incorporated into a political plot. A sign of his madness is that he wants to travel to Hell and bring Revenge back up to earth; he sees such myths with too much concreteness for sanity, and expresses them without concern for social proprieties. On the other hand, Revenge is a figure on the stage that the audience can see, and that validates Hieronimo's vision.

Hieronimo's style, through which pale moral abstractions take on a visionary concreteness, became the hall-mark of mad characters. This is true even of such crude examples of the type as Pasquil in Marston's *Jack Drum's Entertainment* (1600),[44] whose madness over the temporary loss of his sweetheart manifests itself in a series of moral, if incoherent, utterances about the evil with which he is now obsessed:

Vertue shall burst ope the Iron gates of Hell,
Ile not be coop'd up, roome for *Phaeton*.
Lame policy, how canst thou go upright?
O Lust, staine not sweet Love.

(p. 235)

His vision is far broader, less socially concrete, than that of the
more topical satirist (represented in the same play by Planet);
and his arraignments of Justice and Religion have some affinity
with more poetic examples of generalized visionary satire, like
the ravings of Lear on the heath. Madness becomes expressive of
superior vision in such characters because it blurs the usual
distinctions between the figurative and the real.

The development of articulated styles for different types of
melancholy provided the possibility of giving depth to melancholy
characters in tragedy by making them self-conscious role-players.
The colloquial, insulting, and often obscene style of the malcontent
satirist—of Marston's Malevole, or Webster's Flamineo and Bosola
—reveals through its images a heightened awareness of specific
corruptions in those around him:

> And how dost my old muckhill, overspread with fresh
> snow? Thou half man, half goat, all a beast! How
> does thy young wife, old huddle? (*The Malcontent*,
> I, i, 33–6)[45]

This is only one of several possible melancholy styles, as Vindice
and his brother acknowledge in *The Revenger's Tragedy* when
they create melancholy disguises for Vindice, first as blunt critic
and then as a malcontent tool villain suffering from melancholy:

> *Hippolito*   You must change tongue—familiar was your
> first.
> *Vindice*   Why,
> I'll bear me in some strain of melancholy,
> And string myself with heavy sounding wire,
> Like such an instrument that speaks
> Merry things sadly.

(IV, ii, 26–31)

Both the 'familiar' and the sad style involve the conscious adoption of speech-mannerisms or 'tongues'; they are theatrical

39

disguises that are wilfully assumed in order to fool Lussurioso. But (like Hamlet's roles, as we shall see) they are also related to the personality that Vindice displays in his soliloquies, where he inveighs against the corruption of the court and the age. His range of expression is widened by the adoption of theatrical roles that have some relation to his real character, and that, none the less, indicate a flexibility that sets him apart from the other semi-allegorical types in the play.

Webster exploited the familiarity of malcontent styles even more fully to create an illusion of self-consciousness about role-playing. In *The White Devil* Flamineo admits outright that the role of the melancholy malcontent is useful to him because it permits him to talk in certain ways—imagistic, visionary and sententious—that he spells out in an aside to the audience:

> It may appear to some ridiculous
> Thus to talk knave and madman; and sometimes
> Come in with a dried sentence stuff'd with sage.
> But this allows my varying of shapes. . . .
>
> (IV, ii, 243–6)

Although Flamineo is given the biographical features—the poverty and social displacement—of the malcontent type (I, ii, 315–32), his style is really self-justifying, as his tautologous statement here indicates; there is neither a moral nor a strictly practical purpose behind his 'varying of shapes'. One role, the madman's disguise, is assumed on the flimsiest of pretexts: he finds it easier to feign madness than grief over the death of the murdered Duchess (III, ii, 303–8). 'Madness' enables him at this point in the play to vary his punning, obscene manner with a somewhat more generalized satiric one in which he arraigns those ranks of society that have just displayed their corruption in Vittoria's trial:

> O thou gold, what a god art thou! and O man, what a devil art thou to be tempted by that cursed mineral! Yon diversivolent lawyer; mark him, knaves turn informers, as maggots turn flies,—you may catch gudgeons with either. A cardinal;—I would he would hear me,—there's nothing so holy but money will corrupt and putrify it, like victual under the line (III, iii, 21–7).[46]

At another point, Flamineo and Lodovico agree to take on all
the externals of the melancholy pose:

Flamineo Let's be unsociably sociable.
Lodovico Sit some three days together, and discourse.
Flamineo Only with making faces;
Lie in our clothes.
Lodovico With faggots for our pillows.
Flamineo And be lousy.
Lodovico In taffeta linings; that's gentle melancholy,—
Sleep all day.
Flamineo Yes, and like your melancholic hare
Feed after midnight.

(III, iii, 76–84)

The artificiality of the manner, as in the comedies, is revealed
by the wilfulness with which it is adopted, by the open admission
of its contradictions ('let's be unsociably sociable'), and by the
speed with which it is abandoned by Lodovico when he is par-
doned and the two men start fighting:

Flamineo This laughter scurvily becomes your face,—
If you will not be melancholy, be angry.
(*Strikes him.*)
See, now I laugh too.

(III, iii, 122–4)

The context of the scene, however, makes the self-conscious
adoption of the style (a protest against Fortune, as Flamineo
explains, III, iii, 92–7) different here from what we find in the
comedies. It seems inescapable as well as wilful; Lodovico, who
is reprieved from banishment, is able to gloat over his escape from
a game that Flamineo is determined, in some form or other, to
pursue.

Webster went even further with Bosola, in *The Duchess of Malfi*,
in creating a character out of an accumulation of melancholy
roles, and in suggesting a connection between role-playing and
fatalism. As a combination of the neglected scholar, potential
villain and intelligencer, envious railer and 'court gall' (I, i, 23),
Bosola gives expression to most of the varieties of malcontent
style. Like Flamineo, he speaks cynically and satirically, especially
of his own part: 'The provisorship o'th'horse? say then, my

corruption/Grew out of horse-dung: I am your creature' (I, i, 286–7). He embarks with studied emphasis on meditations about the nature of man ('Observe my meditation now,/What thing is in this outward form of man/To be beloved?', etc., II, i, 44–6ff.), and he justifies his melancholy, when he is enjoined by Antonio to give it up, on the grounds of the blunt 'low' style of speech that it enables him to adopt:

> Give me leave to be honest in any phrase, in any compli-
> ment whatsoever—shall I confess myself to you? I
> look no higher than I can reach: they are the gods that
> must ride on winged horses . . . (II, i, 87–90).

Bosola's self-consciousness about the role that he is playing is inseparably bound up with a sense of the limitations of his possibilities.

The other characters in the play speak of Bosola's melancholy as a mask, although they differ in their attitudes towards it. For Ferdinand, the villainous role that he intends to exploit is one that has become almost identical with Bosola's real melancholy nature:

> Be yourself;
> Keep your old garb of melancholy; 'twill express
> You envy those that stand above your reach,
> Yet strive not to come near 'em: this will gain
> Access to private lodgings. . . .
>
> (I, i, 277–81)

Antonio, on the other hand, sees Bosola's melancholy as something poisoning his better nature (I, i, 76–7), and he suggests a distinction between the real man and his evil part:

> Because you would not seem to appear to the world
> puffed up with your preferment, you continue this out-of-
> fashion melancholy—leave it, leave it. . . .
> You would look up to heaven, but I think the devil,
> that rules i'th'air, stands in your light (II, i, 84–6, 94–6).

Yet another distinction between man and mask is made by the Cardinal, who (perverting Antonio's terms) equates Bosola's melancholy with his sardonically expressed moral qualms, and therefore assumes a reality that is worse than the role:

Cardinal   I have honours in store for thee.
Bosola There are many ways that conduct to seeming
Honour, and some of them very dirty ones.
Cardinal Throw to the devil
Thy melancholy: the fire burns well,
What need we keep a stirring of 't, and make
A greater smother? thou wilt kill Antonio?

                                        (V, ii, 304–10)

Webster is able to give Bosola the appearance of profundity because his villainy, his self-deprecation and his remorse can all be seen as possible expressions of a single melancholy character. Most consistently, however, Bosola is pictured as the wearer of a mask that he is powerless to control. His melancholy is 'out of fashion', an 'old garb' or pose that is no longer appropriate to his prosperous circumstances, through the first half of the play, as the Duchess's servant; it is also 'out of fashion' in the sense of being a rather stale theatrical convention by the time the play was written (1612–14). Several years earlier (1605–6) Edmund in *King Lear* had alluded mockingly to his use of its shopworn theatricality: 'Pat! He comes like the catastrophe of the old comedy. My cue is villainous melancholy, with a sigh like Tom o' Bedlam' (I, ii, 128–9). Bosola, none the less, remains the victim of the role, playing his part in the Duchess's murder against his inclinations, until at the end external circumstances (or theatrical precedent) conspire against his plan to atone by saving Antonio. In his dying speeches Bosola refers to the discrepancy between his part and his sense of his real nature, calling himself 'an actor in the main of all/Much 'gainst mine own good nature . . .' and calling the death of Antonio 'Such a mistake as I have often seen/In a play' (V, v, 85–6, 95–6). Even Ferdinand, who has exploited Bosola's malcontent role, finally curses him for having played it so well:

For thee, (as we observe in tragedies
That a good actor many times is curs'd
For playing a villain's part) I hate thee for 't. . . .

                                        (IV, ii, 288–90)

Stereotyped role-playing, of which melancholy villainy is an example, expresses the idea of a sinister fatality in a play which contains many allusions to Fate, to the influence of the stars, and to witchcraft, which robs people's will of control over their destiny.[47] While comic versions of the malcontent are mocked for pretending to have melancholy personalities that transcend the limitations of their role, Bosola's inability to change his constricting mask suggests a painful, cynical self-awareness and a hostile universe.

Melancholy Imagery

The tradition of melancholy not only provided writers with the material for character-types; it also supplied them with a stock of images for the creation of sombre landscapes. The world of the melancholic to which these images were attributed had some coherence even in the crudest and least elaborate of expository descriptions. The melancholy man was always thought to project his feelings on to the world more radically than did other humoral types. The metaphors of some of the expository writers had already gone a long way, therefore, towards expressing connections between the melancholic's physical state, his state of mind and the world that he saw. According to Bright, for example, the melancholic whose mind was literally imprisoned by gross humours saw the world as a prison and all the friends who came to aid him as potential messengers of execution.[48]

Because of its heavy disposition, the melancholy mind was preoccupied with sad and frightening subjects and their symbols. The black bile produced dreams and visions connected with death and evil spirits, with night and with graveyards, and with the plants, animals or other objects that represented or embodied these. Melancholy was, therefore, associated with night and its animals, such as bats and owls, with animals thought to be witches or their familiars, like cats and dogs,[49] or with those that were thought to be solitary, like hares and deer. Plants like yews and cypresses were connected with graveyards, while heavy minerals like lead embodied one of the very qualities of the melancholic. Apart from such specific symbols, moreover, melancholy was connected with the idea of tragedy itself; the imagination that saw the world as tragic could be portrayed as a melancholy imagination, or as Melancholy personified. In Ripa's *Iconologia* the personified image of Tragedy with its bloody sword is dressed in what are described as black 'melancholy' clothes,[50] while Milton's 'Il Penseroso' asks that 'Gorgeous Tragedy/In Scepter'd Pall come sweeping by' (97–8),[51] as opposed to the comedies and romances that are invoked in 'L'Allegro'.

For Elizabethan and Jacobean playwrights, images associated with melancholy served to deepen the tragic atmosphere already established by villainous deeds. The imagery in which the idea of melancholy was projected in drama took a variety of forms, from the most explicit kinds of allegory to the vaguest suggestiveness. In Kyd's *Spanish Tragedy*, for example, Hieronimo's personification of melancholy despair (when he is asked for directions to the villainous Lorenzo) is static and allegorical, in keeping with the context of a play in which Revenge takes personified shape, and in which the principal characters are assigned places at the end in a classical-Christian afterlife:

> There is a path upon your left-hand side,
> That leadeth from a guilty conscience
> Unto a forest of distrust and fear,
> A darksome place and dangerous to pass:
> There shall you meet with melancholy thoughts,
> Whose baleful humours if you but uphold,
> It will conduct you to despair and death:
> Whose rocky cliffs when you have once beheld,
> Within a hugy dale of lasting night,
> That, kindled with the world's iniquities,
> Doth cast up filthy and detested fumes. . . .
>
> (III, xi, 13–23)

Hieronimo incorporates the religious idea of melancholy despair and its affinity with hell, with the solitary rocky caves that were associated with Saturn's imprisonment, or in a transferred sense with the melancholic's withdrawal from society. The cave of Melancholy was often Christianized (or the Christian Hell reclassicized) in just this way in non-dramatic works: the infernal cave of William Rankins's Saturnian satire, equipped with screech-owls and other melancholy beasts, 'Where Melancholly chafes, and madness raves,/Where pain dead torments, torments death begets',[52] provides another instance, as does the 'Stygian cave' of Milton's 'L'Allegro'. An extended example occurs in Thomas Robinson's allegory in Spenserian stanzas, *The Life and*

Death of Mary Magdalene (*c.* 1620), in which the heroine's journey also leads her from Conscience to Melancholy to Hell, the cave of the personified Melancholy being filled with symbolic objects, plants and animals that serve for both infernal and melancholy backgrounds and suggest the relationship between the two:

> Or as the jawes of Scyllas barkinge hounds,
> That aye for greedinesse of booties rave,
> And swallowe all that come within their bounds:
> Such was the gap of Mellancholies cave,
> Where many loose, but few their lives can save;
> Onely for barkinge hounds, the grimme-fac'd cat,
> The slowe-pac'd asse was there, the flutteringe bat,
> The croakinge raven on a slaughtred carcasse sate.[53]

In *The Spanish Tragedy* the stiffness of this kind of imagery is meant to sound deranged in its context of social conversation, even while it receives support from the allegorical machinery of the frame-work.

A less rigidly allegorical use of melancholy symbols in tragedy could create a generalized atmosphere of gloom and tension. One of the ways in which we realize that the tone of Marston's *Antonio's Revenge* will differ from the play to which it is a sequel, *Antonio and Mellida* (1599), and that the second play will provide a more fitting analogue for the hero's melancholy than the more comic play that it follows is that Duke Piero's first speech in *Antonio's Revenge* introduces a number of images connected with melancholy, night and death:

> 'Tis yet dead night, yet all the earth is clutch'd
> In the dull leaden hand of snoring sleep;
> No breath disturbs the quiet of the earth,
> Save howling dogs, nightcrows and screeching owls,
> Save meager ghosts, Piero, and black thoughts.
>
> (I, i, 3–8)

In *The Duchess of Malfi*, Bosola's spying tour of the Duchess's court on the night that she gives birth to her first child is punctuated by abrupt noises, questions and melancholy allusions that all contribute to a portentous mood:

46

Bosola Sure I did hear a woman shriek: list, hah?...
—list again!
It may be 'twas the melancholy bird,
Best friend of silence and of solitariness,
The owl, that screamed so....

(II, iii, 1; 6–9)

Traditionally gloomy and horrifying backgrounds like graveyards or charnel houses could of course also be expanded into
settings for whole scenes, as in *Antonio's Revenge* (III, i, ii) or
Tourneur's *The Atheist's Tragedy* (IV, iii).

It was also possible, however, to create a gloomy landscape
through the ubiquity of melancholy characters, rather than
merely through the use of associative images, and nobody carried
this device further than Webster did in *The Duchess of Malfi*.
Where Kyd had contrasted grief-stricken responses in *The
Spanish Tragedy*—Hieronimo's purposeful madness with his wife's
more uncontrolled ravings, or his contemplations of suicide with
her performance of it—Webster later went much further by
calling every major character in his play 'melancholy'. Bosola,
as we have seen, is an amalgam of melancholy types; the Duchess
is called melancholy by her brothers (IV, i, 11) and by Cariola
(IV, ii, 9), while Ferdinand's melancholy and the Cardinal's are
discussed in the 'characters' that they arc given at the beginning
of the play:

Delio Now sir, your promise: what's that cardinal?
I mean his temper? they say he's a brave fellow,
Will play his five thousand crowns at tennis, dance,
Court ladies, and one that hath fought single combats.
Antonio Some such flashes superficially hang on him,
for form; but observe his inward character:—he is a
melancholy churchman; the spring in his face is
nothing but the engendering of toads; where he is
jealous of any man, he lays worse plots for them than
ever was imposed on Hercules. . . .
Delio You have given too much of him: what's his
brother?
Antonio The duke there? a most perverse, and turbulent nature:
What appears in him mirth, is merely outside;

If he laugh heartily, it is to laugh
All honesty out of fashion.

(I, i, 152–61, 168–72)

Each of the brothers has a courtly or mirthful exterior that belies his melancholy nature. Other characters who either call themselves or are called melancholy in the play are Antonio (I, i, 396) and Julia (II, iv, 28), in neither of whom the condition is developed in any meaningful way. The purpose here is no longer the portraiture of contrasting mental conditions or responses, but rather the establishment of a mood through the repetition of a motif.

Webster uses melancholy as part of his broader imagistic device of working out verbal images intricately in stage action.[54] The allusions to melancholy in the 'characters' at the beginning of the play become progressively realized in action that tends to become frozen in emblematic pictures, so that violence and ineffectiveness of will are portrayed simultaneously. Ferdinand, for example, talks in terms of animal imagery and wolfish violence:

The howling of a wolf
Is music to thee, screech-owl, prithee peace!

(III, ii, 88–9)

The death
Of young wolves [the Duchess's children] is never to be
pitied.

(IV, ii, 258–9)

The wolf shall find her grave, and scrape it up:
Not to devour the corpse, but to discover
The horrid murder.

(IV, ii, 309–11)

At the end of the play he becomes what he has been alluding to, acting out his delusion of being a grave-haunting werewolf, a form of behaviour that the Doctor defines clinically as the type of melancholy known as lycanthropia:

In those that are possess'd with't there o'erflows
Such melancholy humour, they imagine
Themselves to be transformed into wolves,
Steal forth to churchyards in the dead of night,
And dig dead bodies up. . . .

(V, ii, 8–12)

Ferdinand's madness, though placed in the context of melancholy case histories, turns him into an image of the violence that has preoccupied him, and as a fully realized embodiment of his earlier feelings, he seems incapable of further change. In the Cardinal's case, the melancholy that is part of his 'character' finally becomes crystallized in the religious melancholy that takes from him his 'confidence in prayer' and that makes him dwell on images of damnation and see sinister figures in the fishponds of his garden (V, iv, 26–8; V, v, 1–7).

Webster's process of turning character into image has a somewhat different purpose for the Duchess, because she assents to the self-realization it implies from the beginning. When she first marries Antonio, she stages an elaborate emblematic picture:

Duchess   maid, stand apart—
I now am blind.
Antonio   What's your conceit in this?
Duchess   I would have you lead your fortune by the hand,
Unto your marriage bed. . . .
$$(\text{I, i, }493\text{–}6)$$

In her death scene this capacity for 'conceits' becomes more serious. Bosola, in his guise as tomb-maker and teacher, introduces the idea of the Renaissance tomb as an art form connecting melancholy and the death of princes:

. . . princes' images on their tombs do not lie, as they were wont, seeming to pray up to heaven, but with their hands under their cheeks, as if they died of the toothache; they are not carved with their eyes fixed upon the stars, but as their minds were wholly bent upon the world, the selfsame way they seem to turn their faces (IV, ii, 156–62).

The tomb that Bosola describes to convey the idea that death is terrible for princes because their eyes are fixed on the world is like that of Lorenzo de' Medici as 'Il Penseroso' by Michelangelo,[55] an artist who is mentioned elsewhere in the play (III, ii, 52). The pose that Bosola pictures, that of Dürer's Melencolia, became conventional for personifications of Melancholy:

49

> But loe, within, dull Melancholy sits,
> Proppinge with weary hand his heavy head,
> And lowringe on the ground in franticke fits. . . .[56]

Bosola's image is not merely decorative, however. In a play that contains several references to art and to artists, to Michelangelo and to the fictitious 'curious master in that quality, Vincentio Lauriola', and his wax images with which the Duchess is 'plagu'd in art' (IV, i, 111–14), Webster is interested in making his characters' states of mind emblematic. The prayerful posture whose meaning the Duchess explains as she is strangled is in fact not the one that Bosola has suggested in his description of princes' tombs:

> Pull, and pull strongly, for your able strength
> Must pull down heaven upon me:—
> Yet stay; heaven-gates are not so highly arch'd
> As princes' palaces, they that enter there
> Must go upon their knees.—(*Kneels*)
>
> > (IV, ii, 230–4)

One aspect of the Duchess's greatness, then, in contrast to her brothers, is her capacity to turn herself into an image of heroic suffering at the end of the play:

> *Duchess*   . . . who do I look like now?
> *Cariola*   Like to your picture in the gallery,
> A deal of life in show, but none in practice;
> Or rather like some reverent monument
> Whose ruins are even to be pitied.
> *Duchess*   Very proper:
> And Fortune seems only to have her eyesight
> To behold my tragedy. . . .
>
> > (IV, ii, 30–6)

The emblematic process becomes expressive; characters convey their freedom or lack of it by the extent to which they understand and control the meanings of images that represent them. The characters in *The Duchess of Malfi*, all melancholy or called so, themselves partly constitute the imagery of the play, differing in the degree of consent that they can give to the realization of their potentialities.

The uses of melancholy imagery in Elizabethan tragedy, then, ranged from the deepening of gloomy atmospheres and settings through stock symbols associated with death or night, to the transformation of character into image and symbol. But although the imagery of melancholy lent itself most readily to tragedy, with which it had a natural affinity, it could also lend darker tones to plays that were predominantly romantic or comic. The function of 'the melancholy Jaques' in *As You Like It* provides an outstanding example, since, despite the ridicule that is heaped upon him, he gives expression, by his comments and by his very existence, to some of the disharmonies of the forest.

Before Jaques appears on stage he is described by one of the lords as part of a tableau that calls into question the harmony of the pastoral world of the play. The illusion of a natural, unspoiled life for the exiled courtiers in the forest is marred by the fact that they must kill the forest animals for their food, as the Duke regretfully admits:

> *Duke S.* Come, shall we go and kill us venison?
> And yet it irks me, the poor dappled fools,
> Being native burghers of this desert city,
> Should, in their own confines, with forked heads
> Have their round haunches gor'd.
> *1 Lord* Indeed, my lord,
> The melancholy Jaques grieves at that. . . .
> (II, i, 21–6)

While the Duke and the courtiers whose lands and positions have been usurped have fled to the forest as a refuge from the tyranny of men, they exercise the same kind of tyranny, as Jaques also points out, over the animals who have all the rights equivalent to those of property and established society in the forest:

> Thus most invectively he [Jaques] pierceth through
> The body of the country, city, court,
> Yea, and this our life; swearing that we
> Are mere usurpers, tyrants, and what's worse,
> To fright the animals and to kill them up
> In their assign'd and native dwelling-place.
> (II, i, 58–63)

The deer is connected with Jaques by the comments that he makes about its mistreatment by his fellows, by traditional associations between deer and melancholy solitude,[57] and by the tableau that the Lord presents, in which both the wounded deer (or 'hairy fool', II, i, 40) and the philosopher are weeping into a brook, a traditional location for the solitary melancholic, as the 'Author's Abstract of Melancholy' at the front of Burton's *Anatomy* tells us. Though Jaques is mocked for the exaggerated virtuosity and gusto with which he makes his 'thousand similes' comparing the stricken deer's situation with that of the human outcast, he gives the fullest expression in the play to what is false in the idea of pastoral retreat from civilization. The deer who carries his horns on his head is also the natural cuckold or victim of usurpation; tradition associated him with the melancholy of men for that reason,[58] and in a later scene Jaques crowns the deer's slayers with its horns 'as a branch of victory', while the processional song makes the connection with cuckoldry obvious (IV, ii).

Jaques supplies a dissonant note in the forest by his lonely existence as well as by his observations about the necessary artificiality of the human action there. His comment, for example, that Orlando should 'mar no more trees with writing love songs in their barks' (III, ii, 244–5) casts doubt (as Marvell was later wittily to do) on the idea that the imagination of pastoral simplicity could really leave nature natural, and there is a related point in his suggestion that Touchstone and Audrey should get married, not under a tree, but in a church, where 'a good priest . . . can tell you what marriage is' (III, iii, 74–5). But, aside from his remarks, he is himself an image of dissonance, a discordant figure in a sense that is metaphorically connected with his melancholy.

Where comedy projects an idea of harmony of which music is a symbol, the melancholic's humoral imbalance, expressed by his behaviour, strikes a jarring note; as the Duke says of Jaques, 'If he, compact of jars, grow musical,/We shall have shortly discord in the spheres' (II, vii, 5–6). The kind of discord that Jaques' unsociable melancholy symbolizes is expressed also by Malevole in Marston's *The Malcontent* (1604). That play opens with a burst of cacophonous music from Malevole's room: 'The discord rather than the music is heard from the malcontent Malevole's chamber'

(I, ii, 2–3),[59] and Malevole's rudeness of speech and behaviour are connected with his humoral make-up: 'Th'elements struggle within him; his own soul is at variance with herself; his speech is halter-worthy at all hours . . .' (I, ii, 24–6). In Jaques' case the metaphor of disharmony is acted out at the end of the play, when his decision to join the newly religious Duke Frederick in his 'abandoned cave' is also a decision not to enter into the dancing with which the play concludes: 'I am for other than for dancing measures' (V, iv, 197). The romantic comedy is given a somewhat darker dimension by Jaques; its world, until the very end, is large enough to include him as an image of melancholy dissonance that even the ridicule he provokes cannot entirely destroy.

While melancholy could be associated with specific symbols or with characters viewed in terms of a play's imagery, it also had larger associations with dramatic genres themselves. We have already seen the affinity between melancholy and the idea of tragedy; there was also an inverse connection, partly based on medical doctrine and partly metaphoric, between melancholy and comedy. Melancholics were advised by medical authorities to watch dramatic performances and to take part in plays, especially comedies, as a form of recreation to lighten the heavy spirits.[60] This idea found its way into the critical theories of the time. Thomas Heywood, for example, justified comedy in his *Apology for Actors* (1612) partly on the grounds that it alleviated melancholy:

> . . . and these are mingled with sportfull accidents, to recreate such as of themselves are wholly devoted to Melancholly, which corrupts the bloud; or to refresh such weary spirits as are tired with labour, or study, to moderate the cares and heaviness of the minde, that they may return to their trades and faculties with more zeale and earnestnesse, after some small soft and pleasant retirement.[61]

The same justification had been made by Guarini, and, as Madeleine Doran has pointed out, English critics like Puttenham were psychological in their orientation, ascribing therapeutic benefits to drama, even when they did not mention melancholy specifically.[62] A dramatized version of the idea that plays cured melancholy can be found in the Induction to *The Taming of the*

Shrew, where Christopher Sly, the tinker, is to be persuaded that he is a great lord suffering from melancholy, and that the comedians will help him to refresh his spirits:

> Your honour's players, hearing your amendment,
> Are come to play a pleasant comedy;
> For so your doctors hold it very meet,
> Seeing too much sadness hath congeal'd your blood,
> And melancholy is the nurse of frenzy:
> Therefore they thought it good you hear a play,
> And frame your mind to mirth and merriment,
> Which bars a thousand harms and lengthens life.
>
> (Induction, II, 126–33)

The play proper is put on as Sly's 'cure', although that notion is never repeated during its performance.

The idea of comedy as curative of low spirits animates some of the jovial character-types whose function as the embodiment of the comic spirit consists precisely in banishing the melancholy that other characters have generated. Justice Clement in *Every Man in his Humour* is a character of this sort, a merry old soul who defends tobacco and cups of sack, and also the figure who tries to counteract the melancholy of others:

> *Clement* How now, master Kno'well! In dumps? In dumps? Come, this becomes not.
> *Kno'well* Sir, would I could not feele my cares—
> *Clement* Your cares are nothing! they are like my cap, soone put on, and as soone put off . . . mirth's my witnesse, an I had twise so many cares as you have, I'ld drowne them all in a cup of sacke. Come, come, let's trie it. . . .
>
> (III, vii, 82–6, 91–3)

He personifies the comic mirth and festivity of the ending, inviting the wedding party to supper, urging applause and acceptance of the ingenuity of Brainworm's plot, and banishing the humours (melancholy and sadness among them) and their possessors, if only to the kitchen. Another example of the sanguine character who tries (often incongruously) to counteract the melancholy around him with incessant song and mirth is Edward Fortune in Marston's *Jack Drum's Entertainment*, and the type is parodied in the character of Old Merrythought in Beaumont and Fletcher's spoof, *The Knight of the Burning Pestle* (1607).

The idea that comic entertainment counteracted melancholy could be used also to account for the introduction of a play within a play; *The Taming of the Shrew* would provide an instance if its framework were sustained. A more complicated example occurs in *The Duchess of Malfi*, where the supposedly 'comic' entertainment that is provided for the Duchess merely intensifies her tragic situation. Among the tortures that Ferdinand devises to break the will of the Duchess, whose 'melancholy seems fortify'd/With a strange disdain' (IV, i, 11–12), is a masque of madmen,[63] who are to follow the sadistic wax show of her supposedly dead family with which he has already entertained her. Since the sight of madmen and their antics was considered entertaining in an age when visits to Bethlehem Hospital to see the lunatics were a popular amusement,[64] the rationale for the masque is that it will relieve the Duchess's melancholy:

> *Servant*   I am come to tell you
> Your brother hath intended you some sport:
> A great physician, when the Pope was sick
> Of a great melancholy, presented him
> With several sorts of madmen, which wild object,
> Being so full of change and sport, forc'd him to laugh,
> And so th'imposthume broke: the self-same cure
> The duke intends on you.
>
> (IV, ii, 37–44)

Despite these officially benign purposes, Ferdinand has already announced his intention of sending the masque as a way of intensifying the Duchess's misery (for which he is responsible in the first place), alluding sarcastically to its curative powers ('If she can sleep the better for it, let her. . .' (IV, i, 131). The final irony is that the Duchess welcomes the mad show because it actually will offer her the relief that Ferdinand disingenuously ascribes to 'comedy'. Only madness and tragedy can placate her mood:

> *Duchess*   Indeed I thank him: nothing but noise and folly
> Can keep me in my right wits, whereas reason
> And silence make me stark mad;—sit down;

55

Discourse to me some dismal tragedy.
Cariola   O, 'twill increase your melancholy.
Duchess   Thou art deceiv'd,
To hear of greater grief would lessen mine. . . .

                                        (IV, ii, 5–10)

The Duchess's acceptance of her tragedy and her ability to reformulate her experience are voiced in terms of a different if related critical notion: tragedy (not comedy) cures melancholy by driving out lesser griefs with the spectacle of greater ones.[65]

The usefulness of melancholy for Renaissance dramatists, then, consisted partly in the ease with which the psychological condition could be translated into images central to dramatic genres. Comic playfulness counteracted melancholy, as did the festive scenes, dancing and music through which comedy expressed the idea of social harmony. Tragedy, on the other hand, gave expression to the melancholic's sadness or his plotting instincts. The envy and shrewdness which turned people into melancholy schemers also made them in a sense the authors of tragedies. This progression is described in Greene's *Planetomachia*, where '. . . Rodentos baleful mishap spronge from a Saturnine revenge, predominant in the configurations of Valdrackos nativitie, imprinting in his aged minde a melancholie despight, which brought to passe this woefull and unnaturall tragedie'.[66] From bringing a tragedy to pass, as a loose figure of speech, to being the author of it, was a very short step, as the ambiguous possessive of *The Revenger's Tragedy* shows. At the end of that play, Vindice needs to boast of his artistry even if he has to be punished for it: 'This murder might have slept in tongueless brass,/But for ourselves, and the world died an ass' (V, iii, 113–14).

Because there were so many articulated types of melancholy behaviour—the scholar's, the political malcontent's, the lover's—it also became possible to create the impression of complexity and subjectivity in characters composed of a multiplicity of stereotypes and their languages. Webster's Bosola is an example of a disjointed character, the cracks in whose dramatic composition are made to express a painful consciousness. There was another way of enhancing the malcontent's stature, however; this was to place him in a world where his discontents were amply justified by the wrongs he had suffered, where his perceptions were truer than anybody else's, and where his caustic mode of speech was purgative. To the extent that Webster's and Tourneur's malcontent satirists were not only self-serving manipulators but potential heroes, they reflected connections between melancholy and satire of the kind that were established by Marston.

Three

Marston and Melancholy

While Jonson's attitude towards melancholy did not vary appreciably in his humour comedies, Marston never put any of his numerous melancholics into the same literary situation twice. He was fascinated by melancholy and its literary possibilities, and he was continually innovative (if not always successful) in his representations of it—the effort to find appropriate forms for the malcontent's voice or consciousness seems in fact to have been one of his motives for innovation. For this reason, his treatments of melancholy deserve separate consideration. Although the satiric posture that he adopted towards malcontent types like the traveller, Bruto, was conventional,[1] Marston was original in establishing a more positive connection between satire and melancholy, whereby the melancholic's vision was associated with superior insight. In making such connections, he extended the range and flexibility of melancholy as a literary subject, suggesting —as the simpler treatments of stereotypes did not—dimensions beyond those laid down in the expository books.

The distinction in satire between melancholy as an attitude to be condemned and as one to be condoned can be seen, very briefly touched on, in Robert Anton's *Philosophers Satyrs*. Malcontented travellers and scholars are taken to task by Anton, as we have seen, for turning against their society, but when he comes to ask the reason for their apostasy, a note of sympathy comes in:

> Is it because thou hast sung sweete in all
> The liberal *Arts*, and now through *want* doost fall?
> Or doost thou wonder at *pluralities*,

58

Impropriations, or *absurdities*
Of a *lay Patron,* that doth still present
An *asse,* before a grand *proficient?*

(sig. E₃ᵛ)

Such social injustice, as Burton was also to show, could induce justifiable melancholy in the worthy spirits who suffered its effects: 'This makes the worthy Artist, dull and sad,/And rare deserts, most melancholy mad . . .' (sig. E₃ᵛ). Instead of travelling, yielding to passion, or firing his own ambition, however, the discontented author is advised to take a position more appropriate to his profession and more constructive: he should use the specifically artistic means at his disposal, and purge the evils of his time by satire.

The satirist's attempt to differentiate his own anger and discontent from that of the self-seeking and affected malcontents whom he derided was one aspect of a broad theoretical argument about justifiable discontent. In *Christs Teares Over Jerusalem,* for example, Nashe distinguished between proud discontent, sometimes arising from melancholy humour, and good discontent, or anger at wrong:

> There is a tollerable Discontent likewise, which *David* and *Job* had, when they complayned that the Tabernacles of Robbers did prosper, and they were in safetie that provokt God. But so little of this true discontent is there in *London.* . . .²

This was clearly the malcontentedness that a satiric author could use as an appropriate attitude to the world that he was castigating, but for Nashe it had nothing to do with melancholy humour.

On the face of it, melancholy would seem to have several characteristics that would not make it desirable as a quality for a satirist to assume. As an illness, it was associated with a lack of objectivity and sense of reality, as the countless stories that were current about delusions suffered by melancholics show. Even a less violently affected melancholy person was expected to 'see black' as a result of his temperament and physical make-up, rather than as an objective response to the world. It is worth inquiring, therefore, why Marston in particular, since he went further than any writer before Burton in connecting his satiric *persona* with melancholy, should have found such a connection useful even while he was concerned with the rhetorical problem of establishing the validity of his attacks.[3]

Marston began his *Scourge of Villainy* with the Proemium, or invocation to melancholy:

> Thou nursing mother of fair Wisdom's lore,
> Ingenuous Melancholy, I implore
> Thy grave assistance: take thy gloomy seat,
> Enthrone thee in my blood; let me entreat
> Stay his quick jocund skips, and force him run
> A sad-paced course, until my whips be done.
>
> (SV, Proemium to Book I, 9–14)

One function of the invocation is to introduce the appropriate mood for the dark pictures that are to follow. Furthermore, as something that is invoked, a consciously adopted attitude, melancholy in the Proemium is actually used to separate literature from life; its function is exactly the opposite of that often attributed to it of expressing directly the melancholy that Marston the man was afflicted with. The rhetorical illusion (whatever the biographical fact) is that Marston is not temperamentally melancholy at all; his 'blood' and his muse are 'jocund', but he must assume a gloomy attitude, don sad cypress rather than the traditional poetic laurel, in order to attune himself to the dark world that he must unveil (*SV*, Proemium to Book I, 15–18).

The most important point for Marston's satiric *persona* is that the melancholy invoked here is the Aristotelian kind, the temperament of philosophers, rather than the sort that Nashe had associated with bad discontent and that Marston himself, as well as other satirists, had parodied in their portraits of malcontent types. Marston's intention is clarified further by the Preface to the last satire in *The Scourge of Villainy*, where melancholy is expelled:

> Sleep grim Reproof; my jocund muse doth sing
> In other keys, to nimbler fingering.
> Dull-sprighted Melancholy, leave my brain—
> To hell, Cimmerian night! in lively vein
> I strive to paint, then hence all dark intent
> And sullen frowns! Come sporting Merriment,

Cheek-dimpling Laughter, crown my very soul
With jouisance, whilst mirthful jests control
The gouty humours of these pride-swoll'n days,
Which I do long until my pen displays.

(*SV*, Xl, 1–10)

As Milton was to do in 'L'Allegro' and 'Il Penseroso', Marston
is invoking two different aspects of melancholy in these two passages, and Milton's and Marston's invocations throw light on
each other.[4] The melancholy that is to help Marston in whipping
the world, the appropriately sombre attitude for his task, is the
'nursing Mother of faire Wisdom's lore', Milton's 'goddess sage
and holy', while the melancholy that is banished in the last
satire, like that which is banished in 'L'Allegro', has nothing
to do with contemplation or wisdom, but is associated with
mental sluggishness ('Dull-sprighted melancholy'), hell and darkness.

The two moods that the invocation and the banishment of
melancholy represent correspond to the subjects appropriate to
comedy and tragedy in Jonson's distinction, or to comic as opposed to more serious satire.[5] The satire that is preceded by the
banishment of melancholy and the invocation of the mirth that
is sufficient to control 'gouty humours' with jests is entitled
'Humours', and deals mostly with affectations similar to those
ridiculed by Jonson in his humour plays: excessive attention to
dress and to other superficial aspects of being a gentleman—
fencing, aspirations to wit, or attempts at satire without the true
mood or equipment for it. The addresses to melancholy or mirth
try to define the degree of seriousness of Marston's material, and
also point to his difficulty in controlling it. Where the comedian
or tragedian could set his tone at the outset by his handling of
character and event, leading each character to some final and
defining destiny, the formal satirist, like Marston, presenting a
series of semi-dramatized characters and incidents, was faced
with the problem of showing the difference between those to be
loathed and those merely to be laughed at. Since he could not
disappear entirely behind his characters, his own attitude towards
them had to be clarified throughout, and although Marston's
transitional statements about the condition of his 'sprite' are
sometimes jerky, their function is clear. Hall dealt with the same

problem in a similar way when he divided his satires in *Virgi-demiarum* into 'toothless' and 'biting'.

Melancholy had other more specific uses, however, than as a mood to be invoked. The melancholy satirist could first of all make a claim to impartiality because of the traditional associations of both satire and melancholy with Saturn. In the Preface to his translations of Horace's satires (1566), Thomas Drant connected satire with Saturn in two respects, its 'waspishness' and its impartiality:

> Satyre of writhled waspish Saturne may be namde,
>   The Satyrist must be a waspe in moode,
> Testie, and wrothe with vice and hers, to see both blamde,
>   But courteous and frendly to the good. . . .
> As Saturne cuttes of tyme with equall sythe:
> So this man cuttes down synne to coy, and blythe.[6]

The need to establish impartiality had always been a problem for satirists, who were accused of being motivated by personal animosities. Saturnists, as the quotation from Drant's Preface suggests, would have the same lofty impartiality or 'equality' as Saturn in his association with time, destroyer of all things. Marston added to his satiric *persona* another Saturnian attribute, his coldness. Since his rhetorical posture was the Juvenalian one of the man not easily aroused to anger, but unable to remain silent in the face of the evils of the time and the envy directed against him, he used the image of the Saturnist to compare himself with the kind of man least easily moved: 'What icy Saturnist, what northern pate,/But such gross lewdness would exasperate?' (*SV*, II, 19–20). The melancholic was traditionally 'hardly moved to anger, but keeping it long, and not easie to be reconciled . . .'[7]

The spleen, the organ of melancholy, provided another link between melancholy and satire. Because the spleen purged melancholy it was responsible for laughter, but not the joyful laughter of the heart 'tickled' by an abundance of good spirits;[8] splenetic laughter was bitter. Bright described it as 'a kinde of Sardonian, or false laughter', and associated it, as Burton was to do, with the mirthless satiric laughter of Democritus: 'With such kind of laughter did Democritus grieve at the vanities of life: which also moved Heraclitus to weep.'[9] Marston made use of the same associations of Democritic, bitter laughter: 'O if *Demo-*

critus were now alive/How would he laugh to see this devil thrive!'
(*CS*, I, 51–2).[10] Furthermore, to 'vent one's spleen', then as now,
meant to give anger an external object, rather than having it gnaw
at one's insides. Marston used the phrase 'to break one's spleen'
to describe a laughter tinged with anger and exasperation:

> Art thou not ready for to break thy spleen
> At laughing at the fondness thou hast seen
> In this vain-glorious fool. . . .
>
> (*CS*, III, 81–3)

Splenetic laughter was particularly appropriate as a response
to fools or follies which did not need the anger of the satirist's
'whips', and the vices and affectations of the returned traveller
belonged in this class (*CS*, I, 123–4).

A deeper connection, however, between melancholy and Marston's satires, one that affected their tone as well as their substance, was the suggestion that the lofty anger caused by his
contemplation of the evils and unhealthiness of the world had
unsettled his mind. The association of melancholy and anger that
Marston and other satirists transformed was established in both
the religious and medical sources of Renaissance melancholy.
In schemes of the sins, anger was a cause of *acedia*: 'Envye and
Ire maken bitternesse of herte, which bitternesse is mooder of
Accidie. . . .'[11] Dante's treatment of the 'sad' people who occupy
the same region as angry ones in the *Inferno* expressed the same
connection, in images of the sort that would become incorporated,
somewhat more neutrally, in the imagery of melancholy:

> The good Master said: 'Son, thou seest now the souls
> of those whom anger overcame; and I would have
> thee know for sure also that there are people under the
> water who sigh. . . . Fixed in the slime they say: "We
> were sullen [*tristi*] in the sweet air that is gladdened
> by the sun, bearing in our hearts a sluggish smoke;
> now we are sullen in the black mire." '[12]

The medical tradition supplied another connection between
melancholy and anger in the obvious association of black and
yellow bile, and Horace perhaps suggested its possibilities for
satire when he described Orestes' anger, while of 'unsafe mind',
as follows:

He did not dare to attack with the sword Pylades or his sister Electra. He merely threw ill words at both, calling her a Fury, and him by some other name which his gleaming choler prompted.[13]

The 'gleaming choler' or *'splendida bilis'* was the black bile of melancholy, here seen as the moving force behind verbal aggression, which is in turn a major component of satire.

The Renaissance books on the humours saw such verbal aggressiveness, and therefore both the mood and substance of satire, as one of the bad results of humoral imbalance. Lemnius, for example, described the well-tempered man as being 'without byting scoffes, and upbrayding tauntes, without all uncomely and uncivill jesting . . .' and as avoiding the extremes of both Democritus and Heraclitus (fol. 35ᵛ–36ʳ). Walkington makes the same point and the same negative allusions to Democritus and Heraclitus (fol. 80ʳ–80ᵛ). The usual assumption in the expository books, as we have seen, is of a harmonious if fallen world in which the proper attitude, neither satiric nor tragic, but gently didactic, is the one that Fulke Greville described in his 'Treatie of Humane Learning' (*c.* 1605):

> The chiefe Use then in man of that he knowes,
> Is his paines taking for the good of all,
> Not fleshly weeping for our owne made woes,
> Not laughing from a Melancholy gall,
> Not hating from a soule that overflowes
> With bitternesse, breath'd out from inward thrall:
> But sweetly rather to ease, loose, or binde,
> As need requires, this fraile fall'n humane kind.[14]

By overturning the primary assumptions of the expository books, Marston justifies not only his 'Democritic' laughter, but also the imbalance that he displays. The world's disease is identified with a corruption of humours, which the satirist, like a surgeon, will cure: 'Infectious blood, ye gouty humours quake,/Whilst my sharp razor doth incision make' (*SV*, V, 117–18). The image of the satirist as a surgeon or cauterizing agent, purging or burning away the world's impurities, was already present in classical satire, but much more was made of it in the Renaissance.[15] While Marston attacked Hall's abuse of the 'surgical' function ('Thy wit God comfort, mad chirurgion,/What, make so dangerous incision?' *CS*, IV, 93–4) he was at the same time describing his own role. The disease of the world, in Marston's satire, is analogous to the imbalance of the satirist who, contrary to Jonson's well-tempered spokesmen, is maddened by the intensity of his vision, as well as by the futility of his own satire:

> Is not he frantic, foolish, bedlam mad,
> That wastes his sprite, that melts his very brain
> In deep designs, in wit's dark gloomy strain?
> That scourgeth great slaves with a dreadless fist,
> Playing the rough part of a satirist. . . .
>
> (*SV*, X, 10–14)

The very energy that has gone into painting or trying to reform the corrupted world has deranged the satirist, whose mind is a reflection of the world he portrays.

Though Marston's attribution of madness to himself is more a rhetorical device than a statement of fact, it is repeated with great emphasis, and it is heightened by the exclamations and repetitions of a dissonant style:

> Mad world the whilst. But I forget me, I,
> I am seducèd with this poesy,
> And, madder than a bedlam, spend sweet time
> In bitter numbers, in this idle rhyme.
> Out on this humour! From a sickly bed,
> And from a moody mind distemperèd,
> I vomit forth my love, now turn'd to hate,
> Scorning the honour of a poet's state.
>
> (*SV*, X, 65–72)

One of the main advantages of the melancholy or mad pose, as this passage clearly indicates, is that it justifies certain stylistic features of the satires, their mixtures of tones and moods, and their disharmonies, or what Marston refers to as his 'yerking style'. A satire was traditionally rough, metrically and in its diction, 'rude' both in the sense of unpolished and impolite. No flowery 'poetic' phrases, Marston therefore claims in the Proemium to the second book of *The Scourge of Villainy*, will adorn his poems or soothe the world with 'oily flatteries'.

But roughness and unevenness extend beyond metrical irregularities, disdain for 'ballad stuff' and 'riming laws', or Marston's preoccupation with sexual perversion or excremental imagery, to the very rapid changes in mood that he expresses in his 'bitter numbers'. He presents himself in the last six books of *The Scourge of Villainy* as 'heavy' (V, 103–6), scourging and aggressive (V, 117–18), mixing seriousness and jest (Proemium to Book III, 1–3), invoking 'Reproof' (IX, 1–4), and then disowning all seriousness (XI, 1–12, 239–40). The 'moody mind distempered' which he attributes to himself is the organizing principle behind all of these changes of mood and behind the abrupt restatements of his relationship to his material.

Melancholy is also appropriate more specifically to the picture that Marston projects of himself as one who is both self-effacing and insulting, and to the ambiguous relationships that he establishes with his audience. The deluded or perverted types whom he lashes are also the people who will misunderstand his verses;[16] so they are scorned both for what they are and for their supposed scorn of him. He claims to disdain the 'detraction' he fears,[17] while revealing his sensitivity to it continually, defending his verses and then trying to disarm criticism by saying that he does not like them himself (pp. 100–1), that he has been joking all along, and finally dedicating them to Oblivion (p. 175). The melancholy qualities of hostility, defensiveness, fear and self-distrust are all exceedingly obvious in his self-references.[18]

Although Marston appears to the reader as hostile and fearful at the same time, he was not fully aware of the possibilities of associating these melancholy qualities with his satiric personality. This connection between melancholy and satire, only hinted at by Marston, was to be much more fully developed by Burton in 'Democritus to the Reader'. A passage like the following prose piece from *The Scourge of Villainy* points directly to Burton's exploitation of melancholy for his satiric *persona*:

> I cannot, nay, I will not delude your sight with mists; yet I dare defend my plainness against the verjuice-face of the crabbedst satirist that ever stuttered. He that thinks worse of my rimes than myself, I scorn him, for he cannot: he that thinks better, is a fool. . . . If thou perusest me with an unpartial eye, read on: if otherwise, know I neither value thee, nor thy censure (pp. 305–6).

Melancholy was not the substance of discourse for Marston,

and he went no further than to make the idea of derangement, of the 'moody mind distempered', account for the blackness of his pictures and the abruptness of his moods. He found melancholy useful as a way of making his satiric personality appear lofty and gloomy, and as a way of colouring the world that he was portraying and of controlling our attiudes and feelings towards it. That world was supposedly so diseased that it had unbalanced the otherwise jovial satirist; and at the same time it was his moral sensitivity that enabled him to see and paint it as it was.

Marston's repeated attempts to deal with the melancholic in drama avoided the rhetorical difficulties of formal satire—there were many ways, by action or comment from other characters, to establish attitude or point of view—while confronting instead the problem of how to create melancholy characters that were both psychologically consistent and dramatically functional. One of his first efforts, *Jack Drum's Entertainment*, abounds in conventional melancholy types: John Ellis, the love-melancholic;[19] Mamon, the usurer and miser, who has the melancholy of avarice,[20] and finally ends up in Bedlam as a result of his losses; Planet, who considers himself the well-tempered, detached satirist, but is actually an unsociable malcontent scholar; Pasquil,[21] the play's romantic hero, who temporarily becomes a deranged moral seer. The difficulty is that all of these types are held together by a romantic plot that is much too slight to sustain the vision of evil or corruption that several of these figures project.

Marston's sympathetic treatment of the melancholy satirist as one whose imbalance is a reflection of the world's illness carried over, however, to his portrayal of melancholics in drama; Planet's satiric misogyny is supposed to be justified by the faithlessness of the play's anti-heroine, Camelia. Even Marston's most extended comic treatment of a melancholy type, the scholar Lampatho Doria in *What You Will*, is not as consistently ridiculous as Jonson's melancholy-humour characters, because the action of the play to some extent supports the doubts that he voices. On the one hand, as we have seen, Lampatho is a truly comic type, ridiculed for his pretensions, for the mechanical and predictable nature of his meditations, and for the speed with which he can shed what is therefore an obviously artificial pose. His name, furthermore, suggests a bur,[22] or in the context of the play one who is dependent on the courtiers whom his role dictates that he should despise. But the causes of Lampatho's discontent are elaborated at sufficient length to compel serious attention, to some extent justifying the pain that he expresses.

Lampatho is saddened not so much by the physical 'expense of spirit' or loneliness that were supposed to make scholars melancholy (although there is a suggestion of these in his famous speech describing the taxing studies from which he emerged knowing as little as his sleeping spaniel); it is the content of his studies that have depressed him. He has become a sceptic, convinced of the uselessness of medieval metaphysical speculation. His list of scholastic and ancient philosophers and commentators whose varying opinions about the soul have driven him to doubt everything foreshadows some of Burton's catalogues of conflicting authorities, perhaps throwing some light on those:

> I was a scholler: seaven use-full springs
> Did I defloure in quotations
> Of crossed oppinions boute the soule of man;
> The more I learnt the more I learnt to doubt,
> Knowledge and wit, faithes foes, turn fayth about. . . .

> And still I held converse with *Zarabell*,
> *Aquinas*, *Scotus*, and the musty *sawe*
> Of antick *Donate*, still my spaniell slept:
> Still went on went I, first *an sit anima*,
> Then and it were mortall, O hold! hold!

(pp. 257–8)

Lampatho articulates also the problem of the scholar who had no place in the world, describing subjectively the amalgam of scepticism and discontented railing that made up the type of the malcontent traveller:

> A company of odde phrenetici
> Did eate my youth, and when I crept abroad,
> Finding my numnesse in this nimble age,
> I fell a railing, but now soft and slow,
> I know, I know naught, but I naught do know.
> What shall I doe, what plot, what course persew?

(p. 258)

Lampatho's complaints are not entirely laughable because they hint at subjective pain, and also because the scepticism over which he goes through such exaggerated and at times conceited tortures underlies the whole play. The plot deals with the efforts of Albano to establish the identity of which he has been robbed by an impersonator, and his realization that identity depends on sense-impressions or 'opinion'. Quadratus, the philosopher whose name establishes him as the embodiment of humoral and temperamental balance, asserts not the values of reason, but of Epicurean pleasure; his is a libertine response that accepts the proposition that 'Naught's knowne but by exterior sence' (p. 252), and that 'all that exists,/Takes valuation from oppinion' (p. 237). He does not deny Lampatho's view of the world, but only finds a happier solution for dealing with it. Lampatho's intellectual predicament receives enough support from the rest of the play, therefore, that critics have not been able to agree whether he represents one of Marston's enemies or an autobiographical sketch.

In his tragedies and tragicomedies, Marston carried over from satire not only the figure of the melancholy satirist, but also the world of policy, intrigue and lechery from which he drew his perceptions of evil. Arnold Davenport has pointed out that amid Marston's pictures in the satires of lust, perversions and avarice are passages about the helplessness of man's will that express a very pessimistic Calvinism,[23] and that effectively deny the classic moral excuse for satiric aggression, that knowledge of virtue (or pictures of vice) can make men improve. For Marston, the body's grossness or 'slime' could obscure reason as effectively as a perverse will, and, as Davenport puts it: 'Marston at least once [*SV*, VIII, 185ff.] suggests that these obscurations are not merely transient results of disease but the results of having a body at all. . . .'[24] The satirist's own distemper is a reflection and expression of a radically evil world that is not amenable to easy Stoic solutions, or reducible to Jonson's images of reason as ordering a well-tempered physiological system.

The difficulty in drama of making a vision of uncontrollable appetite emanate from a contented or well-tempered man can be seen in the character of the satirist Feliche in *Antonio and Mellida*. Marston goes to great and occasionally awkward lengths to prove that Feliche, as his name suggests, had no connection with melancholy. After a sleepless vigil, for example, in which he tours the court trying to find occasion for satire, he makes a speech about his 'content', and then ostentatiously and inappropriately goes to sleep in order to demonstrate that he does not suffer from the sleeplessness that was a common melancholy symptom:

> Well, here I'll sleep till that the scene of up
> Is past at court. [*Lies down.*] O calm, hush'd, rich content,
> Is there a being blessedness without thee?
>
> (III, ii, 20–2)[25]

While denying that he is motivated by envy of the sort Macilente describes in *Every Man out of his Humour*—the desire to strip others of the goods he craves himself[26]—Feliche only achieves his contentment by what is really another form of envy, seeing everybody else as truly unhappy and proving that his adversaries have nothing that can be called good in the first place. It is clear that because of his function, the happy and contented satirist is really the malcontent under another name. He too 'breaks his spleen' at the sins he sees (III, ii, 180), looking for material for his satiric bent to exercise itself upon, envying the candle that can see more sin and moral disease than he can:

> O, if that candlelight were made a poet,
> He would prove a rare firking satirist
> And draw the core forth of imposthum'd sin.
>
> (III, ii, 12–14)

The 'imposthume', a boil-like eruption, embodies the moral disorder of the world in the same way as the 'gouty humours' which Marston attacks in the formal satires, and Feliche's disgusted excremental imagery has much in common with that of the satires:

> O that the stomach of this queasy age
> Digests or brooks such raw unseasoned gobs
> And vomits not them forth!
>
> . . . . .
>
> O how I hate that same Egyptian louse,
> A rotten maggot that lives by stinking filth
> Of tainted spirits. Vengeance to such dogs
> That sprout by gnawing senseless carrion!
>
> (II, i, 87–9, 121–4)

Although it is at variance with his name and pretensions, Feliche has no other posture as a satirist than the malcontent one.

The *Antonio* plays demonstrate also Marston's difficulty in evolving an appropriate form for another type of melancholy character, the tragic victim. Antonio is a character whose humoral melancholy incapacitates him from fulfilling (at least temporarily) the roles that the plays in which he figures dictate. In the first play, *Antonio and Mellida*, his state of mind is quite unsuitable for the plot, or for his part as the lover in a comedy; the incongruity of his condition in the context of the play is perhaps a good sign of Marston's interest in depicting a case of melancholy for its own sake. At the point in the story where Antonio should be most actively engaged in effecting an escape for himself and Mellida from her tyrannic father, he collapses, strikes the earth, curses the day he was born, and makes general reflections about the miseries of life.[27] Later in the play his melancholy takes a turn for the worse, the ostensible reason being the loss of Mellida (although according to the story, she isn't lost yet and he meets her a few moments later):

> Until the soul return from—What was't I said?
> O this is naught but speckling melancholie.
> I have been—
> That Morpheus tender skinp—Cousin german
> Bear with me good—
> Mellida—Clod upon clod thus fall. [*Falls to the ground.*]
> *Hell is beneath; yet Heaven is over all.*
>
> (IV, i, 23–9)

The mixture of incoherence and sententiousness (each carried here to its separate extreme), and the sporadic addresses and exclamations to non-existent audiences were the hall-marks of mad speeches, as we have seen. Antonio's madness, however, is both more self-conscious than a state like Hieronimo's, as his reference to his 'speckling melancholie' shows, and far less expressive of any moral vision that is relevant to the play. Contrary to Hieronimo's passion, Antonio's melancholy is everywhere excessive and at odds with his situation; fear and sorrow are as causeless in him (and as dramatically unintelligible) as in the definitions supplied by the expository books.

Whatever its flaws, the tragic sequel to *Antonio and Mellida*, *Antonio's Revenge*, provides a more appropriate setting and action for the hero's condition, and it may represent Marston's efforts to find a more suitable form through which to express the idea of melancholy and its relationship to role-playing. The play develops, in ways that are occasionally more schematic than dramatically convincing, two related but contrasting responses to grief, both of which turn out to be false: Antonio, whose father has been killed, is melancholy; Pandulpho, whose son has been killed, is a Stoic. Each adopts the stylized postures that his attitude demands. Antonio wants to sit and wreathe his arms like a melancholic (I, ii, 281–2), enters in black with a book, and promises distractedly that he will follow the standard remedies for melancholy:

> I' faith I will, good friend, i' faith I will.
> I'll come and eat with you. Alberto, see
> I am taking physic, here's philosophy. [*Shows book.*]
> Good honest, leave me; I'll drink wine anon.
>
> (II, ii, 42–5)

He remarks, however, that neither the counsels of friends nor those of Senecan philosophy are adequate to deal with the real sources of his grief (II, ii, 1–6, 47–56). Pandulpho, on the other hand, who condemns melancholy posturing as 'apish action, player-like' (I, ii, 316), enters laughing about the death of his son (I, ii, 294)—Marston's typically clumsy way of depicting the Stoic outlook, which is impervious to the blows of Fortune. Both men drop their postures in order to take a common revenge. Pandulpho comes to see that he has been playing a false part and weeps for his son:

> Man will break out, despite philosophy.
> Why all this while I ha' but play'd a part,
> Like to some boy that acts a tragedy,
> Speaks burly words and raves out passion;
> But when he thinks upon his infant weakness,
> He droops his eye.
>
> (IV, ii, 69–74)

Antonio's progression is somewhat similar: from prostration with grief, to the recognition that the outward signs of melancholy can be player-like ('I will not swell like a tragedian/In forced passion of affected strains', II, ii, 105–6), to the savage irony with

which he attacks his mother and which makes her think, as
Gertrude does in *Hamlet*, that her son is mad,[28] and finally to the
planning and execution of a bloodthirsty revenge. Both men 'act'
openly as players in the end, but in roles that are overtly theatrical
and over which they therefore have more control: Antonio,
ordered by his father's ghost to assume a 'feigned habit' (III, ii,
88), appears in Piero's court as a fool, and both Antonio and
Pandulpho appear 'in masking attire' for the masque with which
the play ends.

The Malcontent solves many of the problems that the *Antonio*
plays suggested, because Marston joins the roles of satirist and
victim, makes their connection spring from their nature rather
than from mere conveniences of plot, and places the malcontent
in a world that makes the enactment of his part credible. Malevole
is the discordant, rude and insulting satirist whose justification is
the consonance of his vision with what is actually going on, and his
antipathy to flattery. As the antithesis of the flatterer against
whom humanist handbooks warned princes, he enacts on the stage
Marston's claims in his formal satires to scourge the world rather
than to soothe it with 'oily flatteries', and one of the ways in which
Duke Pietro shows that he is capable of redemption is that he
encourages Malevole's insults: 'I like him; faith, he gives good
intelligence to my spirit, makes me understand those weaknesses
which others' flattery palliates' (I, ii, 26–8). The world of lechery
and Machiavellian policy that Malevole sees receives external
corroboration from the intrigues of Mendoza, from the appearance
of bawds and self-seeking courtiers, and from the fact that Pietro, as
both a weak Duke and a cuckold, epitomizes the sexual and
political corruption with which Malevole is obsessed. In Antonio
the connection between the melancholic and the bloodthirsty
revenger is somewhat contrived to show the polarity between
passivity and action, and the shift from one response to the other
is jerkily announced in soliloquy and dialogue. Malevole, on
the other hand, acts out the alleged wish of the satirist to scourge
as well as to reform those whom he is attacking, and it is at this
point that the malcontent satirist has a real bond with the
revenger: Malevole's aggressive utterances are themselves the
instruments of his revenge. He gets the same kind of satisfaction
out of telling Pietro of his wife's unfaithfulness that Iago gets from
tormenting Othello:

Duke, I'll torment thee: now my just revenge
From thee than crown a richer gem shall part.
Beneath God naught's so dear as a calm heart.

(I, iii, 167–9)

Though Pietro refers to the disharmony in Malevole (I, ii, 24–5), and he himself speaks about his sleeplessness (III, ii, 1–14), there is a very limited sense in which Malevole is melancholy at all; his imbalance is principally a way of accounting for his attacks and his rudeness. Contrary to Feliche and more believably, he is able to enact the satirist's part as the discontented man; contrary to Antonio, there is no suggestion of psychological complications that have no outlet in action and plot. His most famous melancholy meditation is really functional in that it acts as a kind of sermon to bring about Pietro's repentance:

> Think this: this earth is the only grave and Golgotha wherein all things that live must rot; 'tis but the draught wherein the heavenly bodies discharge their corruption; the very muck hill on which the sublunary orbs cast their excrements. Man is the slime of this dung pit, and princes are the governors of these men. . . .

(IV, v, 107–12)

Pietro is convinced by the point made by Malevole in his role of 'pitiful surgeon' (IV, v, 64)—he renounces his dukedom and promises to devote himself to religion and to the restoration of Altofronto—and although Malevole's temperament is adjusted to the disgust about the world that the speech expresses, the subjective element is not the important one. Malevole's malcontent utterances represent the satirist's viewpoint in a world that corresponds to his vision.

Marston has given Malevole a richer and more interesting nature by joining together two major melancholy roles, that of the malcontent satirist and that of the victim, and making one the logical outgrowth of the other. The deposed Duke whose unsuspecting nature cost him his dukedom ('I wanted those old instruments of state,/Dissemblance and suspect', I, iv, 9–10) becomes the malcontent obsessed by his visions of the Machiavellian policy that he has previously disregarded, while his intention to achieve his revenge through verbal aggression rather than bloodshed,

74

and to effect the moral cure of his enemy, makes his disguise as a malcontent consonant with his moral nature as the idealistic Duke. There are times, as T. S. Eliot pointed out, when Malevole's 'real' nature as Altofronto seems disturbingly similar to his assumed one.[29] If it can be artistically justified, this overlap creates the illusion of depth in a character who seems to be hiding a nature that is not out of keeping, though not identical, with the one that he is revealing most of the time. Marston suggests a more profound nature in his character by juxtaposing the mechanical, expected features of the malcontent role with the man who plays it.

The showy theatricality of Malevole's malcontent role is expressed most obviously by changes of language. One stage direction announces such a change from ordered verse to insulting and obscene prose directly: 'Bilioso *entering*, Malevole *shifteth his speech*' (I, iv, 44).[30] Comments by characters about each others' images—'A hot simile' (I, vi, 41), 'A good old simile, my honest lord' (III, i, 10)—emphasize the self-conscious attention to manner throughout the play. At one point, Malevole describes the content of his bad dreams to Pietro, in a speech that the mad visions of some of Webster's characters (those of Brachiano in *The White Devil*, for example, just before his death) are to resemble:

> Why, methinks I see that signior pawn his footcloth, that *metreza* her plate; this madam takes physic that t'other *monsieur* may minister to her. Here is a pander jewel'd; there is a fellow in shift of satin this day that could not shift a shirt t'other night.
>
> (I, iii, 48–52)

At the end of the whole tirade Pietro says, 'You run' (I, iii, 62). It is a comment on what is clearly viewed as a performance, just as various asides by Vindice's brother in *The Revenger's Tragedy*, 'You flow well, brother' (II, ii, 146) or 'Brother, you've spoke that right' (III, v, 66), serve the same purpose of emphasizing the theatricality of Vindice's vision of evil. In *The Malcontent* the self-consciousness of Malevole's style reinforces the contrast between the actor and his role that Webster's Induction to the play, in which the actors discuss their parts, makes at the outset. There is also a hint, possibly taken from *Hamlet*, but not developed very far by Marston, that this theatricality is itself expressive of a deeper melancholy and a cause of it: 'O God, how loathsome this toying is to me! That a duke should be forc'd to fool it!' (V, iii, 41–2).[31]

The Malcontent expresses more successfully than any play except *Hamlet* the potentiality of the malcontent satirist for heroism and for true vision which Marston suggested in the satires. The rhetorical problems raised by satire, its aggressiveness and excess, arc controlled by manipulation of the world which the malcontent inhabits, and by giving him two main roles to play, one more 'real' than the other. The bad side of Malevole, his antisocial, obscene railing, though justified by the world around him, is none the less (if not always consistently) controlled by another role, that of the deposed Duke whose claim is a rightful one. What Marston is unable to express (as Shakespeare does in *Hamlet*) is that the good and bad aspects of melancholy are inextricably connected. *The Malcontent* reveals, however, the dramatic possibilities of the melancholy satirist as a hero, and the elements of satire, both creative and destructive, that imply a credible rather than a factitious connection between the melancholic, the satirist and the revenger.

Four

Melancholy and *Hamlet*

Shakespeare was familiar with all aspects of melancholy that were current in literature, and we have already seen several examples of the range and diversity of his allusions to it in his earlier plays.[1] Love-melancholics appear (and are usually ridiculed) in *Romeo and Juliet, Love's Labour's Lost, Two Gentlemen of Verona* and *Twelfth Night*; fashionable and affected melancholy is mentioned in *King John* (IV, i, 15–17), while Prince Hal and Falstaff bandy melancholy similes in *1 Henry IV* (I, ii, 71–6). Causeless and debilitating melancholy is the basis of the character of Antonio in *The Merchant of Venice*. Shakespeare also mentions the value, as cures for melancholy, of recreation (*Comedy of Errors*, V, i, 78–82), of music and singing (*All's Well that Ends Well*, III, ii, 3–10), of 'good counsel' (*Romeo and Juliet*, I, i, 139–40), and, as we have seen in the Induction to *The Taming of the Shrew*, of comic entertainment. Melancholy villains are represented by Aaron, the villainous Moor 'born under Saturn' in *Titus Andronicus*, and by Don John, the sullen villain of *Much Ado about Nothing*, whose confederate, Conrade, is also born under Saturn. These are only a few examples; altogether, seventy-one instances of the word 'melancholy' are cited in Bartlett's *Concordance*, and there are many allusions to the condition, and to the roles in which it displayed itself, without the name. In making Timon of Athens the hero of one of his late tragedies, for example, Shakespeare chose a figure whose name was proverbially synonymous with melancholy.[2]

Melancholy is central to *Hamlet* in all of the ways that other dramatists (and Shakespeare himself in other plays) tended to develop separately. As a melancholy character, Hamlet communicates his condition to others in the language of the expository books and in the styles that dramatic stereotypes had made familiar. Settings and symbols confirm or qualify the hero's vision; the graveyard scene, which is elaborately iconographical, contains a variety of melancholy symbols that give support to Hamlet's view of the world, while the images of disease with which the play abounds create a world to which melancholy is akin, and to which it is also an appropriate response. The structure of *Hamlet*, particularly the staging of the Gonzago play, is associated with the relationship that we have seen developed in other plays of the period between melancholy and entertainment or theatricality. While it is useful to separate these elements in the play, it is also highly artificial: melancholy or diseased characters to some extent constitute the 'world' and imagery of the play, just as the melancholic's affinity for role-playing, a feature of his character, has bearing on the shape of the plot.

What makes Shakespeare's treatment of melancholy so much richer and more successful than that of any other dramatist is that in his hands the devices for representing it become expressive as well as dramatically functional. Hamlet's playing of a great variety of stereotyped melancholy parts, for example, is itself symptomatic of a character who refuses to be identified entirely with any of the roles that he plays, and whose real melancholy is made evident through the evasiveness and aggressive wit with which he manipulates such roles. Furthermore, Shakespeare has extended the range and complexity of melancholy as a metaphor by making it include both the good and bad features of the condition; he has fused the seemingly incompatible aspects that were never really joined in the expository tradition (where writers tended to take sides), and has shown their necessary interconnectedness.

Rather than merely portraying Hamlet as a character who has been incapacitated for action by melancholy illness, as so many critics since Bradley have suggested,[3] Shakespeare has associated Hamlet's melancholy with the problem of action in a more fundamental sense: melancholy is the source of Hamlet's superior imagination, and of his awareness of the corroding effects of time or change that make specific actions appear meaningless. Although melancholics were generally considered 'pensive' and contemplative, the idea that they were paralysed by their thoughts, though occasionally mentioned in discursive

1 Dürer 'Melencolia I' (1517)

H EERE *Melancholly* muſing in his fits,
    Pale viſag'd, of complexion cold and drie,
All ſolitarie, at his ſtudie ſits,
Within a wood, devoid of companie:
    Saue Madge the Owle, and melancholly Puſſe,
    Light-loathing Creatures, hatefull, ominous.

His mouth, in ſigne of ſilence, vp is bound,
For *Melancholly* loues not many wordes:
One foote on Cube is fixt vpon the ground,
The which him plodding *Conſtancie* affordes:
    A ſealed Purſe he beares, to ſhew no vice,
    So proper is to him, as *Auarice*.

2 Henry Peacham 'Melancholy' from *Minerva Britanna* (1612)

and literary treatments of the condition,[4] was not always considered central to it. In earlier revenge plays like *The Spanish Tragedy*, Hieronimo's madness or 'melancholy' is never proposed in the play as the cause of his delayed revenge, but is rather associated, by the King and others who know nothing about his plans for revenge, with the wildness of his passionate outbursts.

It is therefore interesting to note that Belleforest's Hamlet story, translated into English in the sixteenth century as 'The Hystorie of Hamblet', connects Hamlet's melancholy, not with inactivity, but with divination and with theories that Saturnists were especially inspired:

> It toucheth not the matter herein to discover the parts of devination in man, and whether this prince, by reason of his over great melancholy, had received those impressions, devining that, which never any but himselfe had before declared, like the philosophers, who discoursing of divers deep points of philosophy, attribute the force of those devinations to such as are saturnists by complection, who oftentimes speake of things which, their fury ceasing, they then alreadye can hardly understand who are the pronouncers. . . .[5]

The question that Belleforest debates is whether Hamlet has obtained his knowledge of the plots against him from divine or infernal sources, and in this Shakespeare seems to have followed Belleforest. Melancholy is not merely an illness that prevents the enactment of the speedy revenge that a 'healthy' person would take; it is both an unsocial, life-negating disease and the source of superior imaginative wisdom.

Shakespeare establishes the complex nature of Hamlet's melancholy from the beginning by showing the differences between its public and private manifestations. The first scene in which Hamlet appears (I, ii) reveals the connections as well as the discrepancies between melancholy and role-playing, between feelings of grief and disgust and their representations in gesture, costume and language. Through the conventional signs of his melancholy, the black clothes, the downcast eye and the isolated posture, Hamlet expresses not only grief, but also hostility to the Court and its present ruler. The clothes and the gestures are analogous to his first spoken words, an 'aside' in which he registers his isolation as well as his bitterness. In the first remark that is actually addressed to another character Hamlet announces the fact of his melancholy:

> *King* How is it that the clouds still hang on you?
> *Hamlet* Not so, my lord; I am too much in the sun.
>
> (I, ii, 66–7)[6]

Melancholics traditionally fled the light and warmth of the sun in order to go (literally or metaphorically) into their cavernous retreats; as Laurentius described the melancholic, 'hee is become a savadge creature, haunting the shadowed places, suspicious, solitarie, enemie to the Sunne . . . .'[7] In his answer to Claudius, therefore, Hamlet makes an open allusion to his melancholic's aversion to the sun (and this is the only meaning that is socially possible) at the same time that his punning answer is covertly aggressive about the King's attempt to call him 'son' three lines earlier, and about the common analogy between the King himself and the sun.

Through Hamlet's display of the public and conventional aspects of melancholy, the scene introduces us to the problem of melancholy style. His postures are 'sincere', in that the soliloquy that concludes the scene reveals the feelings of revulsion, grief and desire for death that the costume properly expresses, but possible discrepancies between style and feeling are indicated in Hamlet's heated denial of them:

> Seems, madam! Nay, it is; I know not seems.
> 'Tis not alone my inky cloak, good mother,
> Nor customary suits of solemn black,
> Nor windy suspiration of forc'd breath,
> No, nor the fruitful river in the eye,
> Nor the dejected haviour of the visage,
> Together with all forms, moods, shapes of grief,
> That can denote me truly. These, indeed, seem;
> For they are actions that a man might play;
> But I have that within which passes show—
> These but the trappings and the suits of woe.
>
> (I, ii, 76–86)

The scenes that follow show Hamlet, until his departure for England, playing a variety of melancholy roles: disillusioned scholar, satirist and misogynist, ambitious political malcontent, melancholy lover, madman. Each is possible (some more than others); each is particularly directed at the character who is most receptive to it, and each is exaggerated and rendered theatrical to the point where it cannot be said to 'denote' him truly.

The first performance that Hamlet puts on after his announcement of the antic disposition to his friends is that of the love-melancholic. Ophelia's account of Hamlet's appearance in her closet (II, i, 74–100) is in itself a plausible one of that condition; the physical details that she describes, the pallor and the disarray, the 'stockings fouled,/Ungart'red and down-gyved to the ankle' (II, i, 79–80), are in accordance with conventional representations. Hamlet's behaviour and appearance are, therefore, susceptible to the interpretation that Polonius gives, and, of course, Hamlet tries to confirm Polonius in his view by 'harping' on Ophelia later (II, ii, 181–90, 398–407). What makes us aware of the implausibility or exaggeration of the pose is our knowledge of the context, a knowledge that Ophelia's language, reminiscent of that in which the Ghost's visits have been described, reinforces.[8] On the one hand, no parts of her account are entirely out of keeping with the language of such expository books as Lemnius's, which describes suffering melancholics

> with countenance & loke so grim and frowninge, as though they were lately come out of Trephonius Denne, or out of some Cave under the ground (such as the fabulous yawning of the Earth in Ireland, commonly tearmed S. Patrickes denne or Purgatory is).[9]

But the Ghost is even more strongly evoked by Ophelia's picture of Hamlet's pallor (cf. I, ii, 232–3), of his departure (like that of the Ghost from Horatio) with his eyes fixed on her as if he did not need them, and of his 'look so piteous in purport/As if he had been loosed out of hell/To speak of horrors' (II, i, 82–4). We are, therefore, aware at the same time of the misinterpretation by Polonius and Ophelia of the conventional aspects of Hamlet's performance, and of the truth that it none the less conveys in terms of his real situation and reasons for melancholy.

Other melancholy or malcontent roles that are to varying degrees made theatrical, often through the use of costumes and props as well as through language, are those of the political malcontent, the scholar and satirist, and the madman. Hamlet's hints that he is a political malcontent are mainly for the benefit of Rosencrantz and Guildenstern, who are the first to interpret Hamlet's behaviour in terms of that convention (II, ii, 252–61), and for Claudius, who fears political danger to himself in Hamlet's melancholy. Again, the role is exaggerated beyond the truth it contains; when Rosencrantz and Guildenstern first attribute his behaviour to ambition, he rejects the suggestion (II, ii, 254–5), only to take it up again himself later when he is questioned about the cause of his melancholy by Rosencrantz ('Sir, I lack advancement', III, ii, 331). His similar hint to Claudius ('I eat the air promise-cramm'd; you cannot feed capons so', III, ii, 91–3) has the same effect of simplifying the battle between them in terms of conventional motivation.

In his role as a melancholy scholar, Hamlet's entrance with a book (II, ii, 167) is a stage convention, as we have seen, and he also registers the disillusioned scholar's weary cynicism about his studies:

> *Polonius*   What do you read, my lord?
> *Hamlet*   Words, words, words.
>
> (II, ii, 190–1)

His satire in this scene, involving an attack on Polonius in terms of the 'satirical rogue' whose book he is reading, is bookish in origin, though personal in application. The same is true of the stock diatribes on female dishonesty and corruption, in the manner of Marston and other satirists, with which he attacks Ophelia:

> . . . the power of beauty will sooner transform honesty from what it is to a bawd than the force of honesty can translate beauty into his likeness. This was sometime a paradox but now the time gives it proof (III, i, 111–15).[10]

The King sees the conscious artifice behind these stock invectives, which communicate a belligerence that has nothing to do with love or madness (III, i, 162–4), even while Polonius is able to persist in his belief in both of these.

Hamlet's postures as a madman involve a dishevelled appearance, the nature of which we can guess at from the King's remark that 'nor th'exterior nor the inward man/Resembles what it was' (II, ii, 6–7). An often-quoted poem of the period about a lover who 'puts off his cloathes, his shirt he onely wears,/Much like mad Hamlet'[11] gives another indication of the extent of Hamlet's disarray in contemporary performances, and of the contrast with the courtier whom Ophelia remembers as 'The glass of fashion and the mould of form' (III, i, 153). The exaggeration of the mad role is evident not only from Hamlet's announced intention at the beginning of putting on an 'antic disposition', but also from his own asides at those points where he is most obviously playing the madman. After comparing the same cloud with a camel, a weasel and a whale, for example, and forcing Polonius into the pretended agreement that expository books recommended for the treatment of deluded lunatics, Hamlet registers his displeasure with the responses that his role evokes: 'They fool me to the top of my bent' (III, ii, 375).

Although none of the melancholy roles whose stereotyped nature Hamlet exaggerates with costumes and with props— the 'inky cloak' of his first scene, the ungartered stockings of the lover, the book of the scholar and satirist, the dishevelled appearance of the madman—is entirely definitive, each is to some extent relevant and possible. The degree to which his public performances are staged is sometimes clearly indicated; in breaking off his reasonable discourse with Horatio for the entrance of members of the Court to the play, Hamlet announces a change to his public manner: 'They are coming to the play; I must be idle' (III, ii, 89). But even if the stereotyped parts exaggerate reality they reflect it through the soliloquies, and through a certain amount of overlap among the roles themselves. The dishevelled madman, for example, sometimes has difficulty in keeping control over his own thoughts in soliloquy: 'Fie upon 't, foh!/About, my brains' (II, ii, 583–4). The stagey scholar also debates to himself academic *topoi* like 'To be, or not to be' and expresses, in conversation with friends from his university, the opinion that 'there is nothing good or bad, but thinking makes it so' (II, ii 249–50). The satirist who berates Ophelia with inappropriate stock sentiments about the corruption of women shows in his first soliloquy the real disgust that his mother's behaviour has inspired in him ('Frailty, thy name is woman!' I, ii, 146), and becomes, in the closet scene, the related kind of satirist whose disgust is connected with a wish for the moral cure of those he attacks: 'I must be cruel only to be kind' (III, iv, 178).

The extent to which public behaviour and private feelings overlap is clearly expressed in Hamlet's speech describing his behaviour as melancholy illness to Rosencrantz and Guildenstern (II, ii, 292–309). He presents his symptoms first in terms of publicly observable behaviour, repeating what he is sure the King and Queen have been saying about him:

> I will tell you [why you were sent for]; so shall my anticipation prevent your discovery, and your secrecy to the King and Queen moult no feather. I have of late—but wherefore I know not—lost all my mirth, foregone all custom of exercises. . . .

The speech reveals the connections between Hamlet's behaviour and his subjective feelings about his 'loss of mirth' by injecting his private perceptions into the King and Queen's supposed public account ('I have of late—but wherefore I know not—lost all my mirth . . .'); their picture merges with feelings about the world of which he alone could know ('why, it appeareth no other thing to me but a pestilent congregation of vapours', II, ii, 300–1), and which are very similar to ones expressed in the first soliloquy, where he sees the world as an unweeded garden.

The close relationship in Hamlet of roles to a character who plays them becomes even clearer through the contrasting portrait of Ophelia. Those situations and verbal echoes which establish a parallel between her and Hamlet also emphasize her greater obedience and passivity: the alacrity with which she reports his visit to her closet to her father, for example, compared with Hamlet's secrecy about the Ghost's visit, or the docile, metaphoric gift of the key of her memory to her brother (I, iii, 85–6), compared with Hamlet's hyperbolic vow to remake his memory in accordance with the Ghost's task. Ophelia's passivity is expressed dramatically by the fragmentation of her roles. We have seen that Hamlet's appearance as a solitary melancholic with a book is related to what we hear in soliloquy, and is not divorced from the idea of a personality that can express itself in this way. When Ophelia appears to Hamlet alone with a book, the pose that signifies prayer and devoutness in women[12] is one that is entirely staged by Polonius with a frank admission of its falseness:

Ophelia, walk you here.—Gracious, so please you,
We will bestow ourselves.—Read on this book;
That show of such an exercise may colour
Your loneliness.—We are oft to blame in this:
'Tis too much prov'd, that with devotion's visage
And pious action we do sugar o'er
The devil himself.

(III, i, 42–8)

The madness from which she finally suffers is therefore not, like
Hamlet's, partly a role that can express a larger personality, but
independent and total, a division 'from herself' as well as from
'her fair judgment' (IV, v, 82).

Hamlet's role-playing becomes expressive of melancholy unwillingness to trust or communicate with others, and of a desire
to hide his true personality from his enemies so that it cannot be
defined and manipulated, or 'played on' (III, ii, 342–63). At
the same time the discrepancy between Hamlet and those around
him appears in their search for conventional causes of melancholy
to explain his behaviour. The effect is therefore the opposite of
that created by such comic characters as Jaques, who have a
conceited illusion, punctured by other characters, that they
transcend the stereotyped roles that they play. Hamlet is set off
from those around him because they take (or, in Claudius's case,
pretend to take) the roles that he plays for the reality.

They also use a different kind of language to talk about his
behaviour than he does himself. If, as Levin has suggested, Hamlet's prose (with its lack of expected order) is one way in which he
expresses his disjunction from those around him,[13] the language
that he uses about his melancholy reveals another difference. The
other characters tend to talk about his condition in the terms that
discursive writing had made conventional. Claudius's description
of Hamlet's illness, for example, is couched in the terminology
of the expository books, when he pretends to hope that a sea-
voyage will expel

This something-settled matter in his heart
Whereon his brains still beating puts him thus
From fashion of himself.

(III, i, 173–5)

A similar description can be found in Batman, who wrote of the consequences 'When any obscure thing beteth the brain (as melancholy fleme) . . .'.[14] Equally well known in medical descriptions of the disease were the melancholy fits to which the Queen refers (V, i, 278–9) when she is trying to preserve Hamlet's protective mask of madness for him in the graveyard scene.[15] The bereavement that she suggests earlier as a partial cause of Hamlet's 'distemper' and the frustrated ambition that Rosencrantz and Guildenstern adduce were also well-attested causes:

> Some be brought into it through long sorowe, and heavy-
> nesse for the death of their Parents, or some great losse
> of worldly wealth, or finally by missing and being
> disappoynted of some great desyre and expectation. . . .[16]

Similarly, Polonius's account of the progress of Hamlet's supposed love-melancholy is substantially the same as one that can be found in Laurentius (p. 118), except for the pedantic manner in which one symptom is joined to the next:

> And he repelled, a short tale to make,
> Fell into a sadness, then into a fast,
> Thence to a watch, thence into a weakness,
> Thence to a lightness, and, by this declension,
> Into the madness wherein now he raves. . . .

(II, ii, 145–9)

The 'declension' that Polonius claims to have noticed applies also to his diagnosis as a verbal formulation.

The cures that are offered or suggested to Hamlet are equally well known in treatises on melancholy; the members of the court, in fact, act out the physician's or friend's roles as these are described in the expository books. The first cure for grief that is offered to Hamlet is the *consolatio philosophiae* spoken by the Queen and amplified by Claudius (I, ii, 68–73, 87–107). The argument here is standard and classical, similar to the one that Cicero advances to demonstrate the unreasonableness of excessive grief in the *Tusculan Disputations*: the death of fathers is part of nature's law, and to persist in mourning and grief is unreasonable and impious. The function of friends, however, was not only to give counsel, but also to enable the melancholic, literally, to unburden his heart—an activity that Hamlet regretfully calls impossible in his first soliloquy ('But break, my heart, for I must hold my tongue', I, ii, 159). Rosencrantz evokes the benefits of such unburdening when he finally makes a frontal attack on Hamlet's secrecy: 'Good my lord, what is your cause of distemper? You do surely bar the door upon your own liberty, if you deny your griefs to your friend' (III, ii, 327–30).

Pleasures and distractions were also recommended as ways of drawing the sufferer's mind from himself. The King gives the appearance of accepting this idea (together with that of the value of companionship) when he asks Rosencrantz and Guildenstern to remain in court, 'so by your companies/To draw him on to pleasures . . .' (II, ii, 14–15), and in his display of satisfaction that Hamlet has become interested in the players (III, i, 24–7). The same notion justifies Claudius's proposal of a sea journey as a distraction, since good sea air as well as 'variable objects' supplied by travel were considered healthful for melancholics:[17]

> Haply the seas and countries different,
> With variable objects, shall expel
> This something-settled matter in his heart. . . .
>
> (III, i, 171–3)

The 'cures' that Claudius proposes are put as exactly in the language of contemporary humoral theory as his analysis of Hamlet's condition.

Hamlet also adopts the language of medicine and humoral theory when encouraging the theories of the others; when he denies Rosencrantz and Guildenstern's first suggestion that his melancholy is caused by ambition, for example, he is quick to counter with another standard symptom, that of bad dreams (II, ii, 251–5).[18] But his own thoughts about his state are more apt to be framed in the language derived from the idea of *acedia* or that to be found in treatises advocating the supremacy of reason over the passions. The words that were traditionally applied to *acedia*, and to the progression of vices that it entailed, can be seen in Chaucer's *Parson's Tale*:

> Thanne cometh sompnolence, that is sloggy slombrynge, which maketh a man be hevy and dul in body and in soule . . . Thanne cometh neclicence . . . Thanne cometh ydleness. . . .[19]

Forgetfulness (especially of one's salvation or the means to bring it about) was also part of the idea of sloth, and so were incapacity for one's business, fear of starting or pursuing good works and weariness of life.[20] The popular medieval formulation of the sins by William Piraldus included under *acedia* all of these concepts and a few more: a kind of stupidity that is the cause and result of idleness and negligence, 'tarditas' and 'inconsummatio', not bringing a work to its conclusion. Under the heading, '*Quomodo acedia auferat homini bona gloriae, gratiae, et naturae*', Piraldus included the idea that *acedia* involves letting one's talents and virtues rot, and failing to accomplish one's task in a more worldly sense also.[21]

The expository books tended to mix the two notions of vice and disease together with varying emphases, as we have seen. The 'heavyness' of which Bright speaks is partly physiological, while Lemnius's picture of the solitary man, bestial and stingy (fol. 146ʳ), is weighted with moral overtones. Particularly apt to see melancholy as a vice, of course, are those authors like Charron who treat it primarily as one of the passions that reason should govern. The duties for which melancholy incapacitates men are not so much religious ones, according to such writers, as those involving self-fulfilment and glory:

> Now it [melancholy] doth not onely alter the visage . . .
> but piercing even to the marrow of the bone, *Tristitia
> exiccat ossa: Heavinesse drieth the bones.* It weakeneth
> likewise the soule, troubleth the peace thereof, makes a
> man unapt to good and honourable enterprises. . . .[22]

In *Hamlet* the vocabulary of melancholy as a vice is employed first of all (though negatively) by the imposer of the task, the Ghost:

> I find thee apt;
> And duller shouldst thou be than the fat weed
> That roots itself in ease on Lethe wharf,
> Wouldst thou not stir in this.

(I, v, 31–4)

The Ghost's terms—aptness, dullness, ease—are exactly those connected with sloth, and so is the idea of forgetfulness which he repeats in his injunctions, 'Remember me', 'Do not forget' (I, v, 91; III, iv, 110), and in his allusion to 'Lethe wharf'. Lemnius uses exactly the same words to describe sufferers from 'cold' melancholy: 'Whereby it cometh to passe that such kinde men (lyke Asses or other brute beastes) be blockish, unapt, dull and forgetfull.'[23] The connection with the frame of reference associated with sloth, here and in other descriptions of 'asinine' melancholy (like Lord North's observation, 'I may bee incorrigibly melancholy, but it is not of the Asinine Kind'), is very clear: the ass was the most common symbol for laziness and often figures in representations of *acedia*.[24]

The language that Hamlet applies to himself in two of his soliloquies echoes that of the Ghost, and of the moral or ethical, as opposed to the purely medical side of melancholy. For him the fear (or, in a better sense, prudence) that is an attribute of melancholy is cowardice (II, ii, 565–75; IV, iv, 43). He also calls himself 'tardy' (III, iv, 106), 'dull', and 'muddy-mettled' (II, ii, 561), or earthy in the worst sense, and an ass (II, ii, 561). The last is admittedly a common term of opprobrium, but it is also a reference to the dull beast whose nature is further discussed in the graveyard scene ('your dull ass will not mend his pace with beating', V, i, 56–7), and it is an insult that Hamlet abruptly stops himself from applying to Claudius after the Gonzago play, possibly because he has just used it to refer to himself.[25] The idea of sleeping while the major business of life remains undone, suggested also in the second soliloquy (II, ii, 561–3), is expanded by Hamlet in the fourth act:

> What is a man,
> If his chief good and market of his time
> Be but to sleep and feed? A beast, no more!
> Sure he that made us with such large discourse,
> Looking before and after, gave us not
> That capability and godlike reason
> To fust in us unus'd. Now, whether it be
> Bestial oblivion. . . .
>
> (IV, iv, 33–40)

The identification of his task as the activity proper to manhood makes the language of *acedia* ('bestial oblivion') appropriate. Hamlet also speaks of the 'fusting' of his reason, and the idea that idleness rusted or destroyed the soul was central to descriptions of sloth, or to moralized accounts of melancholy.[26]

The two principal approaches to melancholy that were combined in the expository books are differentiated in *Hamlet*, not necessarily because Shakespeare made a conscious effort to distinguish between two kinds of language, but because such a differentiation followed naturally from the presentation of a melancholy hero whose subjective views and feelings about himself are markedly distinct from the attitudes of those around him. There is only one point in the play where Hamlet speaks of his melancholy, in soliloquy, as a disease, and this is when he mentions it as a reason for testing the Ghost's story by means of the Gonzago play:

> The spirit that I have seen
> May be a devil; and the devil hath power
> T'assume a pleasing shape; yea and perhaps
> Out of my weakness and my melancholy,
> As he is very potent with such spirits,
> Abuses me to damn me.

> (II, ii, 594–9)

The effect of rationalization is created here as much by the change in terminology as by the context. The argument of the passage is perfectly plausible in Elizabethan terms, as many critics have pointed out—perhaps it is meant to sound excessively so. The devil was thought to take special advantage of the weakened bodies and heightened fantasies of melancholy men, and black melancholy humour was, therefore, '*balneum diaboli*', the devil's bath.[27] But what is striking is that Hamlet should suddenly speak of himself as diseased or temperamentally 'weak', towards the end of a soliloquy in which he has expressed very different attitudes about himself and the causes of his behaviour. The placing of the passage in the soliloquy (the plan for putting on the play precedes the explanation of its necessity) only reinforces the impression created by Hamlet's sole and sudden adoption of conventional speech about melancholy as a humour or temperament. The rest of his private thoughts assume a different frame of reference, and the difference is one more expression of Hamlet's isolation in the play: where the others regard his condition and behaviour from the standpoint of illness and social danger, he sees it in relation to the task that he must perform, and he uses the language of morality to talk about it.

Hamlet's melancholy, which is seen throughout the first part of the play by himself and the others (though in different terms by each) as undesirable rather than in any way creative, is none the less justified by the diseased and rotten world to which it is a response. Since cures for his condition are offered by those who are morally questionable, his isolation, established by the difference between public and private aspects of his performance, or by the differences between his frame of reference and those of other characters, seems virtuous. Furthermore, there is a contrast, created in a variety of ways, between aspects of his nature which are not melancholy at all, and melancholy behaviour which therefore seems forced on him by the exigencies of his situation.[28] The antisocial silence and secretiveness which were characteristic attributes of the melancholy man are painful necessities ('But break, my heart, for I must hold my tongue', I, ii, 159); they become part of the Ghost's command when he makes Horatio and Marcellus swear to silence.[29] But the secretiveness which offends even Horatio (I, v, 120–40) is contrasted with the obvious cordiality with which Hamlet greets the arrival of his friends (I, ii, 161ff.; II, ii, 223ff.). Suspicion and craftiness were also traditional attributes of the melancholy personality; they became stereotyped, as we have seen, in the melancholy machiavels of Elizabethan drama. In Hamlet's case, however, his mistrust of all his interlocutors, his plotting of the play-within-the-play, his adoption of the 'antic disposition' and the element of craftiness in his madness are all contrasted with reminders of a truer personality to which even Claudius attests and which emerges again at the end of the play:

> He, being remiss,
> Most generous, and free from all contriving,
> Will not peruse the foils. . . .
>
> (IV, vii, 134–6)

The same kind of contrast can be seen in Hamlet's treatment of Ophelia. Although there was occasionally some disagreement in the expository books about whether melancholy men could be as susceptible to love as other temperamental types,[30] there was little doubt on this point in the literary tradition: if anybody suffered from melancholy that was not actually caused by love, he was averse to it. This was equally true of melancholy satirists like Marston's spokesmen or Jaques, and of scheming plotters like Don John: solitariness that precluded any interest in love, or intellectual orientations that militated against it, were essential signs of their nature.[31] Marston's Malevole is filled with disgust about women; it is as Altofronto that he is able to love (at least enough for the plot's purposes) the virtuous Maria. In Hamlet both responses appear more complex because they belong to the same person. The cruelty that he shows towards Ophelia is juxtaposed with expressions of tenderness (III, i, 88–9), and with indications that a real love existed before the action of the play began. Misogyny, like other aspects of melancholy behaviour, is seen as a response to a particular situation, involving Ophelia's implication, however innocent on her part, in the evils of the Danish Court.

Finally, the same kind of distinction between melancholy behaviour and a nature that does not really accord with it is made with regard to Hamlet's inability or refusal to play his part as a courtier. Ophelia's speech comparing the social accomplishments that Hamlet used to have with his present 'ecstasy' (III, i, 150–60) is the means, in this case, of showing the past truth behind the present appearances. The original invitation, however, to be 'Our chiefest courtier, cousin, and our son' (I, ii, 117) comes from Claudius, and Hamlet's response is rudeness, idleness and the forgoing of 'all custom of exercises'.[32]

Melancholy in its worst senses—solitude, suspicion, verbal aggressiveness, idleness, unfriendliness—is seen in terms of the diseased society to which it is a response, and which provides some justification even for 'bad' melancholy by corrupting the meaning of sanguine and mirthful activities: love is perverted as lust and incest; courtly entertainment is debased in the King's drinking bouts. The contrasts between the potential courtier, lover, soldier, poet and the disharmonious malcontent roles that Hamlet actually plays are not meant to indicate that the play is a study of sanguine 'melancholy adust';[33] they are rather the image of the discrepancy between what might be and what is.

Hamlet's maladjustment to his world is further expressed by the stylistic discords of the antic disposition. The word 'antic', as the citations in the *OED* show, meant incongruous, grotesque, bizarre, 'uncouthly ludicrous': examples other than the one that is quoted from *Hamlet* associate the word with the unruliness of an anti-masque.[34] The comic and satiric aspects of the antic disposition are inseparable from its stylistic incongruities—Hamlet's prose, his snatches of song and doggerel, the games of hide-and-seek that he plays with the Ghost, and later with Rosencrantz and Guildenstern. Such a variety of tones and styles would have been considered inappropriate in pure tragedy,[35] though Hieronimo's mad speeches and extravagant gestures, or the prose of the crazed Zabina in *Tamburlaine*, provided some precedents. In *Hamlet*, the incongruities express Hamlet's discordant opposition to the tragic action and to his part in it.

A mixture of styles was particularly appropriate for the representation of melancholy, as Burton was also to show. Melancholy was a state that included violent opposites in feeling and behaviour, from total dejection and apathy to hysterical outbursts and frenzy,[36] with swings from one to the other, as the Queen suggests in her descriptions of Hamlet's supposed 'fits' (V, i, 279–282). Lemnius described the variety of melancholy moods and behaviours, the changes (depending on whether the humour was hot or cold) from mirth to sadness,[37] and Bright also gave an account of such diversified moods:

> The perturbations of melancholy are for the most parte, sadde and fearfull . . . sometimes furious, and sometimes merry in apparaunce, through a kinde of Sardonian, and false laughter, as the humour is disposed that procureth these diversities.[38]

The responses that melancholy engendered were not only various, but inappropriate, since they were stimulated by internal disorders:

> Also it commeth of a madnesse, and of disposition of melancholy, when such have lyking and laugh alway of sorrowful things, and make sorrow and dolor for joyful things.[39]

For the representation of such a condition on the stage, the mixture of styles and moods of a performance that was labelled as 'antic' or grotesque, and that had some affinities with the satyr's antics (and therefore with rude satire), had a very obvious appropriateness.

The specific affinity between play-acting and melancholy went further, however, even in non-literary material about the condition. Melancholics were commonly players of roles. Lemnius, for example, discussed the diverse postures of melancholics and drunkards, saying that both had as many affectations, gestures and fancies 'as though they were Stage Players'.[40] Theatrical metaphor entered also into Bright's description of the effects that different kinds of adustion could have in producing varied and inappropriate responses, from 'heavinesse without cause' to rage, frenzy, madness and revenge: 'If bloud minister matter to this fire, every serious thing for a time, is turned into a jest, & tragedies into comedies, and lamentations into gigges and daunces. . . .'[41] Comedy was not only one of the standard cures for melancholy, as we have seen, but, as Bright's analogy suggests, it could also represent, metaphorically, the melancholic's inability to adjust to his situation.

Hamlet's attempt to turn the action of the play into a comedy through the antic disposition can therefore be seen both as the expression of melancholy itself, with its inappropriateness of response, and as an antidote to the melancholy mood. After he has killed Polonius, Hamlet delivers his meditation to Claudius in a tone inappropriate to the immediate confrontation with the King, as well as to his own part in what has just happened:

> *King* Now, Hamlet, where's Polonius?
> *Hamlet* At supper.
> *King* At supper! Where?
> *Hamlet* Not where he eats, but where 'a is eaten: a certain convocation of politic worms are e'en at him. Your worm is your only emperor for diet: we fat all creatures else to fat us, and we fat ourselves for maggots; your fat king and your lean beggar is but variable service—two dishes, but to one table. That's the end.
>
> (IV, iii, 17–25)

The chatty, colloquial tone of this meditation ('Your worm is your only emperor') is disrespectful to its subject as well as to Claudius; the puns and the play of wit that turn emperors who convoke Diets

3 'Inamorato' from the Frontispiece (by C. Le Blon) to Robert Burton's *The Anatomy of Melancholy* (This engraving first appeared in the 3rd edition of 1628)

4 'Democritus Abderites' from the Frontispiece (by C. Le Blon) to
Robert Burton's *The Anatomy of Melancholy*

at Worms into the victims of worms who diet on them are also a way of reducing the importance of Polonius's death by a display of mental and verbal superiority.

The incongruity that is so obvious in the joking that follows Polonius's death is evident from the first assumption of the antic disposition, or just before Hamlet actually announces his intention of assuming it (I, v, 116ff.). His 'wild and whirling words' to Horatio and his levity towards the Ghost after its departure are sufficient indications of the new mood even before he gives it a name; more specifically, he attempts to reduce the Ghost to a stage figure by his reference to it (in terms of the actual stage) as the 'fellow in the cellarage' (I, v, 151), just as later he tries to reduce Polonius to one who 'plays the fool' (III, i, 132) and Claudius to a stock theatrical type, the comic-villainous 'vice' of the late-medieval stage, by referring to him as a 'vice of kings' (III, iv, 97). Hamlet's own comic fooling and his sadness, about which we hear in soliloquies and asides, are meant to bring each other into bitter relief, as his interchange with Ophelia at the play shows:

> *Ophelia* You are merry, my lord.
> *Hamlet* Who, I?
> *Ophelia* Ay, my lord.
> *Hamlet* O God, your only jig-maker! What should a man do but be merry? For look you how cheerfully my mother looks, and my father died within's two hours.
>
> (III, ii, 117–23)

The Gonzago play is one manifestation of the bitter attempt to turn tragedy into comedy that the whole antic disposition represents. In terms of the effect that this interpolated play has on Hamlet's mood, its success and happy result in the achievement of certainty, he is right in calling it a comedy ('For if the King like not the comedy,/Why, then, belike, he likes it not, perdy', III, ii, 287–8), even though it is really a tragedy and called so by the Prologue (III, ii, 144). Hamlet's change of the player's generic designation is reinforced by the fact that he also rewords the original lines from the familiar *Spanish Tragedy*: 'And if the world like not this tragedy,/Hard is the hap of old Hieronimo' (IV, i, 193–4). In the earlier play, Hieronimo insists on staging a tragedy even though he is told that a comedy is more suitable as courtly entertainment, and his triumph consists of turning his interpolated play into a real tragedy for his spectators. Hamlet suggests even more openly by his euphoria after the Gonzago play that for him the King's discomfiture has the effect of comedy.

The Gonzago play works temporarily to transfer melancholy to the King, as Hamlet's first quatrain after Claudius leaves the play indicates:

> Why, let the strucken deer go weep,
>   The hart ungalled play:
> For some must watch, while some must sleep:
>   Thus runs the world away.
>
> (III, ii, 265–8)

The stricken deer was a common melancholy symbol, as we have seen, as well as the symbol for a guilty conscience;[42] it is the King who must now 'watch', because he will be unable to sleep. Hamlet suggests ironically that if the 'comedy' does not do Claudius any good, perhaps another traditional cure, the music provided by recorders, can help him. We see simultaneously Hamlet's desire for music, expressive of his own mood, and the ironic offering of it to the King—the same duality that is evident when Hamlet calls the play a comedy. Appropriately enough, Guildenstern soon enters with talk of the King's 'distemper', and, to make the parallel between Hamlet and Claudius even clearer, Rosencrantz soon again asks Hamlet about the cause of his own 'distemper'. The King's condition[43] reveals itself to be one that writers on melancholy frequently tried to distinguish from the disease, the distress of a guilty conscience.

One achievement of the Gonzago play, then (and one purpose of the 'antic disposition'), is the destruction of Claudius's peace of mind. The remorse to which he is brought is not fruitful for him in the way that Pietro's is in *The Malcontent*, but the two situations are similar. Pietro applies the same image of the stricken deer to himself that Hamlet applies to Claudius:

> *Pietro* I would fain shift place; O vain relief!
> Sad souls may well change place, but not change grief.
> As deer, being struck, fly through many soils,
> Yet still the shaft sticks fast, so—
> *Bilioso* A good old simile, my honest lord.
>
> (III, i, 6–10)

Malevole is even more open than Hamlet in wanting to infect his opponent with his own sleepless melancholy:

> Lean thoughtfulness, a sallow meditation,
> Suck thy veins dry! Distemperance rob thy sleep!
> The heart's disquiet is revenge most deep:
> He that gets blood, the life of flesh but spills,
> But he that breaks heart's peace, the dear soul kills.

(I, iii, 153-7)

Pietro's distemper, like Claudius's, is commented upon by those in court:

> *Bilioso* The Duke is wondrous discontented.
> *Passarello* Ay, and more melancholic than a usurer
> having all his money out at the death of a prince.

(III, i, 129-31)

The transference of melancholy to Claudius is not quite as explicit as the similar transference which occurs in *The Malcontent*, but it is there. Claudius too is a 'stricken deer' who will be sleepless, and Hamlet's ironic offerings of the 'comedy' and of music only emphasize the point. From then on Claudius speaks of Hamlet (as Hamlet does of him) as a disease of which he must rid himself (IV, iii, 9-11; IV, iii, 65-7); like Hamlet he is made to assume an appropriate response to his situation.

Hamlet's own assumption of a manner appropriate to his world is dramatized in the graveyard scene. The antic disposition that begins with his efforts to turn the Ghost into a comic stage ghost and that reaches its climax in the explicit and extended theatricality of the Gonzago play is in obvious contrast with his manner after his return from the sea-journey. If the first part of the play has dramatized the social aspects of melancholy by means of melancholy role-playing, the graveyard scene presents a more objective and impersonal picture of the melancholic as a thinker, by means of the visual impression of the scene and the established meanings of the characters, conversations and actions of which it is composed. Since the subject of contemplative melancholy that is objectively justified does not lend itself easily to action or soliloquy, it is transmitted as an animated and speaking picture, which is similar to many of its details to contemporary representations of Saturnian melancholy, both in literature and in the pictorial arts. Hamlet's advice to the players about the proper deportment of the clowns is suggestive also with regard to the antics of the clown-grave-diggers in the graveyard scene:

> And let those that play your clowns speak no more than is set down for them; for there be of them that will themselves laugh, to set on some quantity of barren spectators to laugh too, though in the meantime some necessary question of the play be then to be considered.
>
> (III, ii, 36–41).

One of the necessary questions to be considered in the graveyard scene is that of heroic or tragic melancholy, and the clowns are actually essential to the statement that is made iconographically as well as verbally.

The graveyard scene, removed as it is (until the arrival of Ophelia's funeral cortège) from the action of the play, provides a kind of emblematic epitome for several of its important themes. The contrast between appearance and reality, for example, which Hamlet has already talked about in terms of women's painting (III, i, 142–3), is epitomized by the discrepancy between 'my lady's painting' and the reality of the skull,[44] just as the presence and talk of rotting bodies renders in a different mode the play's emphasis on decay and disease, the image of Denmark as 'rotten'.[45] The idea of suicide, which has been important in Hamlet's soliloquies and asides, is rendered visually in Ophelia's 'maimed' funeral rites later in the scene, and verbally in the clown's discussion of her end. It is, therefore, not surprising that the subject of melancholy also, used throughout the play to define the distance between Hamlet and the other characters, is here represented in a highly condensed verbal and pictorial form that serves to give objective validity to some of Hamlet's postures and feelings earlier.

The general association of graveyards and melancholy in its worst senses would, of course, have been obvious to Shakespeare's audience, and we have already seen graveyards used in plays like *Antonio's Revenge* to create a general atmosphere of melancholy gloom. Graves and graveyards were traditionally the subject of melancholy dreams, like those described by Nashe in *The Terrors of the Night*, a work that discussed those qualities of churchyards— their affinity with melancholy and night—that made them fitting settings for tragedies. This is the kind of atmosphere that Hamlet briefly invokes earlier in the play as the analogue to conventional dramatic postures of revenge:

> 'Tis now the very witching time of night,
> When churchyards yawn, and hell itself breathes out
> Contagion to this world. Now could I drink hot blood,
> And do such bitter business as the day
> Would quake to look on.
>
> (III, ii, 378–82)

This is the atmosphere associated with the infernal and sinister aspects of the Ghost's visit and the 'eruption' in the state that it signifies, the very opposite of the 'wholesome' nights that are associated with the Christmas season (I, i, 158–64). The 'contagion' that Hamlet later sees hell as breathing out on the world in connection with yawning churchyards and the 'witching time of night' is associated with other diseased contagions and 'blastments', such as Lucianus's poison in the Gonzago play: 'Thou mixture rank, of midnight weeds collected,/With Hecat's ban thrice blasted, thrice infected' (III, ii, 251–2).

The context of verbal imagery and ghostly visitations that has linked the idea of graveyards in the play with that of melancholy in its worst senses—night, witchcraft and disease—makes the graveyard scene itself particularly striking in its clarity and comic detachment. The physical details that the Clowns dwell on, their jokes and quibbles about what they do and about recent events in the play, the way in which the First Clown maintains his verbal positions against Hamlet, all indicate the autonomous character of a scene that is emphatically not a mere projection of a melancholy imagination, or a setting for conventionally gloomy events. The fact that the graves and the skull are actually there makes Hamlet's meditations absolutely just, although the content of his reflections is often similar to what he has said before in other contexts. Melancholy is therefore pictured in the graveyard scene not as excess and incongruity of response, but in its associations with knowledge of the truth. The scene abounds in allusions, visual and verbal, to the 'Children of Saturn', who were so often portrayed in the visual arts, and to the professions and concerns that were associated with Saturn. As a tableau, it presents the idea of melancholy in its Aristotelian sense, and of the melancholic as one whose solitude and alienation are bound up with unusual gifts for contemplation.

The scenic picture in which the central figure is the melancholy man meditating upon a skull is filled out, visually and verbally, by a group of human figures, animals, occupations and professions traditionally associated with melancholy. We have already seen that the occupations that were considered to be governed by Saturn included the highest and lowest, extreme wealth and poverty, authority and command on the one hand, and the humblest services on the other. The grave-diggers represent and talk about most of the lowly Saturnian professions, their particular work, grave-digging, being one of the traditional examples.[46] The earth in which they dig and of which they sing was, of course, the element particularly associated with melancholy, and the pick-axe that comes up in one of the Clown's songs (V, i, 91) was occasionally Saturn's instrument. Almost all of the other occupations, professions and artifacts mentioned in the Clown's quibbles were thought to be governed by Saturn also: the gardeners and ditchers (V, i, 30), the mason, shipwright and carpenter who figure in the riddle about grave-making (V, i, 41ff.), the gallows-maker, and the tanners (V, i, 162–8), as well as the parchments which they produced and which Hamlet mentions (V, i, 110–13).[47] The lowly activities mentioned by the Clowns provide a counterpoint to Hamlet's meditations, even while they amplify the frame of reference that is central to the whole scene.

While the Clowns discuss and represent the lower Saturnian professions, Hamlet himself speaks of the higher ones: the politician who 'would circumvent God' (V, i, 77–9); the lawyer with his cases, tenures and tricks; and the greatest commanders of earthly power: Caesar and Alexander. Melancholics, even when not endowed with the true wisdom that could apprehend the hidden (sometimes occult) reality behind appearances, were thought to have a kind of experiential shrewdness that made them astute politicians, and they had a talent for wielding power.[48] The law, especially with the negative connotations that Hamlet gives it (V, i, 95ff.), also had a connection with melancholy: extensive litigation was thought to be both a cause and an effect of the melancholy disposition.[49] This is the basis of the melancholy personality that Vindice offers to his employer, Lussurioso, in *The Revenger's Tragedy*:

Lussurioso Tell me, what has made thee so melancholy?
Vindice Why, going to law.
Lussurioso Why, will that make a man melancholy?
Vindice Yes, to look long upon ink and black buckram.
I went to law in *anno quadragesimo secundo*, and I waded
out of it in *anno sexagesimo tertio*.
Lussurioso What, three and twenty years in law?
Vindice I have known those that have been five and
fifty, and all about a pullen and pigs.
Lussurioso May it be possible such men should breathe,
to vex the terms so much?

(IV, ii, 48–58)

In the graveyard, Hamlet 'vexes' lawyers' terms ('Is this the
fine of his fines, and the recovery of his recoveries . . .', V, i, 101–2)
to show the vanity of the lawyer's 'quiddities' in this setting. The
only profession mentioned by Hamlet that was not specifically a
Saturnian one is the courtier's, and even this figure is presented
in his most political guise, precisely the aspect of vain courtier-
ship on which Burton was to expatiate in his Preface to the
Anatomy.[50]

The idea of mutability that provides the perspective against
which all these different activities are viewed was also the particular province of Saturn, who was closely associated with time.[51]
The scythe or sickle that he carried was a symbol of the connection, and the story that he devoured his own children was
interpreted allegorically to mean that time was the destroyer of
what it had created. Saturn also represented the sciences of
measurement, which in turn could be associated with time. Clocks
and dials were part of his paraphernalia, and the hour-glass is
prominent on the wall behind Dürer's figure of Melencolia.
The genesis of historical thinking was therefore also attributed to
Saturn; as Cartari put it, '. . . de Saturne l'histoire commença
d'avoir voix, & d'estre cognue: car sans doubte au paravant que
les temps fussent distingués elle ne pouvoit estre sinon muete &
incognue'.[52]

The subject of time in its relation to personal and general
history, as well as to death, is central to the songs and the dialogue
of the graveyard scene. The Clown sings about the passage of time
and the onset of age and of death:

> But age, with his stealing steps,
> Hath clawed me in his clutch,
> And hath shipped me intil the land,
> As if I had never been such.

(V, i, 71–4)

Hamlet meditates on the vanity of all human activities, because death is the end of them, and he and the Clown discuss in some detail the length of time required for the decomposition of a body. The idea of historical time has importance here as well: Hamlet's personal life is now related to the sequence of public events that have been alluded to in the play, and the grave-digger is a measurer in this regard also:

> *Hamlet* How long hast thou been a grave-maker?
> *1 Clown* Of all the days i' th' year, I came to't that day
> our last King Hamlet overcame Fortinbras.
> *Hamlet* How long is that since?
> *1 Clown* Cannot you tell that? Every fool can tell that:
> it was that very day that young Hamlet was born. . . .
> I have been sexton here, man and boy, thirty years.

(V, i, 137–57)

It has been said that Hamlet suffers from a disoriented time sense throughout the first part of the play; one of the many ways in which he is cut off from those around him is that he cannot and does not want to adjust to their time scheme.[53] In his first soliloquy, for example, he seems far more appalled by the speed with which his mother has remarried than by the incestuous nature of her marriage, and he expresses the disproportion between his feelings about time and the actual succession of events in a highly exaggerated form to Ophelia in the play scene:

> *Hamlet* For look you how cheerfully my mother looks,
> and my father died within's two hours.
> *Ophelia* Nay, 'tis twice two months, my lord.
> *Hamlet* So long? Nay then, let the devil wear black,
> for I'll have a suit of sables. O heavens! die two months
> ago, and not forgotten yet? Then there's hope a great
> man's memory may outlive his life half a year. . . .

(III, ii, 120–8)

Time is the source of Hamlet's anxieties about the impermanent motives and unpredictable consequences of action, and about the impossibility of enduring love, problems that the Player King restates in his stylized and archaic couplets:

> I do believe you think what now you speak;
> But what we do determine oft we break.
> Purpose is but the slave to memory,
> Of violent birth, but poor validity. . . .
> What to ourselves in passion we propose,
> The passion ending, doth the purpose lose.
> The violence of either grief or joy
> Their own enactures with themselves destroy. . . .
> This world is not for aye; nor 'tis not strange
> That even our loves should with our fortunes change. . . .
>
> (III, ii, 181–96)

The dialogue with the grave-digger in which Hamlet is placed objectively in time and in relation to his father is the antithesis of the subjectively dislocated time sense we have seen earlier. Hamlet's age is presented with the same detachment as the information about the length of time it will take a tanner's corpse to rot.

Not only death as the end of all, but especially death by suicide (Ophelia's questionable death by drowning), dominates the conversation in the graveyard, and suicide too was the particular province of Saturn, as well as the special preoccupation of melancholics. The 'gallows-maker' whose craft and product are discussed by the Clowns (V, i, 43–9) was shown in many of the representations of the children of Saturn,[54] since the gallows were associated, not only with criminals (who were Saturnian types), but also with suicide: in at least one picture of the gallows tree the victim is a suicide stringing up his own rope.[55] Death by drowning, Ophelia's particular fate, was claimed by Chaucer's Saturn as part of his prerogative and power.[56]

If the first part of the graveyard scene is viewed as a Saturnian-melancholy emblem, its centre is the figure of the thinker, turning the world over for his own inspection, considering the vanity of all human activity against the perspective provided by the skull that he holds. It is in this kind of pose that personifications of Melancholy, whether male or female, were often portrayed in paintings and engravings. The picture of Hamlet as the melancholy thinker, meditating on objects of death and especially on the skull of the Court Jester, contains the same amalgamation of the medieval 'vanity' motif with the more modern one of melancholy that was often seen in the pictorial arts.[57] Where the medieval skull, frequently meditated upon by saints, had pointed a moral about the shortness of life and the transitoriness of all things, the melancholic meditating on a skull was cultivating and dramatizing his own sensibility as much as pointing to any objective lesson. Hamlet's varied imagery throughout the play, but especially in the graveyard scene—the number of ideas and images that the skull gives rise to—characterizes him as a thinker and makes us see that his sensibility is far superior to that of anybody else in the play.[58]

Examples of personified figures of Melancholy brooding over skulls can be found in the collection in *Saturn*, as well as elsewhere: an engraved portrait of a pensive young nobleman with a skull in his hand, made by Lucas van Leyden in 1519, may well be a representation of this subject.[59] The seventeenth-century painting of 'Meditation' or 'Melancholy' by Domenico Feti is another, more certain example.[60] Here a female figure sits resting her forehead on one hand and looks down at a skull; the objects around her include broken columns, a broken torso of a satyr, some books, an hour-glass and artistic implements; a dog is chained up in the corner. The purpose of the picture is to show the vanity of all human activity, the relics of which are surveyed by the thinking figure. An etching of Melancholy by Benedetto Castiglione [61] is even more relevant to the scene from *Hamlet*. In this picture a female figure sits with a skull and a musical scroll in her lap, with various artistic and musical instruments around her. Behind her are a cat and a chained dog. The inscription at the top of the etching, '*Ubi Inletabilitas Ibi Virtus*', makes the subject-matter very clear. The unhappiness of the melancholic— in fact, his incapacity for being cheered up—are the conditions of virtue. Artistic and musical implements, like the statuary relics and scattered books in the Feti painting, are emblematic also of distractions from melancholy: since they are themselves subject to the decay of time, they cannot (and should not) give any solace to the central brooding figures except perhaps by providing the source of their meditations.

The iconographic associations of the graveyard scene give added meaning to Hamlet's manner and behaviour in it—his relinquishment of the madness and the play-acting of the antic disposition. Whereas his earlier levity was often in contrast with the gravity of what was taking place, the discrepancies between his situation and his reactions to it have now disappeared. On entering the graveyard, his first remark (with its obvious pun on 'grave') is tantamount to a denial of his behaviour in earlier episodes: 'Has this fellow no feeling of his business, that 'a sings in grave-making?' (V, i, 64). It is now the Clowns who do most of the fooling, and the quibbles they indulge in, based on their inability or unwillingness to understand what their interlocutor is saying, are not in fact very different from Hamlet's more deliberate quibbling earlier. Yorick's skull, the focus of the early part of the scene, is the most visible token of Hamlet's abandonment of the comic mode. His meditations about death and the passing of all things include thoughts about the transitoriness of the jokes and antics of the Court Jester. To the extent that Hamlet himself has been fulfilling the role of jester,[62] the scene is a comment, visual and verbal, on the whole 'antic disposition'. Melancholy meditation is now explicitly harmonized with the world that gives rise to it.

The importance of the first part of the scene, then, is that it justifies Hamlet's imagination as a melancholic through the dialogues, pictures and contrasts with earlier episodes that it provides. The imagination was the mental faculty that was considered to be particularly associated with melancholy; for this reason, when Spenser allegorized the three faculties of the mind, Memory, Imagination and Understanding, in the second book of *The Faerie Queene*, he portrayed the imagination, Phantastes, as a melancholic who was born under Saturn.[63] Melancholy people were notoriously the victims of 'imaginings', as Laurentius explained:

Their imagination is troubled onely three waies: by nature, that is to say by the constitution of the bodie: by the minde, that is to say, by some violent passion, whereunto they have given themselves: and by the intercourse or medling of evill angels, which cause them oftentimes to foretell & forge very strange things in their imaginations.[64]

Since the corrupted imaginations of melancholics produced delusions and hallucinations, Hamlet says earlier in the play that he fears his imagination: the Ghost that he has seen may be a devil using his melancholy weakness (just as the Ghost's second visit is attributed by Gertrude to Hamlet's mad imagination). The function that he ascribes to the Gonzago play is, therefore, to check on the questionable trustworthiness of his own imagination:

> If his occulted guilt
> Do not itself unkennel in one speech,
> It is a damned ghost that we have seen,
> And my imaginations are as foul
> As Vulcan's stithy.
>
> (III, ii, 78–82)

In the graveyard, however, Hamlet renounces his former fears, and follows his imagination even into paths that are abhorrent to him: 'And now how abhorred in my imagination it is! Here hung those lips that I have kiss'd I know not how oft . . .' (V, i, 180–1). In conversation with Horatio, he is now able to defend the imagination and the 'curiosity' that enable him to trace the dust of Alexander stopping a beer-barrel:

> *Hamlet*   Dost thou think Alexander look'd a this fashion
>   i' th' earth?
> *Horatio*   E'en so.
> *Hamlet*   And smelt so? Pah!
> *Horatio*   E'en so, my lord.
> *Hamlet*   To what base uses we may return, Horatio!
>   Why may not imagination trace the noble dust of
>   Alexander till 'a find it stopping a bunghole?
> *Horatio*   'Twere to consider too curiously to consider so.
> *Hamlet*   No, faith, not a jot; but to follow him thither
>   with modesty enough, and likelihood to lead it, as
>   thus. . . .
>
> (V, i, 192–201)

Horatio is cautious here, as he was in warning Hamlet not to follow the Ghost (I, iv, 62ff.), and in his fears at that point that Hamlet 'waxes desperate with imagination' (I, iv, 87). Again, the graveyard scene clarifies a contrast that is made earlier in the play: Horatio is the admirable, well-tempered man in whom the elements are perfectly mixed (III, ii, 63–72), but he has neither Hamlet's task to perform nor the heightened imaginative faculty which Hamlet is finally able to defend.

The scene in the graveyard consists of two main parts, with the arrival of the funeral procession introducing the second, less emblematic portion. At the very end of the second part, however, Hamlet's weary and ironic couplet, after his unhappy confrontation with Laertes, can be seen as reiterating in symbolic terms the negative connotations of melancholy as a disease or evil which have also been implicit throughout the play:

> Let Hercules himself do what he may,
> The cat will mew, and dog will have his day.
>
> (V, i, 285–6)

The dog and the cat were two of the most common animal symbols of melancholy; we have seen that they served for melancholy background material in many plays and poems, and that they were represented in pictures of Melancholy like Castiglione's.[65] The meaning of the couplet appears to be that even if Hamlet were to attain the heroic stature of Hercules, he cannot entirely overcome the worst kinds of melancholy around him, the melancholy that is involved in the animal imagery that he elsewhere applies to Claudius: 'a paddock . . . a bat, a gib' (III, iv, 190).[66] The cat and the dog symbolize the objectively evil or irreducibly unheroic state of a world that even the hero's efforts cannot correct.

Hamlet's allusion to Hercules at the end of the graveyard scene has considerable significance as an expression of his attitude towards the heroic-melancholy role, since it is not the first reference to that hero in the play. When Hamlet first brings up the comparison of himself with Hercules, it is in order to reject it: 'My father's brother; but no more like my father/Than I to Hercules' (I, ii, 152–3). Since Hercules was a type of heroic virtue in the Renaissance,[67] Hamlet is expressing his reluctance, at the beginning of the play, to assume a heroic role for which he feels inadequate. The second reference is a theatrical one. When Hamlet learns from Rosencrantz and Guildenstern about the arrival of the players, he discusses with them the encroachment of the child-actors on the popularity and reputation of the 'tragedians of the city':

Hamlet   Do the boys carry it away?
Rosencrantz   Ay, that they do, my lord—
Hercules and his load too.

(II, ii, 356–7)

'Hercules and his load', or Hercules carrying the world, was perhaps also the sign of the Globe Theatre where the real play was being performed;[68] if this is so, the hero in this allusion is transformed into a theatrical emblem and subjected to the encroachments of time through the usurpation of the boys just at the point in the action where Hamlet is about to begin his own theatrical venture, the staging of the Gonzago play. In the final allusion in the graveyard, Hamlet no longer rejects the association with Hercules, even though he expresses a sense of its futility.[69]

The shifting comparisons of Hamlet with Hercules also have a specific relevance to the idea of melancholy as virtue. Hercules was the son of Jupiter, a relationship that Hamlet adopts metaphorically when he speaks of his father as Jove-like to Gertrude (III, iv, 56) and to Horatio:

For thou dost know, O Damon dear,
   This realm dismantled was
Of Jove himself. . . .

(III, ii, 275–7)

In the Renaissance Hercules was considered to be the type not only of physical strength, but especially of mental virtue and conquest of the passions. Several of his exploits were allegorized in terms of spiritual significance; the victory over the Nemean lion, for example, could be interpreted as the conquest of anger.[70] None the less, his madness, for which he repented after he came to his senses, caused him to kill his children, and (in Euripides' version of his exploits) his wife Megara as well.[71] Finally, the allegorized legend of 'Hercules at the crossroads', a favourite subject of Renaissance painting,[72] concerned his confrontation with a choice between pleasure and virtue, and had strong similarities, in some of its details, with representations of melancholy.

When Hercules in the paintings chose virtue rather than pleasure, he turned his back on the flowery landscapes, games, social occupations and couples wandering arm-in-arm (in the more religious versions, on the way to hell), and chose the steep and stony path that was travelled by solitary pilgrims. Of the two women personifying 'Voluptas' and 'Virtus', Voluptas, naked or seductively clothed, had much affinity with representations of the sanguine temperament in the complexion books, while Virtus, veiled or dressed like a nun, was sometimes portrayed in the same posture and aspect as Dürer's picture of Melencolia. The background figures behind the two personifications also had much in common with representations of the 'children of Venus' and the 'children of Saturn' respectively.[73]

Hamlet's comparisons of himself with Hercules, therefore, characterize his heroic role as well as his ambivalence about assuming it. Although Hercules was punished with madness, as Hamlet says in the end he himself has been (V, ii, 220–31), his heroic feats were taken to represent spiritual triumphs that were linked with melancholy and solitary refusals to indulge in social pleasures. Hercules chose, in Christian terms, the stony path to heaven to which Ophelia jokingly alludes when saying good-bye to her brother in the first act (I, iii, 46–51), and was a pilgrim, a figure with which she identifies Hamlet in her madness:

> How should I your true love know
> From another one?
> By his cockle hat and staff,
> And his sandal shoon.
>
> (IV, v, 22–5)[74]

Hercules was always also simply the successful performer of tasks, the destroyer of monsters and the purger of rottenness (as in his cleansing of the Augean stables), and the emblem of strength who temporarily carried the world on his shoulders. The final identification with Hercules on Hamlet's part is ironic, however, and reiterates the complexity of the ideas and images of melancholy in the play. The graveyard objectively justifies the vision of mutability that reduces Caesar and Alexander to earth; the histrionics with Laertes that comprise the greater part of the second section of the scene provide an extreme example of the falseness of theatrical heroics, hyperboles and self-assertions. The scene that establishes the validity of Hamlet's melancholy imagination is also one that demonstrates the ultimate absurdity of expressions of Herculean heroism.

The end of the antic disposition in the graveyard scene introduces one of the most noticeable changes in Hamlet's behaviour in the last scene: there is now no effort to theatricalize the action. The 'rash' act that has saved his life on the boat has involved a surrender of such attempts to restructure the play: 'Ere I could make a prologue to my brains,/They had begun the play . . .' (V, ii, 30–1).[75] Claudius is now Hamlet's 'mighty opposite' (V, ii, 62) rather than a theatrical buffoon or 'vice of kings', and Osric, contrary to Polonius, reveals himself to be entirely the comic 'waterfly' that Hamlet makes him to be. The fact of the apology to Laertes (V, ii, 218–36) is as significant as the disowning of previous behaviour as 'madness'; it expresses a renewal of courtesy, and, since the Queen has urged the apology, a return to filial as well as courtly behaviour. In marked contrast to other melancholy revengers like Hieronimo, Antonio or Vindice, Hamlet does not stage a masque or play through which to effect his revenge. He submits himself instead to the scene that his enemies have staged down to its last details—including its time-sequences, placement of characters, sound-effects and fatal props—and expresses his belief in the providential outcome of an action that Claudius does not ultimately control either. Paradoxically, Hamlet becomes the revenger at the point where he accepts again the courtly role that he has given up at the beginning of the play.

We can now see how the devices that convey the idea of melancholy in *Hamlet* are fused so that they express, through their interdependence, the meanings behind the conventions. Hamlet's role-playing conveys what lies behind the melancholic's traditional attributes of shrewdness and secrecy—his sense of a hostile world that makes him unwilling to divulge his identity to others; Hamlet's theatricality and his mixture of styles and modes, all of which are inseparable, express his refusal to accept his situation as it is laid out for him. Disease in *Hamlet*, the parts that the hero plays, and the landscape which he inhabits and which includes the other figures in the drama, are all related but varied manifestations of a single image.

A subordinate character like Ophelia, for example, rather than merely emphasizing the idea of melancholy by accumulation, mirrors (and distorts) those aspects of Hamlet's thought and behaviour that are especially connected with the passive side of melancholy: the part of feeling and memory in responding to loss. Her madness in the fourth act echoes Hamlet's and carries it to uncontrolled extremes in the confusion of styles, the snatches of song and doggerel, the inappropriate remarks, the outrageous costume. She is also to an extent a seer in her madness, expressing her insights in highly symbolic terms, characterizing Hamlet as a pilgrim and identifying the other characters (although it is now difficult for us to determine who is meant in each case) by the flowers that she gives them. Reinforcing her own association with flowers throughout the play, the flowers and herbs that she dispenses, many of them symbolic of melancholy or known as melancholy cures, translate the idea of that disease into a gentler idiom; they express her own nature as an inadequate healer (cf. III, i, 38–42), as well as the pathetic victim of the disease the play deals with. Rosemary, rue, fennel and violets, aside from the meanings that are usually assigned to them, were associated with melancholy cures,[76] while the columbine was the flower of melancholy because its letters (*ancolie* in French) stood in some relation to the word 'melancholy';[77] for this reason it was a common symbol for the sorrows of the Virgin,[78] and may be symbolic of Ophelia's virginal sorrows also. Characterization and symbolism are inseparable in her case, and both are also fused with the idea of melancholy in the play.

For Hamlet himself (as for Marston), melancholy is connected with the diseased world to which it is a response, and which justifies the sufferer's perceptions and actions. The prevalence of disease imagery in *Hamlet* has been well analysed by critics;[79] where the first part of the play contains many generalized allusions to corruption and contagion, the second part abounds in references to specific diseases, such as pleurisy (IV, vii, 117), ulcer (IV, vii, 123), 'canker' (V, ii, 69), 'imposthume' or boil (IV, iv, 27), 'hectic' (fever) (IV, iii, 66). In the loose terminology of contemporary medicine most of these diseases were connected with melancholy,[80] and Shakespeare was drawing on what the medical writers had already suggested: a metaphoric connection of all diseases with melancholy. Disease is not only part of the verbal imagery of the play; it is embodied in some of its main characters, as in Webster's plays (though not merely by attaching the word 'melancholy' to several characters): in Claudius as a 'canker'

(V, ii, 69), in the Queen as hiding the 'ulcerous place' that Hamlet tries to lance (III, iv, 147), in the mad Ophelia, and, of course, in the hero himself.

Although the positive and negative aspects of melancholy are fused in Hamlet throughout the play, the progress of the action is related to a shifting emphasis first on the worse and then on the noble associations of the condition. The first part of the play concentrates on dramatizing the disorders of thought and behaviour, the disjointed soliloquies and self-reproaches, the rudeness and cruelty, though never without a clear sense of the situation that justifies such alienation; the graveyard scene presents the melancholy thinker whose perceptions are entirely borne out by his setting, although again not without reminders that the time-ridden world that supplies the source of melancholy reflection also defines the limitations of heroic action.

Melancholy is integrally related to the progress of the action because the genres and styles which give it literary shape are made to be genuinely expressive of Hamlet's state of mind. Like Burton, Shakespeare uses melancholy stereotypes in order to reveal what went into their creation in the first place: the disgust of the would-be lover whose responses have been poisoned by images of lust, the disillusioned idealism of the satirist, the scepticism of the scholar for whom objective value is meaningless. The perspective provided by the expository books has only a limited usefulness (even though we can discover in them some of the language through which melancholics communicated their condition), because they rest on the very assumptions about health and social conventions that the play questions. For Hamlet, as for Burton, melancholy stereotypes (purposely exaggerated) have only a provisional reality, because melancholy is also connected with the vision that enables each to see the inadequate and temporary nature of such roles.

Five

The *Anatomy of Melancholy* as Literature

Burton and English Literature

The most ambitious literary treatment of melancholy in the seventeenth century was *The Anatomy of Melancholy*, Burton's life's work, which first appeared in 1621 and which he revised continually until his death in 1640. The constant, obsessive revisions of this long work give us one important clue about it: it is highly contrived, and, in its author's eyes, a work of art of very large scope indeed. All of Burton's derogatory remarks about the carelessness of his writing and the raggedness of his form must therefore be interpreted as defining and characterizing the personality that he displays for us in the *Anatomy*, a highly artificial personality, as all are, because style makes the man: 'our style bewrays us' (I, 27).[1]

Though Burton makes melancholy his subject and his text, his intentions are not strictly informative. The philosophical concerns of the literature of the preceding twenty-five years are fully reflected in the *Anatomy*, which expresses a general scepticism extending to all forms of knowledge, ancient and new, Stoic and scholastic, as well as scientific. In associating melancholy with this scepticism and with the shifting viewpoints that go with it, Burton is more closely attuned to the works with which we have been dealing, such as Marston's satires and plays, Jonson's comedies and *Hamlet*, than to the expository treatises that treat melancholy more straightforwardly. This chapter will therefore have two main purposes. The first will be to show how Burton transformed the expository treatment of melancholy, even in its broadest and most humanistic versions, through his knowledge of the literary works dealing with the subject. The second, closely related, aim will be to demonstrate that one of the main achievements of the *Anatomy* as a work of literature is to portray the melancholy mind in action, even while it is occupied with melancholy as a formal subject. This is Burton's stated intention at the outset (I, 21), and its execution marks the difference in kind, not merely in degree, of the literary quality of the *Anatomy* from that of the expository books that preceded it.

One of the difficulties of relating the *Anatomy* to English literature is the scarcity of direct references to English sources, compared with the abundance of quotations, generally identified and explained by Burton's own notes, from classical and medieval ones. Occasional derogatory references to types of modern literature in the vernacular as frivolous and unworthy may partly explain why Burton stressed the sources he did. He defended his stories, for example, as coming from 'worthy philosophers and physicians' rather than from 'circumforanean rogues and gipsies', and expatiated on the dangers of play-books, romances, love-stories and other forms of popular literature (I, 209, II, 93, III, 109).

Despite this disclaimer, however, the *Anatomy* contains many allusions to English literature, some of which Burton acknowledges in his own notes. The authors that Burton identifies include Chaucer (the most often quoted English author), More, Spenser, Sidney, Bacon (*Essays*, and, in later editions, *The New Atlantis*), Marlowe ('Hero and Leander'), Daniel, Drayton, Jonson (*Volpone, Every Man out of his Humour, Epicœne* and lyrics), and Shakespeare. The undoubted Shakespearian references are to 'Venus and Adonis' and 'The Rape of Lucrece', *Much Ado About Nothing* and *Romeo and Juliet*.[2]

A more comprehensive picture of Burton's interests in English literature is provided by the evidence we have of his private library.[3] Among the works listed in his collection are five plays by Jonson not mentioned in the *Anatomy*, *The Spanish Tragedy*, several plays each by Chapman, Beaumont and Fletcher, Middleton, Heywood, Dekker and Shirley, Webster's *The White Devil* and *The Duchess of Malfi*, Ford's *The Lover's Melancholy* (which was indebted to Burton) and Marston's *Parasitaster*. Among the satires and works with satiric elements are five of Nicholas Breton's 'pasquils', Greene's *Groatsworth of Wit* and *Quip for an Upstart Courtier*, Harington's *Metamorphosis of Ajax*, Hall's *Virgidemiarum*, and both of Marston's satires, *Pygmalion's Image* and *The Scourge of Villainy*.[4] The evidence of the library indicates that Burton's apology in the *Anatomy* for writing his own work in the vernacular (I, 30) may be symptomatic of a desire to disclaim what had a great attraction for him.

The library, then, establishes that Burton's knowledge of English literature, and especially of English drama and satire, was far greater than his direct allusions and notes in the *Anatomy* suggest.[5] Burton often embedded snatches and images from English literary sources in his text when they were related by thought or mood to what he was saying, without feeling that he had to take the trouble to identify them. Two lines from one of Ophelia's songs, for example (the first very slightly misquoted), 'Young men will do it when they come to it' and 'tomorrow is St. Valentine's day', were already noted by Shilleto.[6] Burton's protest that his satire is general rather than aimed at any particular person uses the same proverbial tag, in exactly the same context, as Hamlet's ironic version of this traditional disclaimer to Claudius ('Let the galled jade wince, our withers are unwrung', III, ii, 236–7):

> If he be not guilty, it concerns him not; it is not my freeness of speech, but a guilty conscience, a galled back of his own that makes him winch (I, 121).

Furthermore, casual phrases like 'unquiet Hotspurs' (I, 56) (in the section on the uselessness of wars carried on for the personal aggrandizement and glory of the few) or the allusion to a 'Comedy of Errors' (I, 52) indicate the degree to which an English dramatic tradition was a natural part of Burton's consciousness.

The presence of such verbal echoes in the *Anatomy* makes the infrequency of direct quotations especially striking. The explanation for this discrepancy lies only partly in Burton's feelings of literary snobbery (his particular reverence for the classical tradition); frequently plays did not offer the pithy, illustrative maxims that Burton found most quotable. Some knowledge of dramatic context is generally needed in order to make a quotation from a play intelligible, and, more important, most plays were in blank verse and prose, not in sententious epigrams or couplets that made it easy to extract passages. The approximate quotation from

Romeo and Juliet is in fact the verse couplet from the end of the play (III, 187) and attests to Burton's habit of quoting from memory.

The affinities with other English writers, however, go beyond merely verbal echoes or direct quotations. As a satirist, Burton assumes the guises both of the Jonsonian type of detached critic mocking the follies and vices that he professes himself eager to reform, and of the Marstonian type of the melancholy and disgusted man inveighing against evils that he knows cannot possibly be cured. Both types have classical antecedents, as Burton acknowledges when he quotes from Persius and Horace to differentiate his two principal moods of mockery and rage in terms of the humours of black and yellow bile:

> . . . sometimes again I was *petulanti splene cachinno* [with mocking temper moved to laughter loud], and then again, *urere bilis jecur* [my liver was aflame with gall], I was much moved to see that abuse which I could not mend (I, 19).

It is still possible to see that Burton was alluding to more contemporary satire and its problems. Where Erasmus had remarked that the world was so full of folly that a Democritus would be necessary to laugh at other Democrituses, Burton may well have been referring to the contemporary literary scene—to the continual condemnations of bad, irresponsible, self-seeking satirists by supposedly good and disinterested ones that played such a large part in English dramatic and formal satire—in his expansion of the original metaphor:

> Never so much cause of laughter as now, never so many fools and madmen. 'Tis not one Democritus will serve turn to laugh in these days; we have now need of a 'Democritus to laugh at Democritus'; one jester to flout at another, one fool to fleer at another: a great stentorian Democritus, as big as that Rhodian Colossus (I, 52).

Often the process of expansion involves a complicated merger of a classical source with the contemporary idiom of an English satirist. The following passage, for example, recasts a line from

Lucian by introducing an arraignment of the vices and follies of the rich under the heading of Jonsonian 'humours':

> . . . they have most part some gullish humour or other, by which they are led; one is an epicure, an atheist, a second a gamester, a third a whore-master (fit subjects all for a satirist to work upon) . . . one is mad of hawking, hunting, cocking; another of carousing, horse-riding, spending . . . *Insanit veteres statuas Damasippus emendo*, Damasippus hath an humour of his own, to be talked of . . . (I, 115).

The passage indicates Burton's familiarity with Jonson's sense of the 'humours' as a basis for satiric comedy and suggests that Burton's definition of the term, like Jonson's, stresses folly rather than crime. But just as Jonson includes Sordido, the miser and grain speculator who wants to let the poor starve in *Every Man out of his Humour*, in practice stretching his definition of 'humour' to include crimes as well as follies, so Burton goes beyond idle distractions like hawking and hunting, and in his famous, indignant 'Ride on . . . he cares not' passage, castigates the unfeeling rich who trample on the poor (III, 35-7).

Burton's affinity with Marston's type of satiric outlook involves first of all the use of melancholy itself in creating a satiric *persona*. Like earlier satirists, Burton was faced with the problem of distinguishing legitimate satire from railing. Railers, compared by him (as was usual) with barking dogs, are condemned (I, 30); these are the bad satirists, especially those who attack him. On the other hand, satire has a positive function, which is connected with the duty that scholars have as the advisers of princes.[7] This was the kind of duty that Malevole was fulfilling through the insulting remarks that he made to Duke Pietro, and Burton too points out that 'railing' can be honest reproof, opposed to flattery (I, 308).

An even more important connection with Marston's manner than this theoretical justification of the 'railer' is that Burton too is a satirist who tries to defend himself against the attacks of others by all the means at his command, and these include self-depreciation, as well as other melancholy qualities. All of the difficulties of the satirist's position are revealed through his aggressiveness and defensiveness in 'Democritus to the Reader'. The rhetorical

problem of satire is at least as much of an issue here as the personality of Burton the man,[8] and it seems possible that his exagger-
atedly abrupt about-faces at the end of the Preface are meant to
parody those of some of his fellow satirists:

> Take heed you mistake me not. If I do forget myself,
> I hope you will pardon it. . . . I hate their vices, not
> their persons. . . . If any man take exceptions, let him
> turn the buckle of his girdle, I care not. I owe thee
> nothing (reader), I look for no favour at thy hands,
> I am independent, I fear not. No, I recant, I will not,
> I care, I fear, I confess my fault . . . But what needs all
> this? I hope there will no such cause of offence be given;
> if there be, *Nemo aliquid recognoscat, nos mentimur omnia*
> [let no one take these things to himself, they are all
> but fiction]. I'll deny all (my last refuge), recant all. . .
> (I, 121–3).

In particular, his own melancholy, his 'phantastical fit' (I, 122)
and 'perturbations' are presented as causes of his failure to keep
an even tone: '*difficile est satiram non scribere*, there be so many
objects to divert, inward perturbations to molest, and the very
best may sometimes err . . .' (I, 123). The final formulation of the
compulsion to write satire may be taken from Juvenal, but the
preceding vacillations, not really necessitated by the subject-
matter (none of the satire in the *Anatomy* is directed against
individuals, as some of Marston's vignettes or those of the classical
satirists might appear to be) seem to be an exaggeration of contemporary satiric postures. The defensive self-deprecation that is
a feature of some of Marston's writings occurs here in heightened
form, and melancholy in the sense of madness provides the excuse
for offensiveness:

> I have overshot myself, I have spoken foolishly, rashly,
> unadvisedly, absurdly, I have anatomized mine own
> folly. And now methinks upon a sudden I am awakened
> as it were out of a dream; I have had a raving fit, a
> phantastical fit. . . (I, 122).

Burton makes explicit what had only been implicit in Marston's
hints about his own derangement and its relation to his satire.

Similarly, Burton's famous passage on the miseries of scholars

Democritus omnium derisor
in omnium fine defigitur

Salvator Rosa Inv. fecit

5 Salvatore Rosa 'Democritus' (1650)

is very similar, both substantively and verbally, to the complaints vented by Marston's Lampatho Doria. Like Lampatho, Burton's scholar suffers because he cuts a ridiculous figure among gallants:

> Because they cannot ride an horse, which every clown can do . . . *his populus ridet*, etc., they are laughed to scorn, and accounted silly fools by our gallants. Yea, many times, such is their misery, they deserve it; a mere scholar, a mere ass (I, 303).

'A mere scholar, a mere ass', echoes Lampatho's rejection of his scholarly pursuits, 'You made me an Asse, thus shapt my lot,/ I am a meere Scholler, that is a meere sot.'[9] Lampatho has wasted his spirits in fruitless study, without any prospects of a career, 'What shall I doe, what plot, what course persew?' (Wood, II, 258), and Burton's scholar is made to ask the same question: 'For what course shall he take, being now capable and ready?' (I, 306). Quadratus's bitter answer to Lampatho is almost identical with the answer that Burton supplies, and both may partly be responses to observed conditions:[10]

> Well, heer's my Schollers course, first get a Schoole, And then a ten-pound cure, keepe both. . . (Wood, II, 258).

> The most parable and easy, about which many are employed, is to teach a school, turn lecturer or curate, and for that he shall have falconer's wages, ten pound per annum and his diet. . . . (I, 306).

Both then go on to discuss the possibility of simoniacal church careers.

The main similarity between Lampatho and Burton is that both are preoccupied with the futility of scholastic learning. Lampatho, as we have seen (p. 68), 'stufft noting bookes' with contradictory authorities which drove him to doubt everything; Burton can denigrate school divinity, philosophy or the very authorities whom he is so fond of citing. One example occurs at the end of the first partition, where he describes the uselessness of each branch of study, including school divinity, metaphysics '(intricate subtleties and fruitless abstractions') and philosophy ('a labyrinth of opinions, idle questions, propositions, metaphysical terms', I, 366). Both Marston and Burton are painfully aware of the uselessness of the kind of study to which scholars are committed, not only in worldly terms (the poverty-stricken careers to which it can lead), but also as a means of discovering truth. Burton's affinity with Marston's outlook on the scholarly life extends to all features of it, and again there are enough verbal echoes to suggest that Burton was actually familiar with the picture of the scholar that Marston drew in *What You Will*.

The chief manifestation, however, of the malcontent spirit in the *Anatomy* is in the character of Burton himself as he projects it in his work. Like Jaques, Burton is the man who can suck melancholy out of anything; it is a humour that is congenial to him, and he seeks occasions or scenes upon which to exercise it. He uses the word 'melancholize' (e.g. I, 22, I, 247), and he occasionally describes the pleasures of melancholy that accompany, or usually precede, the more acute forms of the disease.[11] In a sense, the whole *Anatomy* is an exercise in 'melancholizing' (from which he says he gets all his knowledge, I, 2); the follies and evils of life are the subject for melancholy reflection, or melancholy, 'Democritic' laughter.

Burton's literary aim, then, is clearly set out in the Preface, 'Democritus to the Reader': the subject-matter in itself, as he explains, is unoriginal and unimportant, while the treatment of it is what matters and what reveals the author (I, 25ff.). His acknowledgment of, and apology for, the 'extemporanean' nature of his style (I, 31), as well as the many unacknowledged echoes from English authors, show how much the *Anatomy* has been inspired by the language of the drama and popular literature, as well as by the learned sources which he quotes so abundantly. He is conveying to the reader, in the idiom of the vernacular literature, pictures and associations of melancholy which the literature of the previous twenty years had made familiar: the conjunction of the melancholy personality with satire and with the playing of roles; the image of the melancholic who luxuriated in his own melancholy and let it feed on all the phenomena that he could observe; the picture of the melancholy scholar which had been given content by being applied to the social life of the time; the conjunction of the idea of melancholy with the intellectual uncertainties and philosophical scepticism of the period. Because the concept of melancholy had been enriched by all of these associations, Burton was able to employ it not only as a metaphor for all of life but also to achieve the aim stated at the beginning of his work, of using melancholy itself for purposes of self-portraiture.

Melancholy Self-portraiture

The main clues to the structure of the *Anatomy* can be found in 'Democritus to the Reader', where Burton describes himself as a sufferer from the malady about which he is writing: 'I write of melancholy, by being busy to avoid melancholy' (I, 20). His is the melancholy mind occupying itself with its own affliction, and the occupation, by providing 'business', is also meant to provide the cure. Although Burton's work is a 'cento' (I, 25), as he tells us, and he often cites authorities for what could well be anybody's observation, he also takes pains to build up a picture of himself, while insisting that he is concealed behind his mask of Democritus. Both the concealment and the self-portrait became more complete as the *Anatomy* went through its six editions. As Babb has pointed out, the allusions to Burton's experiences at Oxford were brought up to date, while a complaint about his lack of preferment was one of the few items that was cut out in the expanded third edition. The picture of himself as looking down at the world from a great height, one that had rhetorical rather than autobiographical importance, was also added in the second edition.[12]

The portrait of himself that Burton gives us is carefully controlled for literary purposes, and when Babb says that the role of Democritus is a mask, but one very similar to what Burton was 'really' like,[13] he is presumably responding to the conformity of man with mask that Burton intended us to see (I, 17). The assumption of a mask that will ensure freedom of speech, but which at the same time is meant to be seen as an extension and elaboration rather than a concealment of the personality beneath, may be Burton's main debt to the dramatic malcontent literature. It might be argued that (as Burton reminds the reader, I, 121) Erasmus, too, pleaded that he was not identical with his personified creations and could not be blamed for what Folly spoke.

But *The Praise of Folly* lacks the element of self-portraiture altogether; no matter whether Folly speaks Erasmus's opinions straightforwardly or ironically, Erasmus himself as a character is outside the picture. This makes possible Folly's joke, 'But I give up proverbializing for fear I shall seem to have rifled the compilations of my good friend Erasmus.'[14] Hamlet, on the other hand, puts on a melancholy show even while he has 'that within which passes show', a feeling that corresponds to but is not identical with its stylized manifestations.

Burton hides behind Democritus: ' 'Tis not I, but Democritus, *Democritus dixit*' (I, 121), and the unmasking that originally took place at the end of the first edition ('The last Section shall be mine, to cut the strings of *Democritus* visor, to unmaske and shew him as he is', with the final signature of 'Robert Burton'), was dropped.[15] But from the outset, although Burton insists that he will remain hidden (I, 15), he draws an elaborate parallel (I, 16–18) between himself and the ancient philosopher whose picture, along with that of Burton as 'Democritus Junior', appears on the Frontispiece. They were both general scholars, divines and physicians, who secluded themselves in order to study the world. They were both anatomizers of melancholy, Democritus in a literal sense, since he was found by Hippocrates under a tree, cutting up animals in order to find where the seat of melancholy was.[16] Democritus was a lawmaker, as Burton pretends to be in his utopia; he was also a scientist whose name is associated with the theory of atomism and with ideas of the infinity of the universe and the plurality of worlds, 'paradoxes' (I, 15) with which Burton was to play, especially in the 'Digression of Air'. In addition to providing a character whose activities and interests formed a parallel with those that Burton wanted to show as his own, Democritus was the type of the melancholy satirist.

Democritus was not only well established as the figure of the sardonically laughing philosopher; he also occasionally represented the healer who dispersed the melancholy humour by his laughter, as Samuel Rowlands's title shows: *Democritus, or Doctor Merry-man his Medicines, against Melancholy humours* (1607). The figure of Democritus as a jester who could dispel the fumes of melancholy occurs in such works as *Tyros Roring Megge, Planted against the walls of Melancholy* (1598), the author of which explains how he tried to cure his own melancholy by calling on Democritus, and Burton may have been referring to this work when he speaks of music as a 'roaring-meg' (cannon) against melancholy (II, 115).[17] Democritus was connected with the English tradition of pills to purge melancholy—an idea that Burton explicitly appropriates when he calls his work on love-melancholy 'gilded pills' to cure mind and body (III, 7)—because he was the purveyor of stories and entertainments that would chase the melancholy humour away.

The figure of Democritus, then, provided Burton with a variety of literary precedents and postures which had already made their way into the expository books.[18] Like Hamlet's antic disposition, the mask of the Democritic satirist enabled the wearer to vent his feelings verbally. Like Hamlet also, Burton is always anxious that his own character should not get lost behind the mask, even while he is claiming the licence of free speech that the mask provides, and asserting that 'I dwell not in this study' (I, 32). There are several references to himself in the *Anatomy*, aside from the extended self-portrait at the beginning that is juxtaposed with the portrait of Democritus. Usually the self-references are inserted to show that he knows at first hand what he is talking about in his descriptions of melancholy; the account of the evils of a harsh education, for example, contains a note of sympathy for those who 'think no slavery in the world (as once I did myself) like to that of a grammar scholar' (I, 333). There are somewhat confused self-exonerations and allusions to his own stand on the question of simony and corruption in the Church, followed by the remark that he would prefer his role of Democritus Junior to that of being a bishop (I, 313–14).[19] His own experience is brought in to illustrate a general point about the corruption of the world, from which retirement is necessary to maintain virtue. His discussion of nobility as distinguished from the mere outward trappings of gentry contains a passage in the same self-defensive tone about his 'worshipful' family, in which he alludes to his own position as a younger brother (II, 142). Again, the personal and the general are combined; what he says about himself ties in with his remarks about the sad fate of younger brothers as one of the world's evils (I, 63), and with his plans for changing their lot in his utopia (I, 101). His references to himself in the section on love-melancholy also establish him as a 'contemplator', not personally involved and yet not entirely inexperienced in what he relates

(III, 184). The result is that Burton appears, as he says, an actor on the stage of melancholy (III, 110) as well as a spectator (I, 18), and the whole *Anatomy*, bookish though it is, seems at least partly to be a projection of his own experience: '*Experto crede Roberto*' (I, 22).

The purpose of Burton's self-portraiture, direct or oblique, is closely connected with what seems to be his general purpose in the *Anatomy*: to show the symptoms, cures and general characteristics of the melancholy mind in action, even while it is busying itself with the subject of melancholy. Burton's famous passage on style restates this two-fold subjective and objective plan. Style must correspond to subject-matter, and the subject-matter is sufficiently diverse to require a multiplicity of styles. This is the idea behind the image of style as a river, in which style is taken to include genre and tone, as well as sentence structure:

> So that a river runs sometimes precipitate and swift, then dull and slow; now direct, then *per ambages* [winding]; now deep, then shallow; now muddy, then clear; now broad, then narrow; doth my style flow: now serious, then light; now comical, then satirical; now more elaborate, then remiss, as the present subject required, or as at that time I was affected (I, 32).

The last phrases are significant: the two determinants of style and of genre are the matter and the author's mood, the objective material and the subjective feeling. The image of the river is a recurrent one for Burton, indicating permanence in flux, the stability of human nature and its follies in the face of changing externals like language, laws and customs (I, 53). It expresses, in the formulation of Democritus's opposite type, Heraclitus, the diversity and likeness of melancholy symptoms, and hence of the activities and characteristics of men:

> There is in all melancholy *similitudo dissimilis*, like men's faces, a disagreeing likeness still; and as in a river we swim in the same place, though not in the same numerical water; as the same instrument affords several lessons, so the same disease yields diversity of symptoms (I, 397).

The subject-matter of melancholy is broadly defined to include its philosophical connotations as well as its purely medical side; melancholy is to be 'Philosophically, Medicinally, Historically, opened & cut up', as the title page puts it. The moods that Burton brings to play upon this subject are the moods of the melancholy man, with all the variety that this by now implied. The matter of each of the first two partitions, then—causes, symptoms and cures of melancholy—is structured in the same way, starting with the most general questions and proceeding to the particular. God is the first cause of melancholy and the most general cure; devils and spirits and the stars are next in order; and so Burton proceeds in each partition through the Galenic six 'non-natural' causes (diet, retention and evacuation, air, exercise, sleeping and waking, and the passions and perturbations of the mind), each of which is 'rectified' in the corresponding section on cures, to the three sub-species of melancholy (head melancholy, hypochondriacal and of the whole body), and *their* causes, symptoms and cures. In the third partition, love-melancholy, a species, is defined as melancholy itself was, divided into kinds, and then analysed as to its causes, symptoms, cures and prognostics. The same is true of its sub-species, religious melancholy.

This highly organized plan is the groundwork upon which Burton's doubtful, or sceptical, or at times contradictory notions operate. Opinions of the *Anatomy* as a random collection of quaint old stories have not yet been dispelled by critics of the work, although Osler defended its structure some time ago and took to task those who regarded it merely as the 'scrapings of the Bodleian'.[20] Jordan-Smith said rather generally that Burton's 'personality' gave the work unity.[21] Critics like Babb and Prawer have seen a radical disjunction between the plan of the work (the 'psychiatric material') and the criticism or commentary that grew around it.[22] They have pointed also to a supposed disunity between Burton as a medical writer and as a raconteur, two activities that were actually not far apart, as earlier writers about melancholy had already made plain. More recently, J. R. King, in an otherwise suggestive essay, has considered the medical framework a hindrance for Burton, interfering with his real 'humanistic' interests, hampering him with a deterministic view of behaviour that was not congenial to him.[23]

However, to view 'psychiatry' (a misnomer under the circumstances in any case) in terms of human behaviour in all its aspects, moral and philosophical, was merely to continue the tradition of Renaissance treatises. Otherwise there was not much to say about melancholy except to list its causes and symptoms, and to give the usual dietary and pharmaceutical remedies. Nor, on the other hand, would Burton's 'critical commentary' or the essays in which he expressed his humanistic interests have been worth preserving in a book, since little of these was original, as he was quick to admit. What was original was the fusion of a great variety of ideas, genres and moods by one large and controlling metaphor. Although Burton says that he will give up the metaphorical meanings of melancholy after the Preface, 'to say no more of such as are improperly melancholy, or metaphorically mad, lightly mad, or in disposition, as stupid, angry, drunken, silly, sottish, sullen, proud . . . etc.' (I, 120)—in other words, not to equate all forms of human behaviour with melancholy as Erasmus does with folly—he obviously continues to play with his terms throughout. One need only think of the section on religious melancholy, where atheism is defined as madness and superstition as a form of melancholy, to realize that the same process of metaphoric extension continues throughout the work, and that the metaphor could not operate if either the framework of melancholy or the humanistic commentary stood alone.

The same play of wit is involved in the way in which the digressions are fitted into the very rigid formal plan. They are far more functional in terms of the plan, and more carefully placed and integrated in it, than their title indicates. The consolatory digression has already been defended critically as part of Burton's design;[24] good counsel was one of the remedies against perturbations, and the digression represents such a remedy. The other digressions are equally functional. The 'Digression of Air', to take another example, is based on a witty elaboration of the Galenic category of air and climate as one of the causes of melancholy, and also on the idea of travel as recreative: 'so will I, having now come at last into these ample fields of air, wherein I may freely expatiate and exercise myself for my recreation, awhile rove, and wander round the world . . .' (II, 34). The medical framework provides points of reference, often metaphorical, for the wide range of subjects treated, all of which are set in relation to it either as causes, symptoms or cures.

The personality, then, that Burton brings to bear on his subject is that of the melancholy man, as he repeatedly says at the beginning (I, 21–2), and he develops this idea, amplifying it by his own performance as the work progresses. One of the well-known characteristics of melancholy men, for example, was their tendency, described by Burton, to belittle themselves or vex or 'macerate' themselves (I, 394); he also recommends as good strategy for anybody who fears that he may have some deformity, to mention it or display it himself, as a way of forestalling criticism (II, 203). Such passages are relevant to Burton's own strategies, to the defensive self-deprecation that reveals itself in his frequent references to his wordiness or tediousness (I, 38, II, 69, III, 100), to his description of himself as full of faults, or as a fool or madman (I, 119–20), and to his allusions to the deformity and unpolished character of his work (I, 25–30), even while its scope and conscious artifice betray his pride in it. In this last connection, Burton admits that like other writers he is a victim of melancholy ambition and desire for fame (I, 22).

Although the digressions are far better integrated into the treatise than is sometimes thought, their name indicates that they are variations or elaborations on the outline plan, which is thereby shown to be more rigid than the actual subject of the book: 'I have thought fit, in this following section, a little to digress (if at least it be to digress in this subject) . . .' (II, 126). Such digressiveness is certainly also intended to be a manifestation of the melancholy character. We have seen that one aspect of melancholy, derived from the medieval idea of *acedia*, was a busyness about everything except one's real work. It is this characteristic, with less of a connotation of sinfulness, that Burton conveys by his image of the ranging spaniel:

> This roving humour . . . I have ever had, and like a ranging spaniel, that barks at every bird he sees, leaving his game, I have followed all, saving that which I should . . . (I, 17).

The image of the roving spaniel, now identified as 'melancholy', recurs at the end of the 'Digression of Air': 'But my melancholy spaniel's quest, my game, is sprung, and I must suddenly come down and follow' (II, 61); it epitomizes Burton's abrupt changes in pursuing a variety of topics in the *Anatomy*.

Restlessness is itself elsewhere defined as a melancholy characteristic and a companion of idleness; it is the basis of Burton's portrait of the traveller, who is always discontented, whether at home or abroad (I, 367), and it is also associated with the sorrow of the melancholic, 'disquieted in mind, with restless unquiet thoughts' (I, 389). The confession of the restlessness that is part of his 'roving humour' also enters into Burton's self-portrait: 'Something I have done . . . out of a running wit, an unconstant, unsettled mind, I had a great desire (not able to attain to a superficial skill in any) to have some smattering in all . . .' (I, 17). Again, an attribute of the melancholy personality displays itself in the method and substance of the book.

The most obvious sign of restlessness in the intellectual sphere (the analogue of the physical wanderings of the traveller) was curiosity, concern about forbidden or useless subjects, or sometimes an overly minute dissection of matters of faith. Curiosity is discussed in the *Anatomy* as the cause of man's original fall and misery (I, 131), as an offspring of pride and self-love (I, 293), as a restless desire to know that which is meant to be hidden (I, 365–6), and as a symptom and cause of melancholy (I, 394). Examples of curious study include the subtleties of school divinity and philosophy, astrology, alchemy and antiquarian study. The idleness of travel is one category of curiosity: 'He travels into Europe, Africa, Asia, searcheth every creek, sea, city, mountain, gulf, to what end?' (I, 366). For Burton, the favourable aspect of curiosity that the Florentine Neoplatonists elaborated upon, and that was stressed by Huarte, is never present when he is talking about it directly:

> Thus through our foolish curiosity do we macerate ourselves, tire our souls, and run headlong, through our indiscretion, perverse will, and want of government, into many needless cares and troubles, vain expenses, tedious journeys, painful hours; and when all is done, *quorsum haec? cui bono?* To what end? (I, 368)

Precisely this itching humour to see what is not to be seen, however, inspires the 'Digression of Air'. Burton's treatment of scientific subjects can probably best be seen as a means of characterizing himself as a melancholic, and of showing how the melancholy mind operates. In the Digression all the geographical, climatic and cosmological paradoxes that he has read about will be clarified on his flight—solved, the implication is, by direct inspection. In fact, he surveys the whole field of natural and social knowledge, including plants, animals and the manners of different nations. Although it has been pointed out that Burton's knowledge of the new science was very up-to-date and kept increasing from one edition of the *Anatomy* to the next,[25] his attitude towards it was far from modern, or at any rate was literary rather than scientific. Theories about the movement of the earth and the planets, or the plurality of worlds, were merely materials for the mind to play with, for making metaphors, or proof of the impossibility of reaching certainty about such matters (II, 58). Almost the whole Digression is a series of questions without answers, a ready demonstration of melancholy 'curiosity', though at the same time of the distractions that the melancholy mind (sometimes legitimately) tries to find:

> Why so many thousand strange birds and beasts proper to America alone, as Acosta demands, *lib. 4 cap.* 36? Were they created in six days, or ever in Noah's ark? If there, why are they not dispersed and found in other countries?
> (II, 43)

In addition to giving expression to the restlessness of the melancholy man, the travel and the studies that are discussed in the Digression can also be recreative (II, 40, 86); like so many other aspects of melancholy, study is at the same time cause, symptom and cure of the disease. The studies and readings that are listed as recreative and rectifying are virtually the same as those condemned as vanity elsewhere:

> In arithmetic, geometry, perspective, optics, astronomy, architecture. . . . In music, metaphysics, natural and moral philosophy, philology. . . . What so sure, what so pleasant? (II, 88)

The list is a long one and includes the 'reading of some enticing story, true or feigned', where men's manners and actions in the past can be seen 'as in a glass' (II, 87), the study of maps, and the reading of travel literature (II, 89).

These two extreme positions about curiosity or study as either vanity or recreation combine to produce a third, that which views the subjects of study as mere toys of the mind, while acknowledging that we need such toys to keep us sane. The necessity of such diversions is only one more proof of the general melancholy of the world, and the reason why the ignorant man is happiest; like Jaques or Lampatho Doria, though without a context of mockery, Burton pretends to envy the happy fool who is not burdened with the concerns that are weighing him down:

> Happy he, in that he is freed from the tumults of the world. . . . He is not troubled with state matters, whether kingdoms thrive better by succession or election; whether monarchies should be mixed, temperate, or absolute . . . he inquires not after colonies or new discoveries . . . what comets or new stars signify, whether the earth stand or move, there be a new world in the moon, or infinite worlds, etc. (II, 153).

Since these are the very questions that he discusses at such length, there is no question but that Burton is characterizing himself as the melancholy man who is preoccupied by such toys, and that he uses exactly as toys, or as images to play with, ideas of the kind that he specifies:

> Copernicus, Atlas his successor, is of opinion the earth is a planet, moves and shines to others, as the moon doth to us. Digges, Gilbert, Keplerus, Origanus, and others, defend this hypothesis of his in sober sadness, and that the moon is inhabited: if it be so that the earth is a moon, then are we also giddy, vertiginous and lunatic within this sublunary maze (I, 78).

The passage is a play of wit and words, recreative perhaps in its execution, but sceptical as far as its content is concerned. Melancholy meditation about the world, 'this playing labour' as he calls it in the Preface (I, 20), emerges as a necessity that has no end in view except to provide the restless mind with the activity it needs.

An attitude of doubt and dependence characterizes Burton's relationship not only to the world he surveys, but also to his sources. Hardly a sentence in the *Anatomy* does not rely on the buttress of previous opinions, while at the same time scholarly controversies, like lawsuits, are seen to be the results of man's fall:

Scarce two great scholars in an age, but with bitter invectives they fall foul one on the other, and their adherents; Scotists, Thomists, Reals, Nominals, Plato and Aristotle, Galenists and Paracelsians, etc., it holds in all professions (I, 267).

Occasionally Burton adjudicates between conflicting authorities (e.g. II, 237), but more often he is content to watch as they fight it out, as in this passage about the chemical cures of illness: 'But what do I meddle with this great controversy, which is the subject of many volumes? Let Paracelsus, Quercetan, Crollius, and the brethren of the Rosy Cross defend themselves as they may' (II, 240). An attack on the Galenic system should, of course, have concerned Burton more actively if he had any real interest in writing a scientific work setting forth the causes and cures of melancholy; authors who did take some kind of stand on this or other matters are mocked by being lumped heterogeneously together, the serious with the ridiculous, in the manner of Rabelais's or Erasmus's treatments of scholastic learning. In Burton's case, dependence on the authorities of whom he is also scornful is analogous to his melancholy attitude towards the world in general, which he scorns and flees (I, 18), but on which he depends for his reflections.

Burton's use of irony against himself goes beyond his attitude towards his sources, however, and extends to his form. Attacks on the form of scholastic discussions, for example, as well as on the futility of their substance, occur several times in the *Anatomy*.[26] Yet the organization of subject-matter in the *Anatomy*, which proceeds in each partition from first causes to particular instances, is patterned on the scholastic one; the 'obs and sols' (objections and solutions) of the schoolmen are a feature of many of his sections. We can easily see, however, that Burton uses their method in an entirely different way, not to prove given assertions, but to give the impression of doubt and dialogue. The aim is to show that life does not conform to precept and theory, and that the whole subject under consideration is far more complicated than might at first appear.[27] Another related effect is to set up a dialogue between melancholic and author (or physician) that shows the doubtfulness of the melancholy mind, corresponding to the complications of the material it deals with.

A section that can be taken as an example, and which is not very different in its form from several others, is Partition II, Section 2, Member 6, Subsection I: 'Perturbations of the Mind, rectified. From himself, by resisting to the utmost, confessing his grief to a friend, etc.' (II, 102–9). The opening proposition is that the chief cure of melancholy is to avoid or rectify perturbations and passions of the mind. Fear, sorrow and all violent emotions must be extirpated, as the Stoics suggested, and various authorities are cited in support of this view. The opposing party ('thou' as opposed to 'I') offers the opinion that this is easier said than done (II, 103–4); everybody, including philosophers and Stoics, is afflicted with passion. The author's or physician's reply to this is then more realistic, and though still offering precepts and advice, it takes some account of the difficulties of the problem. The melancholic is told to extirpate the more dangerous symptoms by avoiding solitude and idleness, by recreation and by fortifying himself with the word of God.

The next objection, on the same lines as the first, is that 'every man, as the saying is, can tame a shrew but he that hath her' (II, 105–6), and the physician immediately acknowledges the justice of it. He exhorts the melancholic, however, not to let his reason be overruled, and to recognize the disproportion between his sickness and its cause (II, 106). The concluding section drops the dialogue altogether; the 'thou' and 'I' become 'we', and the reality of the disease is accepted and seen as universal: 'If then our judgment be so depraved, our reason overruled . . .' (II, 107). If the previous remedies are useless, we should unburden ourselves to friends, a salutary activity in itself, and accept their counsel. The disease is now a fact, and the physician has aligned himself with the sufferer. A very similar structure can be seen in other parts of the *Anatomy*, such as the sermon against despair (which becomes a dialogue between the sufferer and his counsellor) in the section on religious melancholy.

The rhetorical devices that Burton uses to engage the reader as a participant in the *Anatomy*[28] serve also to intensify the effect of the melancholy mind turning on its own problems, or attempting to be cured. Every problem is seen to have two or more sides to it, and the melancholy man finds it especially difficult to decide between them:

Inconstant they are in all their actions, vertiginous, restless, unapt to resolve of any business, they will and will not, persuaded to and fro upon every small occasion, or word spoken; and yet if once they be resolved, obstinate, hard to be reconciled (I, 391).

Because of his fears, the melancholic finds it difficult to undertake any action even when he has promised to do so (I, 386). The process of making decisions in the face of numerous objections to any course of action is well illustrated in several parts of the *Anatomy*, but nowhere so vividly as in that part of the section on love-melancholy dealing with marriage. Rhetorically the process is formalized and reduced to the level of a literary game in the list of twelve reasons for marriage, followed by a corresponding list of twelve reasons against it: 'All this is true, say you, and who knows it not? but how easy a matter is it to answer these motives, and to make an *antiparodia* quite opposite unto it! To exercise myself I will essay . . .' (III, 253). The game or 'exercise', again a recreation for Burton, is the witty end of a long series of arguments and counter-arguments on the subject, which are meant to display, in another way, the melancholy man's characteristics as Burton lists them at the end: 'Be not then so wayward, so covetous, so distrustful, so curious and nice, but let's all marry . . .' (III, 254). The presentation of the same facts from contradictory or divergent points of view, with Burton taking different sides of similar arguments, is carried to an extreme in this section, where, instead of reconciling a melancholy listener with some unwanted fact, Burton is portraying the difficulty of arriving at a decision to act.

In this section also he displays himself particularly as a player of roles, and thereby adds another facet, one that we have seen to be a traditional attribute of melancholics, to his self-portrait. The playing of parts is explicitly mentioned first in the *Anatomy* as one of the more pleasurable aspects of the early stages of melancholy, along with building castles in the air; 'When to myself I act and smile,/With pleasing thoughts the time beguile' is the beginning of one of the verses of the 'Author's Abstract of Melancholy' (I, 11). Specifically, the castle-building that he describes in the Abstract, the visions of 'Towns, palaces, and cities fine' that constitute the pleasures of the imagination in which the melancholic indulges before he suffers the more serious consequences of his condition, are also the pleasures that Burton will indulge in building his utopia:

> I will yet, to satisfy and please myself, make an Utopia of mine own, a New Atlantis, a poetical commonwealth of mine own, in which I will freely domineer, build cities, make laws, statutes, as I list myself (I, 97).

In the love section, Burton associates the playing of roles with different genres, comic or satiric:

> I am resolved . . . boldly to show myself in this common stage, and in this tragi-comedy of love to act several parts, some satirically, some comically, some in a mixed tone, as the subject I have in hand gives occasion, and the present scene shall require or offer itself (III, 10).

In the arguments where Burton takes the satiric part, detraction of the man or woman loved is proposed as a cure for love-melancholy, and the offices of good friends (for whom Burton is the spokesman) can take that form: 'Injuries, slanders, contempts, disgraces . . . are very forcible means to withdraw men's affections . . .' (III, 201). This is the role taken by Romeo's friends when he is suffering from the pangs of love. Aside from specific detractions, friends may enlarge on some of the stock themes of satire by giving general counsel about the faults of men and women, the miseries of marriage, including poverty, shrewish or sluttish wives, and other possible misfortunes, and Burton's extended descriptions of these, like his consolations, appear to form one side of a larger dialogue against an imaginary infatuated opponent who is understood to be defending his beloved. The conclusion of the passage is a praise of the single life:

> Consider withal how free, how happy, how secure, how heavenly, in respect, a single man is . . . consider how contentedly, quietly, neatly, plentifully, sweetly, and how merrily he lives! (III, 223)

The terms of the dialogue are reversed entirely, however, a few pages later, where Burton speaks for marriage and comedy. All who prevent the course of love are now the villains, especially prospective lovers who are too critical and fastidious, and subject those who are drawn to them to the pains of unrequited love. The adjectives that are applied to such critical people are the same ones that describe melancholics generally: 'nice', 'obstinate', 'curious' (III, 232–3). Furthermore, it is melancholic doubt, taking the form of exactly those arguments that Burton has just offered as objections, that makes people foolishly despair of their suit (III, 234), and the preoccupation with possible consequences of one's actions, an impediment to marriage or to any kind of action, shows a mistrust of God's providence:

> Many poor people, and of the meaner sort, are too distrustful of God's providence, 'they will not, dare not for such worldly respects', fear of want, woes, miseries, or that they shall light, as Lemnius saith, 'on a scold, a slut, or a bad wife' (III, 248).

The reversal of the argument involves a shift in the meaning of melancholy from a superficial to a more profound one, and it also involves a change in the author's role. Similarly, the part of the Stoic philosopher that he assumes in the section on poverty is repudiated in other moods, in which the Stoics are treated with irony or scorn (I, 118–19, 165, 172). The result of these shifts is to show that the subject of melancholy is ultimately too complicated to be easily dealt with by precept; precepts and moods continually modify each other, so that in the end some perception of the difficulty of living well can be conveyed.

The shifting of viewpoints and of genres extends beyond the presentation of arguments to the accompanying illustrative allusions. Burton's references to Dido and Aeneas in the section on love-melancholy, for example, may be said to typify his method of presentation, in which the same facts and allusions are continually being repeated from different points of view. At one point 'love-sick Dido' is included as a miserable example of those suffering from love to the detriment of their ordinary business (III, 151). Then, the man who is first told to 'look before he leap, as the proverb is, or settle his affections', to be prudent and consider 'whether it be a fit match for fortunes, years, parentage, and such other circumstances', is also told to follow Aeneas' reasonable example of getting out in time: 'Or if it be not for his good, as Aeneas, forewarned by Mercury in a dream, left Dido's love, and in all haste got him to sea. . . . Let thy Mercury-reason rule thee against all allurements, seeming delights, pleasing inward or outward provocations' (III, 206). Aeneas is here the reasonable man who left the allurements of love. Later, however, for a different persuasive purpose, he is the impetuous lover who met Dido in a cave and 'made a match upon it' (III, 240). As with the final '*antiparodia*' one is meant to see the argumentative mind at work, and the element of sophistry and wit in argument that occupies itself with material seen from opposing viewpoints.

Apart from his shifting roles in the *Anatomy*, Burton expresses his scepticism by the doubts that he casts on his elaborate outlines and partitions, and on the possibility of making categories at all:

> What physicians say of distinct species in their books it much matters not, since that in their patients' bodies they are commonly mixed. In such obscurity, therefore, variety and confused mixture of symptoms, causes, how difficult a thing is it to treat of several kinds apart; to make any certainty or distinction among so many casualties, distractions, when seldom two men shall be like affected *per omnia* [in all respects] (I, 177).

In fact, his own treatment of melancholy calls attention to the overlapping of causes, symptoms and cures.[29] Fear and sorrow, the principal ingredients, are symptoms (the 'inseparable companions' of most melancholy) and causes (in the case of sudden frights or bereavements); jealousy, too, is both a symptom and a cause ('It is most part a symptom and a cause of melancholy, as Plater and Valescus teach us; melancholy men are apt to be jealous, and jealous apt to be melancholy', III, 266); in fact, all the passions of the mind can be seen in this way (I, 271). The outline is simply inadequate to the material, and Burton shows his difficulty at several points in deciding where to include pieces of material.[30] It is in terms of the categories of others that Burton both justifies his own and indicates their provisional nature:

> If you require a more exact division of these ordinary diseases which are incident to men, I refer you to physicians; they will tell you of acute and chronic, first and secondary, *lethales, salutares*, errant, fixed, simple, compound, connexed, or consequent, belonging to parts

or the whole, in habit, or in disposition, etc. My division at this time (as most befitting my purpose) shall be into those of the body and mind (I, 138).

Burton states simply that his categories are a convenience, not part of the nature of things, and even at times ludicrously misleading.

Burton's attitudes towards categorical distinctions are reflected also in the way that (like Dürer's brooding figure with her mathematical instruments scattered about her) he is preoccupied with numbers, statistics and measurements, while expressing scepticism of the truth that they contain or convey. He applies numbers, and the contradictory authorities about them, to precisely the most 'doubtful' subjects, or those most incapable of measurement— events of the remote past, for example, or those of a semi-mythical character:

> The siege of Troy lasted ten years, eight months; there died 870,000 Grecians, 670,000 Trojans at the taking of the city, and after were slain 276,000 men, women, and children of all sorts (I, 56).

An authority is cited for this, of course, and also for the statistics that follow:

> Caesar killed a million, Mahomet the second Turk 300,000 persons, Sicinius Dentatus fought in an hundred battles, eight times in single combat he overcame, had forty wounds before, was rewarded with 140 crowns, triumphed nine times for his good service. M. Sergius had 32 wounds; Scaeva, the centurion, I know not how many. . . (I, 56).

Exactness, buttressed by authorities either included in the text or in footnotes, is exaggerated to the point of mockery, and ridiculed further by anticlimactic phrases ('I know not how many').

The 'Digression of Air' abounds in passages with numbers that function in exactly this way; they include the measurements of mountains (II, 37), of the earth (II, 40), and of hell (II, 42), all linked as in some way comparable subjects by style and allusions to conflicting authorities. The remote in time and space, geographical facts and historical ones that merge with mythical ones (the list of mountains centres on the problem of 'Whether Mount Athos, Pelion, Olympus, Ossa, Caucasus, Atlas, be so high as Pliny, Solinus, Mela relate . . .', II, 37) are given exact if conflicting dimensions that dramatize the problem of knowledge and of image-making, of rendering the infinite or the transcendental in terms of the quantitative. The sun and the moon, Burton says at one point, will hide themselves while men hold controversies about their nature and dimensions:

> But why should the sun and moon be angry, or take exceptions at mathematicians and philosophers, whenas the like measure is offered unto God Himself, by a company of theologasters? They are not contented to see the sun and moon, measure their site and biggest distance in a glass, calculate their motions, or visit the moon in a poetical fiction, or a dream. . . (II, 58).

The difficulty of measuring the unmeasurable in space and time is, of course, the problem of defining and measuring melancholy:

> And I doubt not but that in the end you will say with me, that to anatomize this humour aright, through all the members of this our *microcosmos*, is as great a task as to reconcile those chronological errors in the Assyrian monarchy, find out the quadrature of a circle, the creeks and sounds of the north-east and north-west passages, and all out as good a discovery as that hungry Spaniard's of *Terra Australis Incognita*, as great a trouble as to perfect the motion of Mars and Mercury, which so crucifies our astronomers, or to rectify the Gregorian calendar (I, 38).

The analogy between the unknowable subjects that arouse his curiosity and that he pursues for his recreation and the subject of melancholy itself, unmeasurable and yet to be 'anatomized', is explicit and clear.

Burton reveals the provisional nature of his large metaphor and framework (even while he is emphasizing its fixed and articulated nature) through his style as much as through the use that he makes of numbers and catalogues. The structure of his sentences suggests the movement of a mind in action, rather than the fixed nature of the material with which it is dealing. This is, of course, the effect of the Senecan or anti-Ciceronian style, well described by such scholars as Croll, Williamson and Barish,[31] and evolved during the Renaissance precisely as a means for more fluid and subtle self-expression. Although there are really several styles in the *Anatomy*—hortatory, cataloguing, abrupt or rhetorically repetitive—one or two typical longer sentences can serve to show how Burton creates the effect of transcribing the provisional and fluid nature of thought:

> Yea, even all those great philosophers the world hath ever had in admiration, whose works we do so much esteem, that gave precepts of wisdom to others, inventors of arts and sciences, Socrates the wisest man of his time by the Oracle of Apollo, whom his two scholars, Plato and Xenophon, so much extol and magnify with those honourable titles, 'best and wisest of all mortal men, the happiest, and most just'; and as Alcibiades incomparably commends him; Achilles was a worthy man, but Brasidas and others were as worthy as himself; Antenor and Nestor were as good as Pericles, and so of the rest; but none present, before or after Socrates, *nemo veterum neque eorum qui nunc sunt* [none of the ancients nor of those of our own day], were ever such, will match, or come near him (I, 42).

The sentence is supposed to illustrate that even the best of worldly wisdom is folly ('But the Holy Ghost, that knows better how to judge, He calls them fools'), but it never gets around to making that point, and neither do the two or three that follow. It is not a sentence that indicates its own ending at any point along the way, and it gets caught up in its qualifications about Socrates' greatness without ever returning to the issue that is being qualified. Like the digressions, such a sentence expresses the temperamental qualities that Burton attributes to himself as the man who pursues all subjects but those which he should. Furthermore, it gathers several related but new ideas and comparisons to itself as it goes along, the praise of Alcibiades being incorporated in such a way that it is difficult to tell whether it is he or Burton who is speaking —whether, as the insertion in Latin suggests, Burton is subordinating his voice to another more remote one, or whether, as the distinction between the 'ancients' and moderns indicates, he is incorporating ancient sources into his own.

Another stylistic mannerism, Burton's introduction of 'etc.' into so many of his sentences, serves also to characterize him as somebody who has only a limited amount of faith in the fixity of his material, and who is either emphasizing its banality or else highlighting its provisional nature. Lists of symptoms or authorities, of countries, bridges or towns often end with 'etc.', as if he could have cited these or others—all are equally important or unimportant. Moreover, sentences in which he is imitating particular specialized vocabularies (of which the language of humoral theory is, of course, the most important) also sometimes include 'etc.'. An example is the following sentence in which he describes himself as a melancholic whose stars created his condition:

> Saturn was my lord of geniture, culminating, etc., and Mars principal significator of manners, in partile conjunction with mine ascendant; both fortunate in their houses, etc. (I, 18).

The two 'etc.'s' put the language of astrology, especially words like 'culminating', firmly in quotation marks; they illustrate the fact that Burton's voice is often submerged behind technical vocabularies that he uses, but of which he indicates the inadequacy, the banality or the jargonistic nature. This habit again expresses the idea of melancholy, of disdain for what he is actually dependent on, and of timidity in asserting his own voice while he scorns those that he has borrowed.

Burton defines himself as a melancholic, then, not only by his statements to that effect at the beginning of his work, but by the characteristics that he displays throughout—his ambition and self-deprecation, his curiosity, doubt, restlessness and love of projecting himself into different parts and fantasies. He emerges most clearly as the detached philosopher who surveys the world from a lofty vantage-point, and who needs the world to occupy his restless thoughts. At the same time, he often takes part in debates and dialogues that he sets up between melancholy sufferers and the physician or divine or philosopher who is counselling them, structuring these arguments in such a way that melancholy doubt and scepticism, the reality of suffering and the inefficacy of easy philosophical solutions become very clear. It therefore seems perverse to criticize him for abrupt (and intentional) changes in mood or point of view, or for the failure to achieve a coherent philosophical system.[32] The aim of the work is far more literary, and involves the portrayal of the melancholy mind not only by its ostensible subject-matter, but also by the manner in which Burton introduces himself into it and expresses himself.

The Anatomy of Melancholy *and the Expository Books*

The originality of the *Anatomy* can be seen most readily when it is placed in the expository-book tradition as it had developed in England during the Renaissance. Of the books discussed above in the first chapter, Burton refers specifically to Bartholomaeus Anglicus, Elyot, Wright, Bright, Boorde, Charron, Lemnius and Laurentius, as well as to the *Regimen of the School of Salerno* and of course to Galen and Hippocrates.[33] In accordance with these authorities, Burton is absolutely orthodox in his analysis of the types, causes and cures of melancholy, and nothing that he says on the subject cannot be found in the works of previous authors. In fact, of course, authorities are cited for all his opinions. The innovation of making religious melancholy a separate species of melancholy, to which he draws attention at the beginning of his section on that subject (III, 311–12), is really one of arrangement and classification. As he points out, religious melancholy had been discussed as a symptom or cause of melancholy by others, including his often-cited authority, Felix Plater, and we have seen that Bright discussed in detail the relationship of melancholy to despair. Most of the English treatises omit the subject of love-melancholy, but Laurentius's was an exception, and it was the most commonly treated branch of the subject in literature. Burton's long section on it, while loaded with medical allusions, undoubtedly heightens the literary quality of his work. Other divisions that Burton adopts, like that of head, body and hypochondriacal melancholy, while not used by all writers on the subject, were not new, and the six 'non-natural' causes of melancholy that originated with Galen had been used by English predecessors, such as Cogan.[34]

Like most of his predecessors, Burton actually makes very little of the discrepancy between 'Galenic' melancholy as a dreaded disease, or the worst of humours, and the Aristotelian concept of melancholy as the temperament of gifted people. For one thing, although the horrors of melancholy are vividly depicted ('if there be a hell upon earth, it is to be found in a melancholy man's heart', I, 433), Burton does not go in for the ranking of humours and the definition of ideal temperaments that play such an important part in works like Walkington's or Lemnius's. For him melancholy is the universal disease from which nobody escapes (I, 120), while every effort must be made to keep it in check. Like most of the expository books described above, the *Anatomy* includes the Aristotelian idea of 'witty' melancholy, but merely as one possibility among several less favourable ones. Melancholics are unaffable, surly, complaining and all the rest,

> and yet of a deep reach, excellent apprehension, judicious, wise, and witty: for I am of that nobleman's mind, 'Melancholy advances men's conceits more than any humour whatsoever,' improves their meditations more than any strong drink or sack (I, 392).[35]

He does not continue this thought very far before returning to less favourable characteristics of melancholics. While he extends the subject metaphorically, elevating it by calling it the source of his knowledge, he does not include any persuasive philosophical justification of the wisdom of the melancholy man.[36]

Burton had a precedent, then, for much of his matter in the earlier expository books. We have seen that the earlier works were in varying degrees treatises on behaviour, and that they drew on a cultural tradition beyond any purely medical one. Walkington's *Optick Glasse of Humors* also showed some of the concern with style that Burton does in 'Democritus to the Reader', even though Walkington's florid euphuistic antitheses were far different from Burton's effort to forge a flexible style suited to the changes and mixed natures of his subject, and therefore indicated a radically different conception of melancholy. Walkington declared his purpose, however, to be the mixture of the useful and the beautiful, and the same aim is expressed in the Horatian tag on the title-page of the *Anatomy*: '*Omne tulit punctum qui miscuit utile dulci.*'[37] Burton's formal plan itself, the clear divisions of which are susceptible to outline form and synopsis at the beginning of each partition, was not an unknown feature of medical books of the period.[38]

The differences between Burton and his predecessors are none the less real and very great. Although most of the subjects treated in the *Anatomy* were discussed under the heading of melancholy by earlier writers, Burton's plan is much more systematic and comprehensive than that of any of his predecessors. Melancholy was usually discussed in connection with some larger subject of which it was a part: the whole scheme of knowledge, as in the encyclopedia of Bartholomaeus Anglicus: the passions of the mind, as in Wright's treatise; the subject of 'physic' in Barrough's, or health in Elyot's; or the humours or complexions in Walkington's or Lemnius's; or the mind and soul, as in Melanchthon's *De Anima*. One of the few longer works on melancholy itself is Bright's *Treatise*, the similarity of whose chapter headings to some of those used by Burton was pointed out by Jordan-Smith.[39] Even in organization, however (let alone in scope), Bright's *Treatise* is quite different, since his main purpose is the limited one of distinguishing melancholy from spiritual illness involving conscience and guilt.

In comparison with Burton, Bright's rhetorical and metaphorical simplicity is very striking. The imaginary friend, 'M', for whom Bright's *Treatise* purports to be written, is a rhetorical fiction of the simplest kind: he is the prototype of the well-educated general reader who provides the excuse for writing in a simple, familiar, vernacular style and for the limits that Bright gives to his topic:

> This I have delivered in a simple phrase without any cost, or port of words to a supposed frend 'M' not ignorant of good letters, that the discourse might be more familiar then if it had caried other direction it otherwise would be. Chaunge the letter, and it is indifferent to whome soever standeth in need, or shal make use thereof. I write it in our mother tong that the benefit . . . might be more common . . . ('The Epistle Dedicatorie').

Bright varies his tone appreciably only at the point where, taking the role of counsellor and teacher, he delivers a spiritual consolation to 'M', assuring him of his salvation and of the humoral rather than spiritual causes of his condition. Even this change of stance and tone, though simple compared to all the changes that Burton goes through, is far more complex than what is attempted in most of the other expository books. The same is true of the rhetorical use that Bright makes of the personality of his imaginary friend, whose melancholy attributes are occasionally invoked to justify the length or tediousness of Bright's arguments: 'If yet you be not satisfied, (for melancholicke persons are for the most part doubtfull and least assured) . . .' (p. 69).

Despite such attempts at artistry, the greater simplicity of Bright's form is an expression of his certainty about the nature of the disease with which he is dealing, and of his straightforwardly didactic purpose. His initial proposition that the word 'melancholy' has many applications—his first chapter is entitled 'Howe diverslie the word Melancholie is taken'—is an introduction of complications that he intends to resolve. The contradictory opinions about the origin of melancholy that he goes through and answers ('The answer to the former objections', p. 10) have the function, as in scholastic disputation, of clarifying the truth:

> . . . but as I have set downe these objections, to the end that trueth being compared with untruth may the better appeare by reason of comparison, so marke for your fuller satisfying in this point, howe yet nothing is hereby lost, but sufficiently it maintaineth it selfe: and by strength of reason, the only pillar of humane truthes it is upholden (p. 10).

Bright's confidence in reason is obvious in his entire critical method, which depends on syllogism, abstract logic and analogy.[40] Nor does he overload his treatise with citations of past authorities, indebted though he is to tradition, but maintains his position as the transmitter of truth, even when this requires authoritative adjudication on his part.[41] In fact, the authorities that he does invoke are generally conveniences, providing excuses for not developing parts of his arguments that he considers over-technical or tedious. His discussion of the anatomical bases of melancholy need not be exhaustive, he says, because he will leave 'the large handling thereof to that most excellent hymne of Galen' (p. 47). Authorities are introduced not in order to raise doubts about the subject or to give a sense of its vast difficulties, but rather to buttress arguments and to limit the discussion in ways that Bright finds useful. The aim of the *Treatise* is always primarily informative.

By contrast, Burton's central idea of including all of life under the headings and divisions of melancholy involves literary features that are different in kind from those to be found in earlier expository books. His images and allusions, for example, have a different character from the illustrative use to which similar ones were put in the expository books. Bright's *Treatise* is rich in images, but their function is always to illuminate by commonplace analogies. The role of reason provides the subject of many stock images for Bright: it is like the bridle or reins of a horse, which control the passions; it is like the prince of a kingdom, or the castle of a besieged town. Democritus and Heraclitus are cited as traditional examples of two opposing but related responses to the world (p. 149), but no attempt is made to exploit these figures any further.

The *Anatomy* abounds, of course, with images and stories used in the same way, but there are also many that are used to establish the internal coherence of the work, like the recurrent image of the melancholy spaniel, or the mythological allusions that take on meaning by repetition and variation, as in a literary work. Burton's use of different aspects of the Dido and Aeneas story for various purposes throughout the section on love-melancholy has already been mentioned. The progressive use of the Hercules myth in 'Democritus to the Reader' is another particularly interesting example, in view of the not entirely different uses to which Shakespeare put this figure in *Hamlet*: a 'general visitor' to purge the state would have to be a heroic performer of tasks like Hercules (I, 96); since the task is beyond the capabilities even of a Hercules, Burton will perform it through his imagination instead (I, 97); and in the end, the reformer of the world is just as mad as the world he is trying to cure:

Shall I say Jupiter himself, Apollo, Mars, etc., doted? and monster-conquering Hercules, that subdued the

world and helped others, could not relieve himself in
this, but mad he was at last (I, 117).

Burton's own role is progressively clarified by his use of this heroic
(and anti-heroic) comparison. Moreover, he is literary not only
in his use of specific allusions and images, but in extending
melancholy as a metaphor for a diseased world, where social
institutions—legal, military, economic—are subject to melancholy
illness.

Another hypothesis that is at variance with the aims of the
expository books, at least in the amount of stress which Burton
puts on it, is his assumption, along with that of the generality of
the disease, of the ultimate uniqueness of each melancholy case:

> The four-and-twenty letters make no more variety
> of words in divers languages than melancholy conceits
> produce diversity of symptoms in several persons. They
> are irregular, obscure, various, so infinite, Proteus him-
> self is not so diverse; you may as well make the moon a
> new coat as a true character of a melancholy man; as
> soon find the motion of a bird of the air as the heart of
> man, a melancholy man (I, 408).

The heart of man is the same as the heart of a melancholy man;
there is no real set of distinguishing characteristics, of the sort
presupposed by the creators of types and 'characters', and the
problem of defining melancholy is equated with the problem
of language and communication. Burton's assumptions are, of
course, the opposite of Bright's simple ones that a reasonable
language, directed to the well-educated, could describe the plight
of one melancholic (his friend 'M'), whose symptoms are classi-
fiable, distinct and also applicable to everybody who suffers from
that particular disease.

The hypothesis that every melancholic, like every man, is
unique, goes against the presuppositions, not only of comic
typology, but also of any scientific attitude, and accounts for
Burton's scepticism and his mockery of moral and medical
precepts. Earlier writers had already suggested that every man
should follow the law of his own nature in such matters as diet,[42]
and Burton is following them in saying that 'such is the variety
of palates, humours, and temperatures, let every man observe,

and be a law unto himself' (II, 29). But he pushes the idea much further, first in connection with 'alteratives and cordials' and then by extension in connection with all remedies:

> I conclude, therefore, of this and all other medicines, as Thucydides of the plague at Athens, no remedy could be prescribed for it, *nam quod uni profuit, hoc aliis erat exitio*: there is no catholic medicine to be had: that which helps one, is pernicious to another (II, 248).

The mockery of general precepts goes even further in a passage where homely generalizing proverbs on all subjects, in the manner of Polonius's advice to Laertes, end with the mocking injunction, 'Look for more in Isocrates, Seneca, Plutarch, Epictetus, etc., and for defect, consult with cheese trenchers and painted cloths' (II, 204–5). The assumption of the generality of melancholy and the uniqueness of each particular case, opposite to that of all the other expository books, lies behind the *Anatomy* as a self-portrait also: Burton's own case and the autobiographical references to it are specific, while the melancholy traits that he reveals are typically those of the melancholy man and, therefore, of all men. It is an entirely literary assumption and enables him to hold a mirror up to his readers; as he says about the engravings in his Frontispiece and in his Preface: 'Thou thyself art the subject of my discourse' (I, 16).

Burton exploits the uselessness of melancholy as a medical category in building his very variable *persona*, and his self-portrait as a melancholic, with all of the rhetorical complications that this involves, sets the *Anatomy* off most completely from the expository-book genre. The broadness of his concept of melancholy, combined with its highly articulated system of causes, symptoms, cures and correspondences gives him the basis of his work, but the system provides him with a groundwork that he is in fact always destroying by emphasizing and exaggerating its weaknesses. He is excessively deferential to previous authorities, who provide the basis for the whole framework, while showing the burdensome weight of these authorities by his very deference, and by the frequent contradictions that he notes in them. Where melancholy had already become an enormous catch-all for causes and symptoms of disease, Burton pushes matters a step further, and by calling it the condition of mortality (I, 144) changes the idea to a metaphysical one. The rigidly schematic pattern of the *Anatomy* is called into question by the extent to which it is over-elaborated, by the contradictory and doubtful ideas that are brought to play on it, and by the demonstration that is made throughout of the inadequacy of theory to the complications of life.

The most strikingly artistic feature of the *Anatomy*, however, is its conscious creation of unity out of diversity. Melancholy, broadly defined, serves as a unifying theme for a wide variety of subjects and experiences, and there is a great play of wit involved in ordering all the material under the various headings of melancholy. Burton's method of composition, the fact that he started with the outline of melancholy and expanded the digressive material in subsequent editions,[43] does not alter the result. The reader's pleasure is enhanced by seeing the way the *Anatomy* is all made to fit together, whether on the level of minor points or longer sections, while the subjects themselves are coloured by the general aspect of melancholy under which they are surveyed.

In the end, all of human behaviour as Burton sees it can be viewed and expressed in terms of melancholy; it has become a metaphor large enough to include all of life and to give it artistic shape. Burton could not have stretched the concept as he did if it had not been enriched by the literary treatments of melancholy that preceded him. He creates the content of his *persona* and the texture of his analysis out of the attributes of the malcontent. The activities of melancholy types in the drama—the traveller, the political malcontent, the discontented scholar and all the rest—are presented (as in *Hamlet*) in terms of the melancholy mental attributes that were part of their make-up in the first place, but which occasionally got lost in the flatter stereotypes. The traveller is seen in terms of the curiosity and restlessness of one who travels by 'map or card'; the political rebel is also the critic and builder of utopias; the satirical railer has all the defensively belligerent characteristics of the man who needs the world, but has no active place in it, and the melancholy scholar is pre-occupied by subjects (and by methods of dealing with them) that he recognizes to have little validity. All of these types and their characteristics, which are discussed substantively by Burton, also play their part in the actual organization and presentation of the work.

Six

Epilogue: Milton's 'Il Penseroso' and the Idea of Time

Burton demonstrates in the *Anatomy* that the melancholic is one who has a heightened awareness of time. The idea of time is woven into the very structure and method of the work; the book's form is subject to it. Burton's material, he tells us, is susceptible to changes in the world's knowledge, as well as to the vagaries of his own memory:

> I have mingled *sacra profanis* [sacred with profane], but I hope not profaned, and in repetition of authors' names, ranked them *per accidens* [as they occurred], not according to chronology; sometimes neoterics before ancients, as my memory suggested. Some things are here altered, expunged in this sixth edition, others amended, much added, because many good authors in all kinds are come to my hands since, and 'tis no prejudice, no such indecorum or oversight (I, 34).

It is 'no indecorum' in a work dealing with melancholy to acknowledge, in its continual revisions, the shifting attitudes of the writer, and the changing nature of the subject in the light of new information about it. Even Burton's final decision to end his revisions is presented to the reader as a wilful and arbitrary one: 'But I am now resolved never to put this treatise out again; *Ne quid nimis* [not too much of anything], I will not hereafter add, alter or retract; I have done' (I, 34). There is no illusion of a formal necessity that has governed the shape of the work; merely an acknowledgment of the limits imposed by time, and the need to make an end.

The perception of flux and decay, according to Burton, is one of the 'discontents' that make people melancholy:

> Citizens devour country gentlemen, and settle in their seats; after two or three descents, they consume all in riot, it returns to the city again. . . . A lawyer buys out his poor client, after a while his client's posterity buy out him and his, so things go round, ebb and flow (II, 155).

Playing a variety of parts, Burton displays himself most consistently as the detached observer of the variable behaviour of others. The melancholy philosopher, watching the 'ebb and flow', the Heraclitean flux which gives him food for his reflections, is saddened, embittered or driven to detachment and to the cultivation of his inner resources or dreams by the spectacle. In the same pose, figures of Melancholy in the graphic arts of the seventeenth century, derived not only from Dürer, but also from portrayals of the idea of 'vanity', are surrounded by ruined human artifacts, and, increasingly as the century progresses, with old bones and skulls. Salvator Rosa's 'Democritus in Meditation' broods like Heraclitus, hand on cheek, over a scene that is littered with bones,[1] while his expression (like that of Burton's 'Democritus Abderites' in the Frontispiece of the *Anatomy*, or like earlier figures of Melancholy by Cranach or Dürer) is dreamy and turned inward.

The inwardness of the melancholic and his consciousness of time are central to the most imaginative literary recreation of melancholy after Burton, Milton's companion poems, 'L'Allegro' and 'Il Penseroso'. The complexities of Burton's prose, which presents melancholy both as his Muse, his 'Egeria', and as 'a kind of imposthume in my head' of which he must rid himself (I, 21), are notably lacking from the verses that he attached to the beginning of his work. These jog back and forth pleasantly but mechanically, in doggerel rhythms and with repeated refrains, alternating stanzas that describe the pleasurable reveries of the early stages of melancholy with those that tell of the nightmare horrors of the full-fledged disease. It was Milton who succeeded in translating the complex and contradictory ideas connected with melancholy into lyric poetry.

Milton, too, alludes to two kinds of melancholy, concentrating on one in each poem: the loathsome 'dull' kind with its affinities with hell and darkness, given in the invocation of 'L'Allegro', and the noble kind that is the source of Hermetic and Platonic contemplation.[2] But he also suggests the connections between them by the symmetry of the two poems, by the similar function of both central figures as detached observers, and by imagery that conveys similarities as well as differences in the two speakers' responses. The hellish darkness that is banished at the start of 'L'Allegro', for example, is associated with 'Ebon shades', with '*Cerberus* and blackest midnight', and with the

> uncouth cell,
> Where brooding darkness spreads his jealous wings,
> And the night-Raven sings. . . . (5–7).

The cell or cave, the animals of night and death, and the blackness are all associated with melancholy as a backdrop for tragic melodrama. The word 'uncouth' evokes, for readers familiar with malcontent literature, the rude, antisocial postures of the melancholic, at the same time that it fits easily into the description of horrors suggested in the poem by the cave itself.

In 'Il Penseroso', blackness recurs with different associations. Like Silence (55), blackness now signifies contemplation because it shuts out the distractions and intrusions of the external world; it is also identified, through a familiar paradox, with the brightness of God or of divine wisdom, which is 'o'erlaid' with black so that it can be perceived by men.[3] As a black-cloaked nun, Melancholy is a contemplative herself as well as the object of the speaker's invocation to wisdom. The 'Stygian cave' to which Melancholy is relegated at the beginning of 'L'Allegro' undergoes a transformation similar to that of blackness; it becomes the 'Mossy Cell' and 'peaceful hermitage' of the contemplative at the end of 'Il Penseroso'. The melancholic, it was said, was either an angel or a fiend,[4] and Milton shows the kinship between these opposed possibilities of solitude by variations on similar images in the two poems.

The two poems also give expression then, unobtrusively and effortlessly through syntax and imagery, to one of the melancholic's most essential characteristics, his heightened awareness of time. Among the many parallel and contrasting features of the poems that have been analysed by scholars, one that has not really been examined is that the speaker of 'Il Penseroso' has a sense of time that his counterpart in 'L'Allegro' lacks, or against which he protects himself. This may be the source of the feeling some critics have had that while 'Il Penseroso' displays greater 'maturity', the central figure of that poem is probably not meant to be older than his counterpart in 'L'Allegro'.[5] But the assignment of chronological age is perhaps not so important in the poems as the differences expressed between two types of consciousness, which display themselves in parallel sequences. Of these, only one, 'Il Penseroso', has an imagination of himself as existing in time.

The central figure of 'L'Allegro' lives in a one day's world in which his imagined experiences follow each other as discrete and disconnected events or scenes. His transitions tend to be abrupt:[6] 'Straight mine eye hath caught new pleasures' (69); 'Then to the spicy Nut-brown Ale' (100); 'Tow'red Cities please us then' (117); 'Then to the well-trod stage anon' (131). 'Then' is the most common transitional word, one that postulates no particular relationship between the events and scenes that are described except mere succession.

Conspicuously absent from the body of the poem (and the substitution of 'us' for 'me' in l. 117 only serves to emphasize this) is the first-person singular pronoun, or a sense of a consciousness that provides meanings and relationships beyond what the scenes are made to express independently. The first part of the descriptive section of the poem contains participles that convey the suppression of 'I', which is understood but left out of such verbal forms as 'Oft list'ning how the Hounds and horn' (53); 'Some time walking not unseen' (57). Infinitives also impersonalize the opening activities: 'To hear the Lark begin his flight' (41); 'Then to come in spite of sorrow' (45). A little later the speaker projects himself not as a personality, but as a recording 'eye':

> Straight mine eye hath caught new pleasures
> Whilst the Landscape round it measures. . . .
> (69–70)
> Towers and Battlements it sees. . . .
> (77)

Throughout, the imagined scenes are actualized and take over the poem from the imaginer:

> Hard by, a Cottage chimney smokes. . . .
> (81)

There let *Hymen* oft appear. . . .
(125)
Then to the well-trod stage anon. . . .
(131)
Sometimes with secure delight
The upland Hamlets will invite. . . .
(91–2)

In the last example the 'upland Hamlets' are endowed with the active power to lure the mind. The major portion of the poem, then, portrays a mind that wills scenes into being and into assuming a kind of independent existence, filling the mind and leaving little space for the subjective.

That the omission of the first person is really associated in the poem with a process of self-distraction to ward off melancholy is clear from the two passages after the invocation where the first-person pronoun does appear, at the beginning and end of the round of activities that form the speaker's 'day'. Each passage alludes explicitly to the suppression of melancholy feelings:

Then to come in spite of sorrow,
And at my window bid good-morrow. . . .
(45–6)
And ever against eating Cares,
Lap me in soft *Lydian* Airs. . . .
(135–6)

The last passage, in its wish for pleasurable self-annihilation, also confirms (in a seemingly unending sentence) a desire for the continued present in which the poem has established its images:

And ever against eating Cares,
Lap me in soft *Lydian* Airs,
Married to immortal verse,
Such as the meeting soul may pierce
In notes, with many a winding bout
Of linked sweetness long drawn out,
With wanton heed, and giddy cunning,
The melting voice through mazes running. . . .
(135–42)

The conclusion of the poem therefore conveys ecstasy by fusing opposites; it joins nouns denoting control and mastery ('heed', 'cunning') with adjectives suggesting looseness ('wanton', 'giddy', 'melting'), and it associates music, a temporal activity, with 'immortal verse'.[7] The invocation of music and poetry to conquer 'eating Cares' is itself a sustained verbal feat, and only the final wish to better Orpheus's performance reminds us (even before the next poem banishes 'vain deluding joys' and 'fancies fond') that even that musician could not entirely overcome the forces of the underworld.

The greater 'fluidity' that Professor Allen has noted in 'Il Penseroso', the more gradual changes and modulated transitions, are an expression of the awareness of time, of the continuous rather than discrete nature of experience, filtered through a consciousness of which we therefore become more aware. Although the poet also invoked scenes in the manner of the earlier poem ('Sometime let Gorgeous Tragedy/In Scepter'd Pall come sweeping by', 97–8), the first-person pronoun is far more conspicuous throughout 'Il Penseroso'. At the very start, for example, participial and infinitive phrases are linked subordinately to main clauses in which 'I' is definitely the subject:

> Thee Chantress oft the Woods among,
> I woo to hear thy Even-Song;
> And missing thee, I walk unseen
> On the dry smooth-shaven Green,
> To behold the wand'ring Moon. . . .
>
> (63–7)

The speaker later asks that his lamp be seen in the 'high lonely Tow'r/Where I may oft outwatch the *Bear*' (85–7), that he be hidden from 'Day's garish eye' (141), and, not be 'lapped' in music, but that music accompany his waking ('And as I wake, sweet music breathe . . .', 151), while the last part of the poem is a projection of his life into the future.

The impression that 'Il Penseroso' gives of a speaker with a personality is intensified by words like 'oft' and 'sometimes,' which convey the idea of custom and habit. The words appear infrequently in 'L'Allegro' and at wide intervals, there intensifying by repetition the future pleasures that are envisaged:

> Sometimes with secure delight
> The upland Hamlets will invite
> (91–2)
> There let *Hymen* oft appear . . .
> (125)

In 'Il Penseroso' even a construction like the last one is more explicitly temporal; it relates the progress or the 'career' of the night to a sense of duration in the speaker: 'Thus night oft see me in thy pale career . . .' (121). In the earlier parts of the poem the word 'oft' fixes the experience of the thinking man clearly in time:

> Thee Chantress oft the Woods among,
> I woo to hear thy Even-Song. . . .
> (63–4)
> And oft, as if her head she bow'd,
> Stooping through a fleecy cloud.
> Oft on a Plat of rising ground,
> I hear the far-off *Curfew* sound . . . .
> (71–4)

The experience is seen as forming a pattern in time, and the idea of repetition is projected on to the surrounding mythological imagery, where Cynthia 'checks her Dragon yoke/Gently o'er th'accustom'd Oak' (59–60). Furthermore, where the most common adverbial connective to indicate time in 'L'Allegro' is 'then', 'Il Penseroso' contains a number of different words to indicate the passage of time. Clauses introduced by 'when' (128, 131), 'as' (151), 'while' (126, 142), or 'till' (122) express a three-dimensional view of time, or of events seen not merely in succession, but in a variety of temporal relationships to each other.

The speaker's presentation of himself in 'Il Penseroso' is one that involves not only habit and custom, but also the sense of possibility and choice: time is important because only one sequence of activities or even of imaginations can take place at any moment. This fact is emphasized by continual evocations of different possibilities that convey the idea of imaginative richness and also of actual limitations. In 'L'Allegro' the poet hesitates briefly between two possible scenes only at the point where he can imagine either a summer or a spring landscape ('Or if the earlier

season lead/To the tann'd Haycock in the Mead', 89–90).[8] The
dominant conjunction in that poem is 'and':

> While the Ploughman, near at hand,
> Whistles o'er the Furrow'd Land,
> And the Milkmaid singeth blithe,
> And the Mower whets his scythe,
> And every Shepherd tells his tale,
> Under the Hawthorn in the dale.
> (63–8)

The word 'and', though less rhythmically and emphatically
repeated, is also the important conjunction in the description of
rural dancing (91–8), and in the scene of rural story-telling
(100–16). The effect is that of scene-painting, of the poet as
imagining vivid objective scenes and itemizing their ingredients.

Although there are obviously also many 'and's to be found in
'Il Penseroso', the word 'or' plays a much more prominent part.
The poet first introduces the possibility of different courses of
action after the initial invocation, 'And missing thee, I walk
unseen' (65), and he continues to offer alternatives later: 'Or if
the Air will not permit, Some still removed place will fit' (77–8);
'Or let my Lamp at midnight hour,/Be seen in some high lonely
Tow'r' (85–6). The word 'or' is important in indicating alternatives for the speaker's imaginative excursions as well as for his
actions:

> Sometime let Gorgeous Tragedy
> In Sceptred Pall come sweeping by,
> Presenting *Thebes*, or *Pelops'* line,
> Or the tale of *Troy* divine,
> Or what (though rare) of later age,
> Ennobled hath the Buskin'd stage.
> (97–102)
> Or bid the soul of *Orpheus* sing. . . .
> (105)
> Or call up him that left half told
> The story of *Cambuscan* bold. . . .
> (109–10)

The sense of possibility rather than of actuality that pervades
parts of the poem is expressed not only by the speaker's multiple

imaginings but also by the literary images or allusions that he conjures up; the evocation of Chaucer's romance is muted because that work also was a victim of time and was left unfinished.

As in the graveyard scene of *Hamlet*, the idea of personal time is connected in 'Il Penseroso' with that of historical time. Literary experience, for example, is evaluated in a historical context that makes the tragedies of the contemporary stage rarely as satisfying as those of antiquity. The myths with which the two poems begin, describing the parentages of Mirth and Melancholy, also have very different orientations to time. The opening of 'L'Allegro' states and restates the story of the origin of Mirth, first giving her traditional parents, Venus and Bacchus, then inventing a new set, the west wind and the dawn, and the flowery landscape they inhabit. While the emphasis here seems to be on poetic inventiveness, the opening myth of 'Il Penseroso' is seen in a historical or typological context:

> Thee bright-hair'd *Vesta* long of yore,
> To solitary *Saturn* bore;
> His daughter she (in *Saturn's* reign,
> Such mixture was not held a stain).
> Oft in glimmering Bowr's and glades
> He met her, and in secret shades
> Of woody *Ida's* inmost grove,
> While yet there was no fear of *Jove*.
> (23–30)

The myth is placed in the manner of some of those in *Paradise Lost*; the union of Vesta and her father Saturn is described in terms of a perspective in which such a union no longer has the innocent character that it had when it took place. Jove, who would bring an end to Saturn's Golden Age and of whom there was no fear when the incestuous union took place, is also by implication the Hebraic or Christian God whose moral law would condemn such a union. Later in 'Il Penseroso' the poet's perceptions of nature in terms of mythological images is set even more precariously against the possibility of the destruction of such imaginative forms:

> me Goddess bring
> To arched walks of twilight groves,
> And shadows brown that *Sylvan* loves

Of Pine or monumental Oak,
Where the rude Axe with heaved stroke
Was never heard the Nymphs to daunt,
Or fright them from their hallow'd haunt.
(132–8)

By introducing perspectives of time into 'Il Penseroso' that are missing in 'L'Allegro', Milton has made differences between comic and tragic treatments of melancholy central to poems that belong to neither genre themselves, but that portray the mental landscapes to which each is appropriate. We have seen that the depth of their perceptions of mutability, or the extent to which the settings in which they are placed support such perceptions, distinguishes comic from tragic malcontents, Jaques in the Forest of Arden from Hamlet in the graveyard. Jaques exists in a world that makes his meditation about the ages of man largely (though not entirely) inappropriate. There are no clocks in the Forest of Arden (III, ii, 282–4), and as Orlando's and Rosalind's catechism makes clear, time exists in the forest through a series of analogies involving cultivated and artificial organizations of life:

Orlando I prithee, who doth he [Time] trot withal?
Rosalind Marry, he trots hard with a young maid between the contract of her marriage and the day it is solemnized. . . .
Orlando Who ambles Time withal?
Rosalind With a priest that lacks Latin and a rich man that hath not the gout. . . .
Orlando Who doth he gallop withal?
Rosalind With a thief to the gallows. . . .
Orlando Who stays it still withal?
Rosalind With lawyers in the vacation. . . .
(III, ii, 296–314)

To an extent, the exclusion of time from the forest is as unrealistic for men as their assumption that they are joining rather than controlling or usurping the natural life there, and Orlando implicitly makes this point when he first meets Duke Senior and the lords:

> But whate'er you are
> That in this desert inaccessible,
> Under the shades of melancholy boughs,
> Lose and neglect the creeping hours of time;
> If ever you have looked on better days,
> If ever been where bells have knoll'd to church. . . .
>
> (II, vii, 109–14)

Jaques' remark at the end of the play that Touchstone and Audrey's 'loving voyage/Is but for two months victuall'd' (V, iv, 185–6) therefore questions the pretensions to timelessness of pastoral and comedy by lightly casting doubt on the conclusiveness of the formal happy ending.

The less time-conscious world of the speaker of 'L'Allegro' is similar to the world of the literary genres that he evokes, the romance, pastoral and forms that celebrate 'Hymen', comedy, masque and pageant. The pensive man's sense of himself as having duration, on the other hand, accords with the idea of time we get in the tragedies that he admires, which create heroic destinies out of actions and choices that are, and are realized as being, irreversible. In 'L'Allegro' our sense of time is produced by the framework of the piece, as it is in comedy; the day into which the speaker fits his activities does not have further implications in any life that we are given to see. Professor Allen has pointed out that the milkmaid, mower, shepherd, and ploughman that occur in lines 63–7 of 'L'Allegro' were standard figures to mark the seasons in medieval calendars and books of hours.[9] They are in the poem as scenic vignettes and distractions, and any sense of the passage of time that they create has little influence on the speaker's consciousness of himself as it is displayed for us. The pensive man, by contrast, has a sense of duration that causes him to see the twenty-four hours he traverses as constituting an analogy to the passage of his life. It has often been remarked that the last lines of 'Il Penseroso' have no analogue in the companion poem, which is twenty-four lines shorter. What the end of 'Il Penseroso' provides is an expression of personal commitment:

> But let my due feet never fail
> To walk the studious cloister's pale,
> And love the high-embowed roof. . . .
>
> (155–7)

The fact of the vow, the recognition it implies that only one course of life is possible and the concomitant sense of responsibility for its direction, is as significant as the substantive expression of devotion to a studious or religious and contemplative life. Having a past that makes his evening walks customary, a pattern of actions and responses that make up a personality, he also has a future ('And may at last my weary age/Find out the peaceful hermitage', 167–8), and his old age is analogous to the end of the day's course that he has described.

Milton has created out of images, syntactic connections, modulations and tempos, voices that reveal the sense of self to be inseparable from the idea of time. The melancholy man who is born under Saturn sees literary artifacts as well as human lives as subject to time; just as paintings and engravings of Melancholy showed her surrounded by broken and discarded lutes, statues and books, the pensive man whom Milton depicts is aware of the temporary nature of artifice, which is subject to comparison, change and even destruction. Neither time nor identity is perceptible to the senses; they are intellectual or spiritual constructs. But for the thoughtful man the knowledge that he exists in time, the source of his self-consciousness, also provides the disposition to religious contemplation that is his gift, and that lifts him through 'old experience' to the 'prophetic strain'.

Like *Hamlet*, 'Il Penseroso' mediates between Renaissance conceptions of melancholy and modern ones. The poem is based on a seemingly effortless fusion of traditional images. We know that the melancholic was the haunter of dark and shadowed places, hiding himself from the sun, and this is the source of the twilight and night scenes of 'Il Penseroso' as opposed to the sunlit ones of the companion poem. But Milton makes the melancholic's evasion of day's 'garish eye' more than a stereotyped attribute; it is expressive of his devotion to his inner life (Wordsworth's 'inward eye/Which is the bliss of solitude'), and of the fact that he is the imaginative maker of images, rather than merely the passive recorder of what he sees.

While 'Il Penseroso' draws on established notions of melancholy, then, it recreates them in such a way that the concept has remained meaningful for us. The pensive man with his 'white melancholy' as a nature-lover and the characteristic landscapes that he created remained (largely because of Milton's poems) an important figure in eighteenth-century poetry; from there his influence can be traced in the romantic poet's conception of himself. In the meantime the word 'melancholy' has become narrower, partly in accordance with Milton's lyric emphases: it now refers to feeling rather than to thought or behaviour, and to the gentler states of despondency rather than to the pathological ones. We have other ways than the Renaissance had of talking about genius, creativity or mental disorders, although we have inherited some sense of their interdependence. But even though the 'matter' of melancholy is now obsolete, the greatest Renaissance writers used it to shape patterns so vivid, so coherent, and at the same time so capable of expressing a complicated view of life that they have permanently shaped our literary consciousness.

Notes

Preface

[1] Northrop Frye, *The Anatomy of Criticism* (Princeton, 1957), 160–1.

[2] Erwin Panofsky and Fritz Saxl, *Dürers 'Melencolia I': eine Quellen- und Typen-Geschichtliche Untersuchung, Studien der Bibliothek Warburg*, II (Leipzig, 1923). This study was expanded and translated into English: Raymond Klibansky, Erwin Panofsky and Fritz Saxl, *Saturn and Melancholy* (New York, 1964).

[3] Lawrence Babb, *The Elizabethan Malady* (East Lansing, Mich., 1951).

Chapter One

[1] Hippocrates, *Works*, ed. and trans. W. H. S. Jones (Loeb Classical Library, New York, 1923), IV, 11–13.

[2] Hippocrates, IV, 185.

[3] Among the numerous modern accounts of the humoral theory, a good one can be found in A. C. Crombie, *Augustine to Galileo: the History of Science A.D. 400–1650* (Cambridge, Mass., 1953), 131ff.

[4] Galen, *De atra bile, liber*, trans. from Greek by Guinterius Ioannus Andernacus (Paris, 1529), fol. 5ff. and *passim*.

[5] E.g., 'Now vitelline [yellow] bile also may take on the appearance of this combusted black bile, if ever it chance to be roasted, so to say, by fiery heat.' (Translator's brackets.) Galen, *On the Natural Faculties*, with an English trans. by A. J. Brock (Loeb Classical Library, New York, 1916), 211.

[6] Galen, *De temperamentis et de inequali intemperie, libri tres*, trans. from Greek by Thomas Linacre (facsimile of the 1521 ed., London, 1881), esp. sig. E2^r. On Galen's theory of temperaments, see George Sarton, *A History of Science through the Golden Age of Greece* (Cambridge, Mass., 1952), 330ff.

[7] The Problems have generally been attributed to Aristotle, although they are not certainly by him. For a discussion of this Problem and its background, see Raymond Klibansky, Erwin Panofsky, and Fritz Saxl, *Saturn and Melancholy* (New York, 1964), 15–41; this work will hereafter be referred

to as *Saturn*. The authors reprint the entire text of Problem XXX, 1, in Greek and English, 18–29.

8 Morton Bloomfield, *The Seven Deadly Sins: An Introduction to the History of a Religious Concept, with Special Reference to Medieval English Literature* (East Lansing, Mich., 1967), 35–6. The mythological and astrological backgrounds are fully discussed in *Saturn*, 127–95.

9 On the use of stones, talismans, colours, etc., which could bring the influence of more favourable planets to bear, see Frances A. Yates, *Giordano Bruno and the Hermetic Tradition* (London, 1964), 6off., 331. Miss Yates points to the use of astral anti-Saturnian magical notions like Ficino's in such Renaissance paintings as Botticelli's 'Primavera', and she explains Dürer's 'Melencolia I' as a Saturnian talisman, an engraving that tries to attract Saturnian qualities just as the 'Primavera' tries to attract Venereal ones (p. 146 and n.).

10 Cicero, *Tusculan Disputations*, with an English trans. by J. E. King (Loeb Classical Library, New York, 1927), 237.

11 See Bloomfield, 54–121, 219, and *passim*.

12 *Saturn*, 300–3.

13 'Une double inspiration anime cette œuvre et en fait la curiosité. Par son sujet, les sept péchés capitaux, elle est médiévale et chrétienne; elle veut être antique par l'expression. L'acedia, mal monastique, y prend la forme de la mélancolie saturnienne; l'orgueil a des trompettes romaines [etc.] . . .', Guy de Tervarent, *Les enigmes de l'art: l'art savant* (Paris, 1946), 20 and the discussion on pp. 13–20.

14 The only exception, Coeffeteau's *Un tableau des passions humaines* (Paris, 1620), did appear in English as *A Table of Humane Passions* (1621), but the translation was not available to me. The dates in the text are of the first editions as listed in the *Short Title Catalogue*; footnote and bibliographical citations are to the editions I have used.

15 Fifteen editions of this work appeared between 1539 and 1610.

16 This work appeared in stages; the first book came out in 1586, the second and third in 1594, and the last not until 1618.

17 Pierre Charron, *Of Wisedome Three Bookes*, trans. from French by Samson Lennard (London, 1640), 99.

18 The *OED* lists the last example of 'accidie', the most common English form of the word, for 1520, with a rare, re-etymologized form, 'acedy', in the seventeenth century.

19 Charron, 100–1.

20 *Ibid.*, 559.

21 Coeffeteau, 316.

22 Levinius Lemnius, *The Touchstone of Complexions* (London, 1581), fol. 145^r–145^v.

23 Thomas Wright, *The Passions of the Minde in Generall* (London, 1621), 62.

24 M. Andreas Laurentius (du Laurens), *A Discourse of the Preservation of Sight*, trans. Richard Surphlet (London, 1599; London Shakespeare Association Facsimile, 1938), 94.

25 Timothy Bright, *A Treatise of Melancholie* (London, 1586; New York, Facsimile Text Society, 1940), 130–1.

[26] *Ibid.*, 199.

[27] Wright, 310–14.

[28] Andrew Boorde, *The Breviarie of Health* (London, 1587), fol. 78ʳ.

[29] Charron, 503. 'Science' in this context appears to mean practical knowledge of nature rather than knowledge of human nature and conduct.

[30] *Saturn*, 251–4.

[31] John Huarte, *Examen de Ingenios, The Examination of Mens Wits*, trans. R(ichard) C(arew) (London, 1594), 67.

[32] *Ibid.*, 59.

[33] Laurentius, 82.

[34] Morris W. Croll, *Style, Rhetoric and Rhythm*, essays, ed. by J. Max Patrick, *et al.* (Princeton, 1966), 216.

[35] Bright, 67ff.

[36] For the physiological basis of Shakespeare's portrayal of emotion, see Ruth L. Anderson, *Elizabethan Psychology and Shakespeare's Plays* (Iowa City, 1927), or John W. Draper, *The Humors and Shakespeare's Characters* (Durham, North Carolina, 1945).

[37] Coeffeteau, 315–16, 329–30.

[38] E.g., Thomas Walkington, *The Optick Glasse of Humors* (London, 1607), fol. 67ᵛ–68ʳ; Laurentius, 82, 89.

[39] Bright, 100, 233.

[40] For other entertaining works that justified themselves as cures of melancholy, see Louis B. Wright, *Middle-Class Culture in Elizabethan England* (Ithaca, 1959), 410–17.

[41] Laurentius, 101; or see Walkington, fol. 69ᵛ.

[42] Walkington, 'Epistle to the Reader'.

Chapter Two

[1] Sir John Harington, *A New Discourse on a Stale Subject Called The Metamorphosis of Ajax*, ed. Elizabeth Story Donno (New York, 1962), 250–1.

[2] Dudley North, 3rd Baron North, *A Forest of Varieties* (London, 1645), 118–19.

[3] Quoted by Robert S. Brustein, 'Italian Court Satire and the Plays of John Marston', unpublished Ph.D. dissertation (Columbia, 1957), 44. See also the connection that Nashe makes between the court, melancholy and malcontentedness in *Christs Teares Over Jerusalem. The Works of Thomas Nashe*, ed. Ronald B. McKerrow (Oxford, 1958), II, 130–2.

[4] Quoted in G. B. Harrison, ed., *The Elizabethan Journals. Being a Record of Those Things Most Talked of During the Years 1591–1603* (Michigan, 1955), II, 132.

[5] See L. C. Knights, '17th-Century Melancholy', in *Drama and Society in the Age of Jonson* (London, 1957), 315–32; F. P. Wilson, 'Some Notes on Authors and Patrons in Tudor and Stuart Times', *Joseph Quincy Adams Memorial Studies* (Washington, D.C., 1948), 553–61; and J. W. Saunders, 'The Stigma of Print: A Note on the Social Bases of Tudor Poetry', *Essays in Criticism*, I (April, 1951), 139–64.

⁶ McKerrow, I, 158.

⁷ *Ibid.*, 169–70.

⁸ *Ibid.*, 170.

⁹ *The Life and Complete Works in Prose and Verse of Robert Greene*, ed. Alexander B. Grosart (London, 1881–6), XII, 172–3.

¹⁰ Edward Guilpin, *Skialetheia, or A Shadow of Truth* (Shakespeare Association Facsimile, Oxford, 1931), sig. B₄ʳ.

¹¹ On this interesting portrait, discovered in 1959, and on several other examples of the vogue for melancholy portraiture in Renaissance England, see Roy Strong, *The English Icon: Elizabethan and Jacobean Portraiture* (London, 1969), 35–9, 352–3. Understandably, men who went to the trouble of having their portraits painted in this style did not conceal their faces with the hats they wore. The pulled-down hat so often mentioned in literature is reserved for satiric drawings of types like 'Inamorato' in the Frontispiece of Burton's *Anatomy of Melancholy*, or Samuel Rowlands's *Melancholie Knight* (London, 1615).

¹² Quoted in Rosemary Freeman, *English Emblem Books* (London, 1948), 203.

¹³ For categories of malcontent types, see, e.g., Theodore Spencer, 'The Elizabethan Malcontent', in *Joseph Quincy Adams Memorial Studies* (Washington, D.C., 1948), 523–35; Lawrence Babb, *The Elizabethan Malady* (East Lansing, Mich., 1952), Ch. IV; or John B. Bamborough, *The Little World of Man* (London, 1952), Ch. IV.

¹⁴ William Rankins, *Seven Satires*, ed. Arnold Davenport (Liverpool, 1948), 15–16.

¹⁵ Robert Anton, *Philosophers Satyrs* (London, 1616), 18–19.

¹⁶ Anton makes this connection, sig. E₄ʳff. For analyses of the traveller, see Z. S. Fink, 'Jaques and the Malcontent Traveler', *PQ*, XIV (July, 1935), 237–52; and Oscar James Campbell's analysis of Jaques in *Shakespeare's Satire* (New York, 1943), 49–57.

¹⁷ Marston, *Certain Satires*, II, ll. 133–9. References to Marston's two groups of formal satires, the *Certain Satires* (referred to as *CS*) attached to his erotic poem, *The Metamorphosis of Pygmalion's Image*, and *The Scourge of Villainy* (*SV*), both of which appeared in 1599, are to the third volume of A. H. Bullen, *The Works of John Marston* (London, 1887), which has modernized the spellings.

¹⁸ Once a lover had been smitten by the object of his desire, his emotional state did cause the kind of humoral imbalance and symptoms connected with other kinds of melancholy, but humoral imbalance was not primary. See John Livingston Lowes, 'The Loveres Maladye of Hereos', *MP*, XI (April, 1914), 491–546.

¹⁹ 'Matthew: I am melancholy my selfe divers times, sir, and then doe I no more but take pen, and paper presently, and overflow you halfe a score, or a dozen sonnets, at a sitting', Jonson, *Every Man in His Humour*, III, iii, 89–93. All references to Jonson's plays are to the edition of the *Works* by C. H. Herford and Percy Simpson (Oxford, 1925–52).

²⁰ Rudolf and Margot Wittkower, *Born Under Saturn* (New York, 1963), especially Ch. V.

[21] *The Englishmans Doctor. Or The Schoole of Salerne*, trans. Sir John Harington (London, 1607), sig. C₄ʳ.

[22] George Chapman, *An Humourous Day's Mirth* in *The Plays of George Chapman: The Comedies*, ed. Thomas Marc Parrott (New York, 1961), Vol. I.

[23] John Marston, *Antonio's Revenge*, ed. E. K. Hunter (Lincoln, Nebraska, 1965).

[24] John Webster, *The Duchess of Malfi*, ed. John Russell Brown (Cambridge, Mass., 1964).

[25] Harry Levin, *The Question of Hamlet* (New York, 1959), 118.

[26] *Every Man in his Humour*, III, iv, 20–2. There is another longer definition in *Every Man out of his Humour*, 'After the Second Sounding', 88ff., which develops the idea of a dominant trait of character, or what would later become the 'ruling passion' of Pope's satire.

[27] The background of Jonson's humours is described in Charles Reed Baskerville, *The English Elements in Jonson's Early Comedy* (Austin, Texas, 1911), 34–75, and Herford and Simpson, I, 339ff. On whether Jonson used the word to denote affectations or deeper psychological tendencies, see H. L. Snuggs, 'The Comic Humours: A New Interpretation', *PMLA*, LXII (March, 1947), 114–22.

[28] The idea of 'satiric landscape', of a crowded, turbulent scene as an element in satiric literature and painting, is developed by Alvin Kernan, *The Cankered Muse: Satire of the English Renaissance* (New Haven, 1956), 4ff.

[29] *Every Man out of his Humour*, 'After the Second Sounding', 143–6; V, iv, 25–7.

[30] A classic example of the comic elevation of melancholy as a courtly word and illness occurs in Lyly's *Midas* (1592), V, ii, 99–110, where the barber, Motto, is taken to task for saying that he is melancholy rather than 'heavy', 'dull', 'doltish', or 'lumpish', because 'melancholy is the creast of Courtiers armes'. *The Complete Works of John Lyly*, ed. R. W. Bond (Oxford, 1902), Vol. III; or see Herford and Simpson, IX, 353.

[31] See Jonas A. Barish, *Ben Jonson and the Language of Prose Comedy* (Cambridge, Mass., 1960), especially 100–4.

[32] *Every Man out of his Humour*, 'Characters of the Personae', 423.

[33] Bright, 124.

[34] John Earle, *Microcosmography: or A Piece of the World Discovered;* in *Essays and Characters* (1628; London, 1897), 19.

[35] All references to this play are to the edition of H. Harvey Wood (London, 1934–9), Vol. II. This edition has no line numbers, and I have, therefore, used page numbers.

[36] Tom Lehrer, *That Was the Year That Was* (Reprise Records, 6179).

[37] Walkington, fol. 66ᵛ.

[38] *The First Part of Hieronimo*, ed. Andrew S. Cairncross (Lincoln, Nebraska, 1967). This play, which exists in a corrupt text, may be based on a longer, original version by Kyd; see the editor's introduction, pp. xv–xix.

[39] See E. E. Stoll, *John Webster: The Periods of his Work as Determined by his Relation to the Drama of his Day* (Cambridge, Mass., 1905).

[40] Cyril Tourneur, *The Revenger's Tragedy*, ed. R. A. Foakes (Cambridge, Mass., 1966).

[41] Bright, 200.

⁴² Thomas Kyd, *The Spanish Tragedy*, ed. Philip Edwards (Cambridge, Mass., 1959).

⁴³ This was one of the passages added in Pavier's edition of 1602, but it is not out of keeping with other passages, e.g. III, xii, 7–9.

⁴⁴ E. K. Chambers listed this play as doubtfully by Marston, but said that Marston had a hand in it: *The Elizabethan Stage* (Oxford, 1923), III, 434. Most critics include it among Marston's works; see, for example, Anthony Caputi, *John Marston, Satirist* (Ithaca, New York, 1961), 259–60. I am quoting from Wood's edition of the plays (Vol. III).

⁴⁵ John Marston, *The Malcontent*, ed. M. L. Wine (Lincoln, Nebraska, 1964).

⁴⁶ John Webster, *The White Devil*, ed. John Russell Brown (Cambridge, Mass., 1960).

⁴⁷ See M. C. Bradbrook, 'Fate and Chance in *The Duchess of Malfi*', in Max Bluestone and Norman Rabkin, eds., *Shakespeare's Contemporaries* (New York, 1961), 210–22.

⁴⁸ Bright, 107.

⁴⁹ On cats, dogs, owls, crows and hares—all 'melancholy' animals—as witches and evil spirits, see Burton's *Anatomy of Melancholy*, I, 183, 193, 195, 210, 286.

⁵⁰ Cesare Ripa, *Nova Iconologia* (Padua, 1618), 527.

⁵¹ *John Milton: Complete Poems and Major Prose*, ed. Merritt Y. Hughes (New York, 1957).

⁵² William Rankins, *Seven Satires*, ed. Arnold Davenport (Liverpool, 1948), V, 3–4.

⁵³ Thomas Robinson, *The Life and Death of Mary Magdalene*, ed. H. Oskar Sommer (London, 1899), Stanza 72.

⁵⁴ See H. T. Price, 'The Function of Imagery in Webster', *PMLA*, LXX (September 1955), 717–39.

⁵⁵ On this statue as a representation of melancholy, see Erwin Panofsky, *Studies in Iconology* (New York, 1962), 210–11.

⁵⁶ Robinson, *The Life and Death of Mary Magdalene*, Stanza 75. In Lomazzo's *A Tracte Containing the Artes of Curious Paintinge, Carvinge, and Buildinge*, tr. R(ichard) H(aydocke) (London, 1598), painters are advised to depict melancholy 'with declined countenances, and eies fixed on the earth, bowing the head, with one elbow resting on the knee, and the hand under the cheeke . . .', p. 25.

⁵⁷ A deer and a stag appear on the Frontispiece of Burton's *Anatomy* under the heading of 'solitudo'. For the deer as a symbol of melancholy solitude, see also Guy de Tervarent, *Attributs et symboles dans l'art profane: 1450–1600* (Geneva, 1958), I, col. 67.

⁵⁸ See, for example, Brown's edition of *The White Devil*, II, i, 93–4, and II, i, 323–9, and the editor's notes to these lines. The stag becomes a melancholy haunter of shadowed places when he loses his horns and men become melancholy by receiving them; therefore the emblem of the weeping stag that is thrown into Camillo's window has the legend, '*Inopem me copia fecit*'.

⁵⁹ See Christian Kiefer, 'Music and Marston's "The Malcontent"', *SP*, LI (1954), 163–71.

⁶⁰ Huarte, for example (pp. 324–5), spoke of participation in plays in connection with kinds of mirth that are antidotes to melancholy. However, since

melancholy had such positive meaning for him, he added that indulgence in plays leads to stupidity.

61 Thomas Heywood, *An Apology for Actors*, introduction and notes by Richard H. Perkinson (Scholars' Facsimiles and Reprints, New York, 1941), sigs. F₃ᵛ–F₄ʳ.

62 Madeleine Doran, *Endeavors of Art: A Study of Form in Elizabethan Drama* (Madison, Wisconsin, 1963), 90, 362, 452n. Miss Doran also discusses the Heywood passage.

63 This device was reattached to the psychological theory that had originally produced it by Ford, in the masque of melancholics (types taken from Burton) which entertains the sick prince in *The Lover's Melancholy* (1628).

64 See Robert Rentoul Reed, *Bedlam on the Jacobean Stage* (Cambridge, Mass., 1952), Ch. I, 'Bethlehem Hospital and its Background'. The idea that mad people and lunatic asylums provided amusement found its way into several plays, including Part I of Dekker's *The Honest Whore* (1604) and Middleton and Rowley's *The Changeling* (1622).

65 This medical theory of catharsis, propounded by Continental critics of the Renaissance like Minturno and Castelvetro, influenced Milton's conception of *Samson Agonistes*. See Hughes's edition of the *Complete Poems*, 543–4.

66 Grosart, V, 99.

Chapter Three

1 See p. 24.

2 McKerrow, II, 131.

3 There is a useful discussion of this question in Lila H. Freedman, 'Satiric Personae: A Study of Point of View in Formal Verse Satire in the English Renaissance from Wyatt to Marston', unpublished Ph.D. dissertation (Wisconsin, 1955). See also Caputi, Ch. II.

4 The verbal parallels between Marston's invocations and Milton's have, of course, been noticed; see, e.g., Lawrence Babb, 'The Background of "Il Penseroso"', *SP*, XXXVII (April, 1940), 257–73.

5 See the famous distinction in the Prologue to *Every Man in his Humour*:

> And persons, such as Comoedie would chuse
> When she would shew an image of the times
> And sport with humane follies, not with crimes. . . .
> I meane such errors, as you'll all confesse
> By laughing at them, they deserve no lesse. . . .

6 This passage is quoted with commentary by Mary Claire Randolph, 'Thomas Drant's Definition of Satire, 1566', *Notes and Queries*, CLXXX (1941), 416–18. See also Freedman, Ch. V, and Caputi, 24–5.

7 Bright, 124.

8 *Ibid.*, 99.

9 *Ibid.*, 102, 149.

10 The first part of this verse is a translation from Horace, *si foret in terris, rideret*

Democritus (*Epistles*, II, i, 194), and Burton makes repeated use of the phrase in 'Democritus to the Reader' (*Anatomy*, I, 53ff.).

11 Chaucer's *Parson's Tale*, in F. N. Robinson, ed., *The Poetical Works of Chaucer* (Cambridge, Mass., 1961), 249.

12 Dante, *Inferno*, with an English translation by John D. Sinclair (New York, 1961), 105.

13 Satire II, ii, 139–41. '*Splendida bilis*' is glossed by the editor of the Loeb edition as the black bile of melancholy. Horace, *Satires, Epistles and Ars Poetica*, with an English translation by H. Rushton Fairclough (Cambridge, Mass., 1961), 165.

14 Geoffrey Bullough, ed., *Poems and Dramas of Fulke Greville, First Lord Brooke* (New York, 1945), I, 189.

15 Mary Claire Randolph, 'The Medical Concept in English Satiric Theory: Its Possible Relationships and Implications', *SP*, XXXVIII (April, 1941), 125–57.

16 See, e.g., *SV*, '*In Lectores prorsus indignos*', IV, 167–70; VI, 101–10.

17 *SV*, 'To *Detraction* I present my *Poesie*', or VI, 101–12.

18 See the descriptions of the melancholy personality by Bright, 'The perturbations of melancholy are for the most parte, sadde and fearefull, and such as rise of them: as distrust, doubt, diffidence, or dispaire . . .' (p. 102), or his description of 'those stormes of outragious love, hatred, hope or feare, wherewith bodies so passionate are here and there, tossed with disquiet' (pp. 93–4).

19 Caputi points out (pp. 123–4) that John Ellis is directly related to such figures in the satires as Briscius (*CS*, I) or 'Inamorato Lucian' ('I approach'd the ass,/And straight he weeps, and sighs some sonnet out/To his fair love!' *CS*, III, 62–4).

20 The connection of melancholy with miserliness was traditional, and is indicated by the purse in representations of the melancholic by Ripa (pp. 92–3) or Peacham (*Minerva Britanna*, London, 1612, p. 126, and see above, facing p. 79). A literary example of the connection is Spenser's Malbecco (*The Faerie Queene*, III, x, and especially Stanza lix).

21 For the association of the word 'pasquil' with satire, see Kernan, 53. Another satirist in the play is Brabant Sr, the bad satirist who uses the follies of others as a way of bolstering his own sense of superiority.

22 For the associations of 'Lampatho Doria' with the Italian word *lampazzo*, or bur (and possibly with *dorio*, 'a musician who plays grave music'), see Caputi, 168.

23 Arnold Davenport, ed., *The Poems of John Marston* (Liverpool, 1961), 19–27. See also John Peter, *Complaint and Satire in Early English Literature* (Oxford, 1956), which deals with the often contradictory assumptions of Renaissance satire, especially Marston's.

24 Davenport, 19.

25 Marston, *Antonio and Mellida*, ed. G. K. Hunter (Lincoln, Nebraska, 1965).

26 On Aristotle's definition of envy and its relevance to satire, see O. J. Campbell, *Comicall Satyre and Shakespeare's Troilus and Cressida* (San Marino, Calif., 1959), 6ff.

27 Philip Finkelpearl suggests that Antonio's excesses of language and action

are being satirized here; see *John Marston of the Middle Temple: An Elizabethan Dramatist in his Social Setting* (Cambridge, Mass., 1969), Ch. IX.

28 The plot of *Antonio's Revenge* has many similarities to that of *Hamlet* and has,
therefore, raised questions as to which play came first. The two parts of
Antonio and Mellida were entered in the Stationers' Register in 1601 and
Hamlet in 1602, but neither of these dates is conclusive. G. K. Hunter points
out in the Preface to his edition of *Antonio's Revenge* that there are no verbal
parallels between the two plays, and suggests tentatively that they were
both derived from the same source. Finkelpearl (Appendix C, pp. 268–71)
summarizes the scholarly literature on this subject. He argues that *Hamlet*
precedes both *Antonio* plays.

29 T. S. Eliot, 'John Marston', in *Essays on Elizabethan Drama* (New York, 1932),
171. An example of such confusion of roles is the soliloquy on sleeplessness,
III, ii, 1–14.

30 See Levin, 117–18.

31 The date of *The Malcontent* (1600 or 1604), and therefore its relation to
Hamlet, have long been a matter of dispute. Finkelpearl (pp. 178–9n.)
briefly and convincingly argues for the later date of Marston's play.

Chapter Four

1 For a list of Shakespeare's allusions to melancholy see G. A. Bieber,
Der Melancholikertypus Shakespeares und sein Ursprung (Heidelberg, 1913),
47ff.

2 For Timon as the prototypical melancholy misanthrope, see, for example,
Lemnius, fol. 143ʳ.

3 The first critical article to observe that Hamlet was melancholy actually
appeared in 1780, as L. L. Schücking observed (1922) in his own analysis
of Hamlet's melancholy: *Character Problems in Shakespeare's Plays* (Gloucester, Mass., 1959), 147–76. Bradley's influential argument (1904) was
that Hamlet, who would have been capable of performing his task of ven-
geance at any other time, was called upon to perform it just when the shock
of discovering the truth about his mother's nature had paralysed him with
melancholy: *Shakespearean Tragedy* (London, 1957), 70, 85ff.

Among other critics who have analysed Hamlet's ailment in terms of
Renaissance psychology are Lily B. Campbell, *Shakespeare's Tragic Heroes:
Slaves of Passion* (New York, 1952), Ch. XII; John W. Draper, *The Hamlet
of Shakespeare's Audience* (Durham, North Carolina, 1938); Oscar J. Campbell,
'What is the Matter with Hamlet?', *Yale Review*, XXXII (December, 1942),
309–22. The connections between *Hamlet* and Bright's *Treatise* are listed in
Appendix E (pp. 309–20) of J. Dover Wilson, *What Happens in Hamlet*
(1935; New York, 1959). An attempt to reconcile Renaissance and modern
psychology is made by Paul A. Jorgensen, 'Hamlet's Therapy', *HLQ*,
XXVII (May, 1964), 239–58.

4 Overbury's 'character' of the melancholy man, for example (1614), includes
inactivity as an identifying trait, as Schücking points out (pp. 154–5, 159).

5 H. H. Furness, ed., *A New Variorum Edition of Shakespeare: Hamlet* (1877;

New York, 1963), II, 104. For the instances of melancholy in Belleforest's *Hamlet*, see A. P. Stabler, 'Melancholy, Ambition and Revenge in Belleforest's Hamlet', *PMLA*, LXXXI (June, 1966), 207–13.

6 In the First Quarto, Claudius phrases his question as follows: 'And now princely Sonne Hamlet,/What meanes these sad and melancholy moodes?', *Variorum*, II, 43 (I, ii, 166–7).

7 Laurentius, p. 82. See also Vindice in *The Revenger's Tragedy*, 'I dare not look till the sun be in a cloud' (IV, ii, 117), and Schücking, p. 155.

8 Kenneth Muir, ed., *Shakespeare: Hamlet* (London, 1963), 25.

9 Lemnius, fol. 146ʳ–146ᵛ. The parallel is interesting because St Patrick's Purgatory is apparently where the Ghost is understood to have come from (I, v, 136).

10 This was a standard topic; see, e.g., Burton, II, 153, where he quotes a phrase from Plutarch about the incompatibility of beauty and honesty.

11 See Schücking, pp. 164–5. For a discussion of Hamlet's costumes, see Maurice Charney, *Style in Hamlet* (Princeton, 1969), 186–90.

12 Cf. Flamineo's comments about Vittoria's entrance in *The White Devil*, V, vi, 1.

13 Levin, 117.

14 Batman, fol. 33ʳ; and see Thomas Wright, 61, for the melancholy blood around the heart.

15 For references to such fits, see Laurentius, 103, and T. Wright, 143; for melancholy men as particularly subject to 'furious fits', see Walkington, fol. 66ʳ.

16 Lemnius, fol. 143ᵛ.

17 See *The Winter's Tale*, IV, iv, 751–2: 'The King is not at the palace; he is gone aboard a new ship to purge melancholy and air himself. . . .' See also Coeffeteau, pp. 326–7, on 'variable objects' and good air as healthful, or Barrough, 36.

18 Another clue that Hamlet tosses out is his remark to Guildenstern: 'I am but mad north-north west; when the wind is southerly I know a hawk from a handsaw' (II, ii, 374–5). As Dover Wilson has shown, the remark may have a relationship to a statement of Bright's, 'The ayre meet for melancholicke folke, ought to be thinne, pure and subtile, open and patient to all winds: in respect of their temper, especially to the South, and Southeast', *What Happens in Hamlet*, 311.

19 Robinson, 265.

20 *Ibid.*, 249–51. In this analysis of *acedia*, the word 'thoughtful' is used in a pejorative sense (p. 296).

21 William Piraldus, *Summae virtuum ac vitiorum tomus secundus* (Lyons, 1668), 164–207, especially 171–3.

22 Charron, 102.

23 Lemnius, fol. 148ᵛ.

24 Lord North, 108. See de Tervarent, *Attributs*, I, cols. 28–9 for a list of examples of the ass used as a symbol of *acedia* and laziness, and Ripa, *Nova Iconologia*, under 'Pigritia', 7, 415–17, where the association is traced back to Egyptian sources and where the connection with melancholy is also made.

[25] 'Ass' is the word left out of the last line of Hamlet's quatrain:

> *Ham* For thou dost know, O Damon dear,
> This realm dismantled was
> Of Jove himself; and now reigns here
> A very, very—peacock.
> *Horatio* You might have rhym'd.

(III, ii, 275–9)

[26] Eighteenth-century editors changed the word 'fust' to 'rust' (*Variorum*, I, 345), but the idea of 'fusting' or mouldering is in any case very similar. For sadness as rusting the soul, see Charron, 99; and for an example of the idea of rusting or mouldering in Hamlet's sense, see Henry Howard, Earl of Northampton, *A defensative against the poyson of supposed Prophesies* (London, 1583). In refuting those who exalted melancholy by associating it with prophecy, Howard used the language that connected melancholy most closely with sloth: '. . . melancholy seeketh ease and shunneth exercise . . . so by the rust of idleness, the sharpest edge of wit is taken off', memory weakens, reason decays (sig. Iᵛ).

[27] See Primaudaye, II, 380, or Huarte, 92–4. On why the devil usually took the likeness of one's parents or relatives, see Nashe's *The Terrors of the Night*, McKerrow, I, 348. On the plausibility of this passage in Elizabethan terms, see, e.g., Lawrence Babb, 'Hamlet, Melancholy, and the Devil', *MLN*, LIX (February, 1944), 120–2.

[28] The fact that we are always being shown pictures of what Hamlet was like before the beginning of the play has often been commented upon; see, e.g., Bradley, 86ff., or O. J. Campbell, 'What is the Matter with Hamlet?', 313–14.

[29] For the association of melancholy and silence see, for instance, 'Malinconio per la Terra', a picture of a man with a gag over his mouth, in Ripa's *Iconologia*; the text explains the connection between silence and coldness (pp. 92–3).

[30] Generally, sanguine temperaments were lovers and melancholics were not; according to Elyot (fol. 8ʳ), for example, and Huarte (p. 313), melancholics were more or less incapable of love because of their physiological make-up. Bright, on the other hand (p. 134), thought they were very prone to love and to idealize others because of their bad opinion of themselves. Burton discusses these contradictions, I, 393. As lovers, melancholics sometimes showed their characteristic possessiveness in morbid jealousy; see Burton, I, 257–9.

[31] Occasionally a Saturnine character like Aaron in *Titus Andronicus* would get involved with a woman, but his love was really subordinated to the villainy that he wanted to perpetrate. The mistress whom Vindice avenges in *The Revenger's Tragedy*, already dead when the play begins, is obviously a mere excuse for the revenge that follows.

[32] Hamlet's return to proficiency in former courtly skills at the end of the play reveals some inconsistency; when he agrees to fence with Laertes, he tells Horatio that he has been in constant practice since Laertes went to France (V, ii, 202–3).

[33] See Lily B. Campbell, Ch. XII.

[34] See, for instance, the quotation from Marlowe's *Edward II*, I, i, 167: 'My men, like satyrs. . . Shall with their goat-feet dance the antic hay.' Levin discusses the word and the comic aspect of the antic disposition, pp. 111–26, 128 n.16.

[35] George Puttenham, 'The Arte of English Poesie', in G. Gregory Smith, ed., *Elizabethan Critical Essays* (London, 1959,) especially II, 158–9.

[36] See, e.g., Boorde, fol. 13ᵛ and 92ᵛ, and *The Taming of the Shrew*, Induction, II, 130, where melancholy is called the 'nurse of frenzy'.

[37] Lemnius, fol. 147ᵛ–148ᵛ.

[38] Bright, 102.

[39] Batman, fol. 33ʳ.

[40] Lemnius, fol. 149ᵛ.

[41] Bright, 111.

[42] See above, pp 51–2, and p. 167, nn. 57, 58; and Peacham's *Minerva Britanna*, 4, for the connection of the stricken deer with a guilty conscience.

[43] The King is distempered with choler (III, ii, 296), and Hamlet remarks sarcastically that he might not be the right person to 'put him to his purgation' (III, ii, 297–9). Although the four temperaments each had different characteristics, the diseases caused by each tended to be subsumed under the heading of melancholy. See *Saturn*, 88–9.

[44] This was a common subject in paintings and engravings; Death was depicted as holding a mirror up to a woman, and showing her a skull instead of her own face. See Samuel C. Chew, *The Pilgrimage of Life* (New Haven, 1962), 77.

[45] See Alan Downer, 'The Life of Our Design: The Function of Imagery in the Poetic Drama,' *Hudson Review*, II (Summer, 1949), 242–63.

[46] *Saturn*, 131, gives two quotations from astrological sources about gravedigging as one of the lowly professions over which Saturn presided. Diggers in the earth in general were thought to be Saturnian types; see Pl. 40 for a picture of Saturn himself as a digger.

[47] Dürer's *Melencolia* is surrounded with the appurtenances of carpentry, and stone-masonry as well as carpentry are occupations in the big fresco of Saturn's children in the 'Salone' of Padua; see *Saturn*, 307–14, Pls. 32–3, and de Tervarent, *Attributs*, I, cols. 101, 412. For Saturn as the patron of sea-journeys, see *Saturn*, 130–1, see also p. 204 for 'working in leather' and p. 190 for a description by Guido Bonetti of Saturn's children as leather and parchment workers, and of the conjunction of Saturn with other planets as determining what subjects workers on parchments would be gifted for—juridical, business deeds etc.

[48] 'The melancholicke are accounted as most fit to undertake matters of weightie charge and high attempt', Laurentius, 85. For rulers as born under Saturn, see Greene's *Planetomachia*, Grosart, V, 46.

[49] There is an extended discussion of this subject in Burton's *Anatomy*, I, 62–5; and see also Nashe's *Christs Teares Over Jerusalem*, McKerrow, II, 130.

[50] Burton, I, 66.

[51] Vincent Cartari, *Les images des dieux anciens* (Lyons, 1581), 35–6; and see also Panofsky, 'Father Time', in *Studies in Iconology*, especially 73–5.

173

[52] Cartari, 35–6. For the association of Saturn and melancholy with measurement, geometry, and the like, see *Saturn*, Pls. 1, 115, 118, 132 *inter alia* and pp. 332–45.

[53] See Wyndham Lewis, *The Lion and the Fox: The Role of the Hero in the Plays of Shakespeare* (London, 1927), 36.

[54] *Saturn*, Pls. 38, 39 and 43 all contain hanged men on the gallows.

[55] *Ibid.*, Pl. 52: Maarten van Heemskerck, 'Saturn and his Children'.

[56] Robinson, 41.

[57] *Saturn*, 388ff.

[58] See Wolfgang Clemen, *The Development of Shakespeare's Imagery* (Cambridge, Mass., 1951), 111.

[59] See Maria Fossi Todovow, *Mostra delle incisioni di Luca di Leida* (Florence, 1963), 27, and the comments to the effect that the subject of this unidentified portrait may well be allegorical (pp. 24–5).

[60] *Saturn*, Pl. 134. The painting (significantly, as the authors note, pp. 388–9) is known in its several copies by both names.

[61] *Ibid.*, Pl. 135. For a brief analysis of another drawing of Melancholy by Castiglione, see Richard Bernheimer, 'Some Drawings of Benedetto Castiglione', *The Art Bulletin*, XXXIII (March, 1951), 47–51. The Feti painting dates from around 1614 and the Castiglione etching was influenced by it; there is no question, therefore, of any direct influence on Shakespeare, only of similarity of intention.

[62] Levin, 123.

[63] For a discussion of this passage in *The Faerie Queene* (II, ix, 50–2) and of the general connection between melancholy and the imagination see Northrop Frye, *Fables of Identity: Studies in Poetic Mythology* (New York, 1963), 154–61.

[64] Laurentius, 100.

[65] See above, p. 104, and *1 Henry IV*, I, ii, 83: 'I am as melancholy as a gib cat.' For cats as melancholy, see also, e.g., the 'melancholly Pusse' in Peacham's emblem of melancholy (facing p. 79). For dogs as melancholy (and the possible explanation that their sad faces and their propensity to madness were the reasons), see de Tervarent, *Attributs*, I, cols. 94 and 431. For both animals, see Burton's *Anatomy*, the Frontispiece and Argument to the Frontispiece, and I, 79.

[66] Bats, as night creatures, were emblematic of darkness and melancholy, and a bat is the bearer of the title of Dürer's Melencolia. Both the cat and the bat figure in a much later version of melancholy (based, however, on the earlier symbolism), Goya's 'Caprichio 43', see Folke-Nordström, *Goya, Saturn and Melancholy* (Uppsala, 1962), Pl. 62 and p. 119. Frogs are among Nashe's melancholy night animals (McKerrow, I, 386), and see the connection between melancholy and toads (cold-blooded creatures who were associated with stagnating ponds) in *The Duchess of Malfi*, I, i, 157–9, and the further references in the editor's note to these lines.

[67] See, for instance, Ripa, 567–8, for Hercules under the heading of 'Virtù Heroica'.

[68] This traditional interpretation of these lines (see the *Variorum*, I, 168) has recently been questioned; see Ernest Schanzer, 'Hercules and his Load', *RES*, XIX (February, 1968), 51–3.

[69] There is some dispute about who is meant by Hercules in this passage; Dover Wilson, for example, annotates this in his edition of the play (Cambridge, 1961), 241, as a reference to Laertes. For an interpretation of the lines in the sense in which I take them ('Hamlet's last allusion, the last of his several allusions to Hercules . . . is a quietly ironic acceptance of his inability to set the world right') see Douglas Bush, 'Classical Myth in Shakespeare's Plays', in *Elizabethan and Jacobean Studies Presented to F. P. Wilson* (Oxford, 1959), 75.

[70] Eugene Waith, *The Herculean Hero* (New York, 1962), 39ff. Hamlet refers to the Nemean lion, I, v, 83.

[71] Waith, 19, 30–1.

[72] This version of the Hercules story originated with the Sophist Prodicus; its representation in art is discussed by Erwin Panofsky, 'Hercules Am Scheidewege', *Studien der Bibliothek Warburg*, XVIII (Leipzig-Berlin, 1930).

[73] Panofsky, 'Hercules', 58, 102, and *passim*. The nun-like, virtuous Melancholy would, of course, eventually be celebrated in Milton's 'pensive nun, devout and pure' ('Il Penseroso', l. 31).

[74] For identifications of this as a picture of Hamlet as a pilgrim, see the *Variorum*, I, 329–30.

[75] Anne Righter, *Shakespeare and the Idea of the Play* (London, 1962), 154–64.

[76] For rosemary as good against 'all cold maladies' and against 'cold passions of the heart', see Primaudaye, III, 345. Rue, which Burton lists as beneficial against love-melancholy, was also according to him considered by Lemnius 'to expel vain imaginations, devils, and to ease afflicted souls' (Burton, II, 192, 217). On fennel and fennel seed, see Burton, II, 25, 26, 241, 255, or Bright, pp. 270, 273. Violets and oil of violets are listed by Bright, pp. 273, 275, and by Burton (e.g. II, 217, 248–9, 251).

[77] Rabelais expressed scorn for this symbol and others like it that had their origin in purely verbal similarities: 'En pareilles ténèbres son comprins ces glorieux de court et transporteurs de noms, lesquelz, voulens en leurs divises signifier *espoir*, font portraire, une *sphère*, des *pennes* d'oiseaulx pour *poines* [= peines], de *l'ancholie* pour *mélancholie* . . .', Rabelais, *Œuvres Complètes*, ed. Boulenger et Scheler (Pléiade edition, Paris, 1955), 32.

[78] Erwin Panofsky, *Early Netherlandish Painting: Its Origins and Character* (Cambridge, Mass., 1953), I, 146, 416 n.6.

[79] See especially Clemen, 112–18, and the list of disease images in Caroline Spurgeon, *Shakespeare's Imagery and What It Tells Us* (London, 1935), 316ff.

[80] For examples of such loose terminology, see the *Regimen sanitatis Salerni*, trans. Thomas Paynell (London, 1528), sig. xii; 'A canker is a melancolye impostume/eatinge partis of the bodye/as well fleshye as senowy', or Boorde, fol. 92ᵛ, where frenzy or madness are called 'imposthumes' of the brain. For a long list of diseases connected with melancholy, including fevers, stomach troubles, jaundice, epilepsy, cancer, etc., see Greene's *Planetomachia*, Grosart, V, 51.

Chapter Five

1 All quotations from the *Anatomy* will be from the 3-volume Everyman's Library edition edited by Holbrook Jackson. Bracketed insertions in the quotations are those of the editor. Lawrence Babb has pointed out that this version, based on the sixth edition (the last that Burton revised himself), conforms more closely to what Burton left than does the 'standard' edition, based on the seventh, of A. R. Shilleto (1883). However, I have occasionally made use of Shilleto's notes. For Babb's opinion, see his *Sanity in Bedlam: A Study of Robert Burton's Anatomy of Melancholy* (East Lansing, Mich., 1959), 29.

2 See Babb's list in *Sanity*, p. 48. Paul Jordan-Smith lists three quotations from Shakespeare, *Bibliographia Burtoniana* (Stanford, Calif., 1931), 26 and n.

3 Jordan-Smith (p. 26) commented upon the discrepancy between the few English works quoted by Burton and the large number of English books in his library. On the books found in the library, see 'Two Lists of Burton's Books', ed. S. Gibson and F. D. R. Needham, *Oxford Bibliographical Society Proceedings and Papers*, I (1922–6), 222–46, which lists some of the books that Burton left to the Bodleian and Christ Church libraries.

4 Gibson and Needham, 'Two Lists of Burton's Books'.

5 Furthermore, not all the books that Burton owned are in the Bodleian and Christ Church collections that have been itemized. According to his will, his English medical books were given away, as were one or two folios to each of his fellow masters of arts. There was also much more vernacular literature; Sir William Osler, who gathered the Burtonian collections together, pointed out that the original list of Rous, the Keeper of the Bodleian, added the note, 'Porro [dono dedit] comoediarum, tragediarum, et schediasmatum ludicrorum (praesertim idiomate vernaculo) aliquot centurias, quas propter multitudinem non adjecimus'. Besides, the Bodleian apparently sold some of Burton's volumes if they had duplicates of them. Osler, 'Robert Burton: The Man, His Book, His Library', *Oxford Bibliographical Society Proceedings and Papers*, I (1922–6), 185–98.

6 Shilleto, III, 246, 291. Burton might, however, have known this song independently.

7 Siegbert Prawer stressed Burton's humanistic bias in dwelling on the proper duties of scholars in the commonwealth, and pointed out that the *Anatomy* itself was meant to be a useful work, 'paying', as it were, for Burton's position at Christ Church: 'Burton's "Anatomy of Melancholy" ', *The Cambridge Journal*, I (August, 1948), 671–88.

8 For a psychologically slanted analysis of Burton's mixture of truculence and defensiveness, see Bergen Evans, *The Psychiatry of Robert Burton* (New York, 1944), Ch. I, 'The Man'.

9 Wood, II, 278. In both cases the scholar, placed in a social situation, proves his ineptitude by withdrawing into a futile meditation on 'nothing': Burton quotes Persius's satire, 'They meditate the dreams of old sick men/ As "Out of nothing nothing can be brought;/And that which is, can ne'er be turn'd to nought" ' (I, 303). Similarly, Lampatho, in his first venture

into female society, answers inappropriately to Meletza's question of how he will respect her: 'Why just as you respect me, as nothing, for out of nothing, nothing is bred, so nothing shall not beget anything, any-thing bring nothing [etc.]', Wood, II, 280.

10 See L. C. Knights, *Drama and Society*, 325–6.

11 Author's 'Abstract of Melancholy', I, 11–13, I, 406, II, 104. This subject was not unknown in the earlier expository books, e.g. Lemnius, fol. 150ʳ.

12 Babb, *Sanity*, 15–16, 19–20. Also cut out after the first edition was the reference to the physicians who had helped Burton. On these changes see Edward Bensly, 'Some Alterations and Errors in the Successive Editions of *The Anatomy of Melancholy*', *Oxford Bibliographical Society Proceedings and Papers*, I (1922–6), 198–215 (especially p. 203).

13 Babb, *Sanity*, 37.

14 Erasmus, *The Praise of Folly*, ed. Hoyt Hopewell Hudson (Princeton, 1941), 103.

15 Bensly, *loc. cit.*, 203–4.

16 For an account of the 'hippocratic' letters about Democritus, now known to have been spurious, from which most of Burton's portrait is taken, see Babb, *Sanity*, 32–3.

17 N. T. Tyro, *Tyros Roring Megge, Planted against the walls of Melancholy* (London, 1598), sig. A₂ᵛ. This work was among Burton's books, and the relevance of the Tyro passage for the *Anatomy* was commented on by Osler, 'Robert Burton: The Man, His Book, His Library', *loc. cit.*, 189–90.

18 See, e.g., Bright, 149.

19 Burton did in fact have two church livings that he held as an absentee, one in Lincolnshire and one in Leicestershire. The facts of Burton's life are fully summarized in the first chapter of Robert Simon, *Robert Burton (1577–1640) et l'Anatomie de la Mélancolie* (Paris, 1964).

20 Osler, *loc. cit.*, 175.

21 Jordan-Smith, 7.

22 See Babb, *Sanity*, 28, and Prawer, *loc. cit.*

23 James Roy King, *Studies in Six 17th-Century Writers* (Athens, Ohio, 1966), Ch. II, especially 89–91.

24 John V. Lievsay, 'Robert Burton's *De Consolatione*', *South Atlantic Quarterly*, LV (July, 1956), 329–36. Rosalie L. Colie suggests that the entire *Anatomy* is a *consolatio philosophiae*: see *Paradoxia Epidemica* (Princeton, 1966), 437–8.

25 Robert M. Browne, 'Robert Burton and the New Cosmology', *MLQ*, XIII (June, 1952), 131–48.

26 III, 369; and the attacks against the schoolmen of Vives, Erasmus and other humanists are quoted, I, 111, II, 102.

27 A. E. Malloch has shown that this was the aim of such paradoxes as Donne's *Biathanatos*: 'A Critical Study of Donne's Biathanatos', unpublished dissertation (Toronto, 1958). For the *Anatomy* as a paradox, see the chapter on Burton in Colie, 430–60.

28 See Joan Webber's chapter on Burton in *The Eloquent 'I': Style and Self in Seventeenth-Century Prose* (Madison, Wisconsin, 1968).

29 See Colie, especially 446–60.

30 King has pointed out that there is a possibility of parody in the outlines

(p. 79), and that they were taken in this spirit by Burton's biographer in the *DNB* (A. H. Bullen).

31 Croll, *Style*; Barish *Ben Jonson*; George Williamson, *The Senecan Amble: A study in prose form from Bacon to Collier* (Chicago, 1951).

32 King, for example, p. 64, criticizes Burton's 'inability to sustain a single point of view'.

33 See Jordan-Smith, 40–1.

34 These and several other good points about Burton's relationship to the expository books are made by Naomi Loeb Lipman, 'Robert Burton's *Anatomy of Melancholy* and its Relation to the Medical Book Tradition', unpublished M.A. thesis (Columbia, 1952).

35 The nobleman whose opinion on noble melancholy is taken out of context is Henry Howard, Earl of Northampton (see p. 172 n. 26), whose point is exactly the opposite of what Burton implies; Howard says that melancholics are not the prophetic people they are reputed to be (sigs. I_i^r–I_{ii}^v).

36 Other references to the idea of noble melancholy in the *Anatomy* are no more insistent and generally qualified (I, 385, 401, 422–3). In the section on religious melancholy, divine ecstatic melancholy is considered as a possibility, but the bad kind of melancholy is thought to be a more usual danger of fasting and other austerities (III, 343). While Ficino is mentioned several times, he is never fully discussed in terms of a theory of noble melancholy. Burton was familiar, however, not only with Ficino's work, but also with Dürer's engraving (I, 392).

37 This appeared on the title page of the third and subsequent editions. Bensly, *loc. cit.*, 200.

38 Osler (*loc. cit.*, 175) made this point and cited Wecker's *Medicae Syntaxes* (1582) as a precedent. Jordan-Smith (p. 46) proposed Jones's *The Bathe of Bathes Ayde* (1572), a work that is mentioned by Burton and that has synopses like the ones in the *Anatomy*, as a possible source.

39 Jordan-Smith, 163–5.

40 See, for instance, his criteria of knowledge, which include both observation and syllogistic reasoning, at the beginning of Ch. XIV.

41 See his description of the operation of the three bodily spirits, pp. 146–7. Although Lipman (Ch. VI) notes that other expository writers, such as Elyot, expressed less certainty about conflicting authorities than Bright did, it was still not their intention to dramatize the problem.

42 E.g. Elyot, fol. 17^r.

43 Babb, *Sanity*, 18. King has speculated that the original basis of the work was a series of humanistic essays that were eventually fitted into the framework of melancholy (pp. 80–2), but the process he describes would have taken place before the first edition. The revisions of the six editions which Burton made follow the course Babb describes.

Chapter Six

1 Richard Wallace, 'Salvator Rosa's *Democritus* and *L'Umana Fragilità*', *Art Bulletin*, L (March, 1968), 21–32. Rosa's Democritus (1650–1) was influenced by Feti's Melancholy (see p. 104) and posed, as Wallace notes, as Democritus' opposite, Heraclitus. The same is true, however, of the much earlier cut of Democritus in Burton's Frontispiece, which first appeared in the third edition of 1628.

A famous example of a brooding Heraclitus occurs in Raphael's 'School of Athens' (1509–11) in the Vatican. This is now thought to be a portrait of Michelangelo as a melancholic. See Wittkower, *Born Under Saturn*, opposite p. 88.

2 Milton's use of the two traditions, and his indebtedness to Burton, are discussed by William J. Grace, 'Notes on Robert Burton and John Milton', *SP*, LII (July, 1955), 578–91. For some perceptive observations about 'Il Penseroso' in terms of Renaissance concepts of noble melancholy, see Rosemond Tuve, *Images and Themes in Five Poems by Milton* (Cambridge, Mass., 1957), 24–32.

3 Henry Vaughan's 'The Night' is an example of a poem built on this paradox.

4 Walkington, fol. 64ᵛ: 'The melancholick man is said of the wise to be *aut Deus aut Damon*, either angel of heaven or fiend of hell: for in whomsoever this humour hath dominion, the soule is wrapt into an *Elysium* and Paradise of blesse [*sic*] by a heavenly contemplation, or into a direfull hellish purgatory by a cynicall meditation. . . .'

5 See, e.g., Marjorie Nicolson, *John Milton: A Reader's Guide to His Poetry* (New York, 1963), 60, or Don Cameron Allen, *The Harmonious Vision: Studies in Milton's Poetry* (Baltimore, 1954), 11.

6 Allen (p. 10) noted that there is much more fluidity in the transitions of 'Il Penseroso'.

7 For the pejorative implications of 'wanton' and 'giddy' and of Lydian music, considered the degenerate mode in the Platonic musical hierarchy, see Louis L. Martz, 'The Rising Poet' in *The Lyric and Dramatic Milton* (New York, 1965), 18–19. Miss Tuve points out, however (p. 29), that such philosophers as Cornelius Agrippa considered Lydian music Jovial.

8 The alternatives presented in ll. 47–8, of vines outside his window, and in ll. 132–3, of Jonson's or Shakespeare's comedies are very quickly passed over, and do not pose serious imaginative choices.

9 Allen, 6.

Bibliography

ALLEN, DON CAMERON, *The Harmonious Vision*. Baltimore, 1954.

ALLEN, MORSE S., *The Satire of John Marston*. Columbus, Ohio, 1920.

ANDERSON, RUTH L., *Elizabethan Psychology and Shakespeare's Plays*. Iowa City, 1927.

ANTON, ROBERT, *The Philosophers Satyrs*. London, 1616.

BABB, LAWRENCE, 'The Background of "Il Penseroso" ', *SP*, XXXVII (1940), 257–73.

The Elizabethan Malady. East Lansing, Mich., 1951.

'Hamlet, Melancholy, and the Devil', *MLN*, LIX (1944), 120–2.

Sanity in Bedlam. East Lansing, Mich., 1959.

BAMBOROUGH, JOHN B., *The Little World of Man*. London, 1952.

BARISH, JONAS A., *Ben Jonson and the Language of Prose Comedy*. Cambridge, Mass., 1960.

BARROUGH, PHILIP, *The Methode of Phisicke*. London, 1583.

BASKERVILLE, CHARLES REED, *The English Elements in Jonson's Early Comedy*. Austin, Texas, 1911.

BATMAN, STEPHEN, *Batman uppon Bartholome, His Booke De Proprietatibus Rerum*. London, 1582.

BENSLY, EDWARD, 'Some Alterations and Errors in the Successive Editions of *The Anatomy of Melancholy*', *Oxford Bibliographical Society Proceedings and Papers*, I (1922–6), 198–215.

BERNHEIMER, RICHARD, 'Some Drawings of Benedetto Castiglione', *Art Bulletin*, XXXIII (1951), 47–51.

BIEBER, G. A., *Der Melancholikertypus Shakespeares und sein Ursprung*. Heidelberg, 1913.

BLOOMFIELD, MORTON, *The Seven Deadly Sins*. East Lansing, Mich., 1967.

BOORDE, ANDREW, *The Breviarie of Health*. London, 1587.

BRADBROOK, M. C., 'Fate and Chance in *The Duchess of Malfi*', in *Shakespeare's Contemporaries*, ed. Max Bluestone and Norman Rabkin. New York, 1961.

BRADLEY, A. C., *Shakespearean Tragedy*. London, 1957.

BRIGHT, TIMOTHY, *A Treatise of Melancholie*. London, 1586; New York, Facsimile Text Society, 1940.

BROWNE, ROBERT M., 'Robert Burton and the New Cosmology', *MLQ*, XIII (1952), 131–48.

BRUSTEIN, ROBERT S., 'Italian Court Satire and the Plays of John Marston.' Unpublished Ph.D. dissertation, Columbia University, 1957.

BURTON, ROBERT, *The Anatomy of Melancholy*, ed. Holbrook Jackson. 3 vols, New York, 1964.

The Anatomy of Melancholy, ed. A. R. Shilleto. 3 vols, London, 1927.

BUSH, DOUGLAS, 'Classical Myth in Shakespeare's Plays', in *Elizabethan and Jacobean Studies Presented to F. P. Wilson*. Oxford, 1959.

CAMPBELL, LILY B., *Shakespeare's Tragic Heroes: Slaves of Passion*. New York, 1952.

CAMPBELL, OSCAR J., *Comicall Satyre and Shakespeare's Troilus and Cressida*. San Marino, Calif., 1959.

Shakespeare's Satire. New York, 1943.

'What is the Matter with Hamlet?', *Yale Review*, XXXII (1942), 309–22.

CAPUTI, ANTHONY, *John Marston, Satirist*. Ithaca, New York, 1961.

CARTARI, VINCENT, *Les Images des dieux anciens*. Lyons, 1581.

CHAMBERS, E. K., *The Elizabethan Stage*. 4 vols, Oxford, 1923.

CHAPMAN, GEORGE, *The Comedies*, ed. Thomas Marc Parrott. 2 vols, New York, 1961.

CHARNEY, MAURICE, *Style in Hamlet*. Princeton, 1969.

CHARRON, PIERRE, *Of Wisedome*, trans. Samson Lennard. London, 1640.

CHAUCER, GEOFFREY, *The Poetical Works*, ed. F. N. Robinson. Cambridge, Mass., 1961.

CHEW, SAMUEL C., *The Pilgrimage of Life*. New Haven, 1962.

CICERO, *Tusculan Disputations*, English trans. J. E. King. New York, Loeb Classical Library, 1927.

CLEMEN, WOLFGANG, *The Development of Shakespeare's Imagery*. Cambridge, Mass., 1951.

COEFFETEAU, F. N., *Un Tableau des passions humaines*. Paris, 1620.

COLIE, ROSALIE L., *Paradoxia Epidemica*. Princeton, 1966.

CROLL, MORRIS W., *Style, Rhetoric, and Rhythm*, ed. J. Max Patrick *et al.* Princeton, 1966.

CROMBIE, A. C., *Augustine to Galileo*. Cambridge, Mass., 1953.

DANTE ALIGHIERI, *Inferno*, English trans. John D. Sinclair. New York, 1961.

DORAN, MADELEINE, *Endeavors of Art*. Madison, Wisconsin, 1963.

DOWNER, ALAN, 'The Life of Our Design: The Function of Imagery in the Poetic Drama', *Hudson Review*, II (1949), 242–63.

Bibliography

DRAPER, JOHN W., *The Hamlet of Shakespeare's Audience*. Durham, North Carolina, 1938.

The Humors and Shakespeare's Characters. Durham, North Carolina, 1945.

EARLE, JOHN, *Microcosmography*. London, 1897.

ELIOT, T. S., *Essays in Elizabethan Drama*. New York, 1932.

Elizabethan Critical Essays, ed. G. Gregory Smith, 2 vols, London, 1959.

Elizabethan Journals, ed. G. B. Harrison. 2 vols, Ann Arbor, Mich., 1955.

ELYOT, SIR THOMAS, *The Castel of Helth*. London, 1541.

ERASMUS, DESIDERIUS, *The Praise of Folly*, trans. Hoyt Hopewell Hudson. Princeton, 1941.

EVANS, BERGEN, *The Psychiatry of Robert Burton*. New York, 1944.

FINK, Z. S., 'Jaques and the Malcontent Traveler', *PQ*, XIV (1935), 237–52.

FINKELPEARL, PHILIP, *John Marston of the Middle Temple*. Cambridge, Mass., 1969.

FOREST, LOUISE C. TURNER, 'A Caveat for Critics Against Invoking Elizabethan Psychology', *PMLA*, LXI (1946), 651–72.

FREEDMAN, LILA H., 'Satiric Personae: A Study of Point of View in Formal Verse Satire in the English Renaissance from Wyatt to Marston.' Unpublished Ph.D. dissertation, University of Wisconsin, 1955.

FREEMAN, ROSEMARY, *English Emblem Books*. London, 1948.

FRYE, NORTHROP, *The Anatomy of Criticism*. Princeton, 1957.

Fables of Identity. New York, 1963.

GALEN, *De atra bile, liber*, trans. from Greek by Guinterius Andernacus. Paris, 1529.

On the Natural Faculties, English trans. A. J. Brock. New York, Loeb Classical Library, 1916.

De temperamentis et de inequali intemperie, libri tres, trans. from Greek by Thomas Linacre. London, 1521; facsimile London, 1881.

GIBSON, S., and F. D. R. NEEDHAM, eds, 'Two Lists of Burton's Books', *Oxford Bibliographical Society Proceedings and Papers*, I (1922–6), 222–46.

GRACE, WILLIAM J., 'Notes on Robert Burton and John Milton', *SP*, LII (1955), 578–91.

GREENE, ROBERT, *Life and Complete Works in Prose and Verse*, ed. Alexander B. Grosart. 15 vols, London, 1881–6.

GREVILLE, FULKE, *Poems and Dramas*, ed. Geoffrey Bullough. 2 vols, London, 1945.

GUILPIN, EDWARD, *Skialetheia*. London, 1598; Oxford, Shakespeare Association Facsimile, 1931.

HARINGTON, SIR JOHN, trans., *The Englishmans Doctor, Or the Schoole of Salerne*. London, 1607.

A New Discourse on a Stale Subject Called the Metamorphosis of Ajax, ed. Elizabeth Story Donno. New York, 1962.

HEYWOOD, THOMAS, *An Apology for Actors*, intro. Richard H. Perkinson. London, 1612; New York, Scholars' Facsimiles and Reprints, 1941.

HIPPOCRATES, *Works*, ed. and trans. W. H. S. Jones. 4 vols, New York, Loeb Classical Library, 1923.

HORACE, *Satires, Epistles and Ars Poetica*, English trans. H. Rushton Fairclough. Cambridge, Mass., Loeb Classical Library, 1961.

HOWARD, HENRY, EARL OF NORTHAMPTON, *A defensative against the poyson of supposed Prophesies*. London, 1583.

HUARTE, JOHN, *Examen de Ingenios, The Examination of Mens Wits*, trans. R[ichard] C[arew]. London, 1594.

JONSON, BEN, *Works*, ed. C. H. Herford and Percy Simpson. 11 vols, Oxford, 1925–52.

JORDAN-SMITH, PAUL, *Bibliographia Burtoniana*. Stanford, Calif., 1931.

JORGENSEN, PAUL A., 'Hamlet's Therapy', *HLQ*, XXVII (1964), 239–58.

KERNAN, ALVIN, *The Cankered Muse*. New Haven, 1956.

KIEFER, CHRISTIAN, 'Music and Marston's "The Malcontent" ', *SP*, LI (1954), 163–71.

KING, JAMES ROY, *Studies in Six 17th-Century Writers*. Athens, Ohio, 1966.

KLIBANSKY, RAYMOND, ERWIN PANOFSKY and FRITZ SAXL, *Saturn and Melancholy*. New York, 1964.

KNIGHTS, L. C., *Drama and Society in the Age of Jonson*. London, 1957.

KYD, THOMAS, *The First Part of Hieronimo*, ed. Andrew S. Cairncross. Lincoln, Nebraska, 1967.

The Spanish Tragedy, ed. Philip Edwards. Cambridge, Mass., 1959.

LAURENTIUS, M. ANDREAS (André du Laurens), *A Discourse of the Preservation of Sight*, trans. Richard Surphlet. London, 1599; London, Shakespeare Association Facsimile Text Society, 1940.

LEMNIUS, LEVINIUS, *The Touchstone of Complexions*. London, 1581.

LEVIN, HARRY, *The Question of Hamlet*. New York, 1959.

LEWIS, WYNDHAM, *The Lion and the Fox*. London, 1927.

LIEVSAY, JOHN V., 'Robert Burton's De Consolatione', *South Atlantic Quarterly*, LV (1956), 329–36.

LIPMAN, NAOMI LOEB, 'Robert Burton's *Anatomy of Melancholy* and its Relation to the Medical Book Tradition.' Unpublished M.A. thesis, Columbia University, 1952.

LOMAZZO, GIOVANNI, *A Tracte Containing the Artes of Curious Paintinge, Carvinge, and Buildinge*, trans. R[ichard] H[aydocke]. Oxford, 1598.

LOWES, JOHN LIVINGSTON, 'The Loveres Maladye of Hereos', *MP*, XI (1914), 491–546.

LYLY, JOHN, *Complete Works*, ed. R. W. Bond. 3 vols, Oxford, 1902.

MALLOCH, A. E., 'A Critical Study of Donne's *Biathanatos*.' Unpublished Ph.D. dissertation, University of Toronto, 1958.

MARSTON, JOHN, *Antonio and Mellida*, ed. G. K. Hunter, Lincoln, Nebraska, 1965.

Antonio's Revenge, ed. G. K. Hunter. Lincoln, Nebraska, 1965.

The Malcontent, ed. M. L. Wine. Lincoln, Nebraska, 1964.

Plays, ed. H. Harvey Wood. 3 vols, London, 1934–9.

Poems, ed. Arnold Davenport. Liverpool, 1961.

Works, ed. A. H. Bullen. 3 vols, London, 1887.

MARTZ, LOUIS L., 'The Rising Poet', in *The Lyric and Dramatic Milton*, ed. Joseph H. Summers. New York, 1965.

MILTON, JOHN, *Complete Poetry and Major Prose*, ed. Merritt Y. Hughes. New York, 1957.

MUIR, KENNETH, ed., *Shakespeare: Hamlet*. London, 1963.

NASHE, THOMAS, *Works*, ed. Ronald B. McKerrow. 5 vols, Oxford, 1958.

NICOLSON, MARJORIE, *John Milton: A Reader's Guide to His Poetry*. New York, 1963.

NORDSTRÖM, FOLKE, *Goya, Saturn and Melancholy*. Uppsala, 1962.

NORTH, DUDLEY, 3RD BARON NORTH, *A Forest of Varieties*. London, 1645.

OSLER, SIR WILLIAM, 'Robert Burton: The Man, His Book, His Library', *Oxford Bibliographical Society Proceedings and Papers*, I (1922–6), 185–98.

PANOFSKY, ERWIN, *Early Netherlandish Painting*. 2 vols, Cambridge, Mass., 1953.

'Hercules Am Scheidewege', *Studien der Bibliothek Warburg*, XVIII. Leipzig-Berlin, 1930.

Studies in Iconology. New York, 1962.

and Fritz Saxl, 'Dürers "Melencolia I"', *Studien der Bibliothek Warburg*, II. Leipzig-Berlin, 1923.

PEACHAM, HENRY, *Minerva Britanna*. London, 1612.

PETER, JOHN, *Complaint and Satire in Early English Literature*. Oxford, 1956.

PIRALDUS, WILLIAM, *Summae virtuum ac vitiorum tomus secundus*. Lyons, 1668.

PRAWER, SIEGBERT, 'Burton's "Anatomy of Melancholy"', *Cambridge Journal*, I (1948), 671–88.

PRICE, H. T., 'The Function of Imagery in Webster', *PMLA*, LXX (1955), 717–39.

PRIMAUDAYE, PIERRE DE LA, *The French Academie*. 4 vols, London, 1594–1618.

RABELAIS, FRANÇOIS, *Oeuvres Complètes*, ed. Jacques Boulenger and Lucien Scheler. Paris, 1955.

RANDOLPH, MARY CLAIRE, 'Thomas Drant's Definition of Satire, 1566', *Notes and Queries*, CLXXX (1941), 416–18.

'The Medical Concept in English Satiric Theory: Its Possible Relationships and Implications', *SP*, XXXVIII (1941), 125–57.

RANKINS, WILLIAM, *Seven Satires*, ed. Arnold Davenport. Liverpool, 1948.

REED, ROBERT RENTOUL, *Bedlam on the Jacobean Stage*. Cambridge, Mass., 1952.

Regimen sanitatis Salerni, trans. Thomas Paynell. London, 1528.

RIGHTER, ANNE, *Shakespeare and the Idea of the Play*. London, 1962.

RIPA, CESARE, *Nova Iconologia*. Padua, 1618.

ROBINSON, THOMAS, *The Life and Death of Mary Magdalene*, ed. H. Oskar Sommer. London, 1899.

ROWLANDS, SAMUEL, *Democritus, or Doctor Merry-man his Medicines, against Melancholy humours*, London, 1607.

SARTON, GEORGE, *A History of Science through the Golden Age of Greece*. Cambridge, Mass., 1952.

Saturn, see KLIBANSKY.

SAUNDERS, J. W., 'The Stigma of Print: A Note on the Social Bases of Tudor Poetry', *Essays in Criticism*, I (1951), 139–64.

SCHANZER, ERNEST, 'Hercules and his Load', *RES*, XIX (1968), 51–3.

SCHÜCKING, L. L., *Character Problems in Shakespeare's Plays*. Gloucester, Mass., 1959.

SHAKESPEARE, WILLIAM, *Hamlet: A New Variorum Edition*, ed. H. H. Furness. 2 vols (1877), New York, 1963.

Complete Works, ed. Peter Alexander. 4 vols, London, 1951.

SIMON, ROBERT, *Robert Burton (1577–1640) et l'Anatomie de la Mélancolie*. Paris, 1964.

SNUGGS, H. L., 'The Comic Humours: A New Interpretation', *PMLA*, LXII (1947), 114–22.

SPENCER, THEODORE, 'The Elizabethan Malcontent', in *Joseph Quincy Adams Memorial Studies*, ed. James G. McManaway *et al.* Washington, D.C., 1948.

SPURGEON, CAROLINE, *Shakespeare's Imagery and What It Tells Us*. London, 1935.

STABLER, A. P., 'Melancholy, Ambition, and Revenge in Belleforest's Hamlet', *PMLA*, LXXXI (1966), 207–13.

STOLL, E. E., *John Webster*. Cambridge, Mass., 1905.

STRONG, ROY, *The English Icon*. London, 1969.

TERVARENT, GUY DE, *Attributs et symboles dans l'art profane: 1450–1600*. Geneva, 1958.

Les Enigmes de l'art: l'art savant. Paris, 1946.

TODOVOW, MARIA FOSSI, *Mostra delle incisioni di Luca di Leida*. Florence, 1963.

TOURNEUR, CYRIL, *The Revenger's Tragedy*, ed. R. A. Foakes. Cambridge, Mass., 1966.

Bibliography

TUVE, ROSEMOND, *Images and Themes in Five Poems by Milton*. Cambridge, Mass., 1957.

TYRO, N. T., *Tyros Roring Megge, Planted against the walls of Melancholy*. London, 1598.

WAITH, EUGENE, *The Herculean Hero*. New York, 1962.

WALKINGTON, THOMAS, *The Optick Glasse of Humors*. London, 1607.

WALLACE, RICHARD, 'Salvatore Rosa's *Democritus* and *L'Umana Fragilità*', *Art Bulletin*, L (1968), 21–32.

WEBBER, JOAN, *The Eloquent 'I'*. Madison, Wisconsin, 1968.

WEBSTER, JOHN, *The Duchess of Malfi*, ed. John Russell Brown. Cambridge, Mass., 1964.

The White Devil, ed. John Russell Brown. Cambridge, Mass., 1960.

WILLIAMSON, GEORGE, *The Senecan Amble*. Chicago, 1951.

WILSON, F. P., 'Some Notes on Authors and Patrons in Tudor and Stuart Times', in *Joseph Quincy Adams Memorial Studies*, ed. James G. McManaway et al. Washington, D.C., 1948.

WILSON, J. DOVER, *What Happens in Hamlet*. New York, 1959.

WITTKOWER, RUDOLF AND MARGOT, *Born Under Saturn*. New York, 1963.

WRIGHT, LOUIS B., *Middle-Class Culture in Elizabethan England*. Ithaca, N.Y., 1959.

WRIGHT, THOMAS, *The Passions of the Minde in Generall*. London, 1621.

YATES, FRANCES A., *Giordano Bruno and the Hermetic Tradition*. London, 1964.

Index